THE DIS-EASES OF SECRECY

THE DIS-EASES OF SECRECY

Tracing history, memory and justice

Brian Rappert & Chandré Gould

This book is not about Dr Wouter Basson, nor have we sought to highlight his role in Project Coast. Basson has, however, become the public face of the apartheid chemical and biological warfare programme, and is the only person who has been formally held to account for activities undertaken in its name. His image has been widely used in the media over a number of years and is familiar to South Africans and those who have followed the revelations of Project Coast internationally. As such it made sense for the publishers to use his image on the cover of this book. I found this choice difficult to accept. This book seeks to disrupt the ways in which we have come to think about and make sense of Project Coast and resists the 'Bassonification' of the programme. Having his image on the front cover is counter to that intent. While I remain discomforted by the use of his image here, and would have preferred us to have avoided it altogether, compromises are a necessary part of any publishing process, and perhaps his image will serve to draw readers to the book.

– Chandré Gould

First published by Jacana Media (Pty) Ltd in 2017
10 Orange Street
Sunnyside
Auckland Park 2092
South Africa
+27 (0)11 628 3200
www.jacana.co.za

ISBN 978-1-4314-2485-6

Cover design Shawn Paikin
Set in Stempel Garamond 10/14pt
Printed and bound by ABC Press, Cape Town

See a complete list of Jacana titles
at www.jacana.co.za

CONTENTS

ACKNOWLEDGEMENTS

THE WORK ON THIS BOOK could not have been undertaken without the assistance and inspiration of many people. Our thanks to Catelijne Coopmans, Malcolm Dando, Alastair Hay, Elis Jones, Rebecca Langlands, Richard Moyes, Khaya Gould, Lyle Lennox and Michael Schillmeier.

Brian Balmer and Verne Harris read early drafts of the book. We are grateful for their time, insights and helpful commentary. Chandré has had the pleasure of hours of debate and discussion with Verne, much of which is woven into her reflections about memory work and transitional justice, and this has informed the search for liberatory ways of working with the memory of violence and harm. The team at the Nelson Mandela Foundation have worked with us in various ways to generate material for this book and the exhibition – for their contribution and support we are most grateful.

Our publisher at Jacana, Sibongile Machika, has been a kind, efficient and valued guide through the publication process for this book. Thank you also to Bridget Impey and Maggie Davey, who believed in the value of this book and have developed a uniquely supportive and engaging publisher.

Kathryn Smith has brought a new dimension to the work that we have done together. Her creativity, intellect and friendship enabled the exhibition *Poisoned Past,* traces of which you will find throughout the book.

We are also grateful for all those who agreed to have their thoughts quoted. Our thanks also go to all those who asked not to be named but who are represented in this book as anonymous voices.

Giovanna Colombetti and Helèt Theron have been extremely patient with us, spending many hours working through this material, for which we are grateful. Helèt has accompanied Chandré on her 20-year journey with Project Coast; I am grateful for her reminders not to take myself too seriously and for her ability to find beauty in the world.

Sections of *The Dis-eases of Secrecy* are reworked reformulations of parts of an earlier publication. Kind permission was given by the Institute for Security Studies to draw on elements of Rappert, B and Gould, C (2014) Biological Weapons Convention: Confidence, the prohibition and learning from the past. ISS Paper No. 258 (July).

The development of this book was aided by the decision of the Nelson Mandela Foundation to support and house a temporary exhibition on Project Coast in 2016–2017 titled *Poisoned Pasts* (curated by Kathryn Smith and the authors).

Activities underpinning elements of *The Dis-eases of Secrecy* were supported by an ESRC, Dstl and AHRC award, 'The Formation and Non-formation of Security Concerns' (ES/K011308/1), as well as a British Academy Newton Advanced Fellowship, 'Cataloguing Secrets, Transforming Justice' (SL-06825).

ACRONYMS

AHRC	Arts and Humanities Research Council
ANC	African National Congress
BWC	Biological Weapons Convention (also often referred to as the Biological and Toxins Weapons Convention [BTWC])
BWWC	Biological Weapons Working Committee
CBM	confidence building measure
CBW	chemical and biological warfare
CCB	Civil Cooperation Bureau
CDU	Chemical Defence Unit
CIA	Central Intelligence Agency
CMC	Coordinating Management Committee
CR	dibenz[b,f]-1,4-oxazepine
CS	o-Chlorobenzylidene malononitrile
CSI	Chief of Staff Intelligence
CSIR	Council for Scientific and Industrial Research
CWC	Chemical Weapons Convention
Dstl	Defence Science and Technology Laboratory
ESRC	Economic and Social Research Council
FAPLA	Military wing of the Popular Movement for the Liberation of Angola
FBI	Federal Bureau of Investigation, United States
FRELIMO	Front for the Liberation of Mozambique

HPCSA	Health Professionals Council of South Africa
NIA	National Intelligence Agency
NP	National Party
NPC	Council for the Non-proliferation of Weapons of Mass Destruction
OSEO	Office for Serious Economic Offences
PLAN	People's Liberation Army of Namibia
RRL	Roodeplaat Research Laboratories
SACBC	Southern African Catholic Bishops Conference
SACC	South African Council of Churches
SADF	South African Defence Force (before 1994)
SAHA	South African History Archive
SAMDC	South African Medical and Dental Council
SAMS	South African Medical Service
SANDF	South African National Defence Force (after April 1994)
SAP	South African Police (before 1994)
SAPS	South African Police Service (after 1994)
SAVC	South African Veterinary Council
SIPRI	Stockholm International Peace Research Institute
SWAPO	South West African People's Organisation
TRC	Truth and Reconciliation Commission
UN	United Nations
UNIDIR	United Nations Institute for Disarmament Research
UNITA	National Union for the Total Independence of Angola
ZANU	Zimbabwe African National Union
ZAPU	Zimbabwe African People's Union
ZIPRA	Zimbabwe African People's Revolutionary Army

INTRODUCTION

Under the code name 'Project Coast', between 1981 and 1995 a chemical and biological warfare programme was established and maintained in apartheid South Africa. Through the endeavours of the Truth and Reconciliation Commission (TRC), the most extensive legal post-apartheid trial of a member of the security forces, and many other investigations, the activities of the project became treated as emblematic of the perversities of a former time – one that should never be repeated.

And yet, each attempt to determine and remember Project Coast has been structured and limited by the very conditions that enabled it. Documentary traces and fragments compiled to date signal that much remains unknown and perhaps will never be widely appreciated. Despite widespread public discussion about the project, its offensive intentions have never been acknowledged officially by South Africa and other nations.[1] Many have found reason to call for the past to be left in the past.

In short, Project Coast is situated between revelation and concealment, remembering and forgetting, the past and the future. In this it shares much with other transgressions elsewhere.

In these conditions, *The Dis-eases of Secrecy* is not simply or even primarily intended to set the record straight. Instead, this study was undertaken in the spirit of investigating possibilities for understanding ourselves and the world; because a danger in examining an activity like

Project Coast is getting swept away by the mystique and spectacle that defines it. Secrecy was not only central to how the programme was justified, undertaken and covered up, it continues to be central to how it is milled, ignored and mystified today. Rather than being swept away, our hope is that we might become receptive to the wantings, aversions, commitments and fascinations associated with attempts to reveal what was hidden.

These points are particularly relevant because the history of Project Coast is not something that can be neatly viewed as 'over there'. For over 20 years, as a reporter, TRC investigator, PhD student and policy analyst, Chandré Gould has been deeply involved in efforts to document the dealings of the programme. At each stage, the question 'What for?' has loomed large, and remains unresolved. Today, the fraught experiences with transitional justice in South Africa – and elsewhere – suggest that pinning down more details about yesterday may not build a more just tomorrow. These experiences also suggest that 'truth-telling' is not a neat, simple process, and even less so when mediated through legalistic channels. We find resolution ephemeral, and knowing about what happened is not as clearly associated with 'healing' as we may have presumed.

But if this is the case, what kind of history should be written?

To this question, *The Dis-eases of Secrecy* offers a stay: we cannot say for certain. Responses to this question turn on the reasons for asking it and these cannot be set in stone – certainly not by us alone, and not now for all time. Rather than establishing a definite history, we are concerned with promoting sensitivities for approaching the question of 'What history?'; sensitivities that promote alertness to our expectations and suspicions. To put it in other terms, the attention we wish to foster is more aligned with receptiveness than focus, and inquiry rather than resolution.

The Dis-eases of Secrecy does this not only through its content but also through its structure, which promotes the experiential dynamics of the interwoven web of claims and unknowns surrounding Project Coast. Through an argument in which what is missing is intended to be as much a feature as what is given, readers are encouraged to participate in a process of investigation – with the lures, frustrations and effects that this can entail. To put it in words borrowed from the philosopher Alfred N Whitehead, we have sought to assemble material in such a way as to provide an antidote to the occlusions of notionally systematic analysis, even while recognising that we are indebted to (and constrained by) the legacy of previous studies, which were intended to set the historical record straight.

The term 'tracing' from the subtitle has varied relevancies for this book. *The Dis-eases of Secrecy* recounts the investigative paths that were previously taken to understand Project Coast. These sought to discover the origins and make-up of South Africa's chemical and biological warfare programme through searches for documentary evidence. With the appreciation that such recountings never amount to mere repetition of the same story, we try to foster an awareness of commitments and consequences of accounts of the past. Through the physical process of page turning, we invite the reader to participate in these tracings.

Tracing implies following a series of marks or clues left behind after something has passed, but also never actually catching up with that which is being pursued. What is known often amounts to an incomplete vestige, which points to somewhere else for a fuller account.[2] In the case of Project Coast, much chasing has been done to establish what took place, but it is also frequently contended that much remains shrouded. And yet, in other respects, the difficulty of investigating Project Coast relates to the overabundance of stories and evidence. An avalanche of information has the potential to render some matters obscure. *The Dis-eases of Secrecy* endeavours to engage with how what is hidden, reveals and what is revealed, hides.

Perhaps more fundamentally though, we want to call into question what is sought from the basic desire to offer a full picture of what took place. *The Dis-eases of Secrecy* marks various courses for inquiring about the past. One goal is to engender sensitivities with the investments in the telling of history. We write with absences and secrecy to alert readers to the processes that produce absences and secrecy. If we have done our job properly, the further you read, the further you should come to a sense of what is outside of these histories of the past. Yet, this will leave you with more rather than less – not in a territory of 'post-truth' but it in an affective state of heightened awareness.

We hope that, between the traces and fragments of our accounts, readers will be able to question themselves and others about the purposes of history and the potential of memory.

HOW TO READ THIS BOOK

THIS BOOK IS INTENDED TO SIMULATE an investigation. In an investigation, the order in which you make meaning is not pre-determined, and the process of making sense of what you are seeing and beginning to know is gradual and iterative.

While it is possible to read *The Dis-eases of Secrecy* from front to back in a conventional fashion, we would encourage you to not to confine yourself to this approach. As shown in the graphic opposite, there are several ways in which you can read the text. *The Dis-eases of Secrecy* has no chapters in the standard manner of books of this kind. It has none of the packaging and trappings of chapters either: neat conclusions that tidy up what is meant or section titles that parse out ideas. This is so as to allow you to draw your own conclusions, make your own meaning, and hopefully arrive at new insights, not only about the chemical and biological warfare programme, but also about how we make sense of complex, secret pasts.

Here are few things to keep in mind as you read this book.
- The themes covered in this book are called Sutras and there are 11 of them.
- The numbers running down the left of the page in red are called Entries.
- Entries are nuggets of information. They are numbered from 1–548 in the order that the investigators encountered them.

- Sewn threads on pages xxiii–xxiv give the order of Entries to follow if reading a particular Sutra.
- Two ways to read this book are: chronologically by going through Entries in the order they are presented or thematically by following the Sewn threads sequence of Entries according to each Sutra.

Some ways to read The Dis-eases of Secrecy

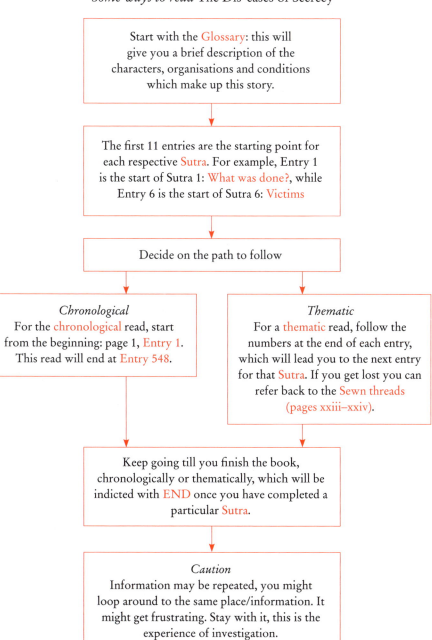

Start with the Glossary: this will give you a brief description of the characters, organisations and conditions which make up this story.

The first 11 entries are the starting point for each respective Sutra. For example, Entry 1 is the start of Sutra 1: What was done?, while Entry 6 is the start of Sutra 6: Victims

Decide on the path to follow

Chronological
For the chronological read, start from the beginning: page 1, Entry 1. This read will end at Entry 548.

Thematic
For a thematic read, follow the numbers at the end of each entry, which will lead you to the next entry for that Sutra. If you get lost you can refer back to the Sewn threads (pages xxiii–xxiv).

Keep going till you finish the book, chronologically or thematically, which will be indicted with END once you have completed a particular Sutra.

Caution
Information may be repeated, you might loop around to the same place/information. It might get frustrating. Stay with it, this is the experience of investigation.

GLOSSARY

WHAT WAS PROJECT COAST? Who was integral to its operations? How far did its breadth extend? These are matters central to debates about its proper history and contemporary relevance. They are also matters varyingly conceived and – at times anyway – much contested.

The threads of this book offer ways to work through these and other questions. They must be worked through because of what is still unknown, but also because a fixed set of answers would be unsuitable. How one might approach and answer the question 'What was Project Coast?' differs markedly between 1997 and 2017. As primer and reference, this glossary offers snapshots of a few elements that recur in accounts of the programme.

PEOPLE

Dr Wouter Basson – In the public imaginations about Project Coast in South Africa and elsewhere, Basson has become singularly synonymous with the programme. This is hardly surprising given that he was its Project Officer between 1981 and 1992, and endowed with extensive operational discretion. Moreover, this is a positioning that Basson himself has appeared to cultivate. He was the only person in South Africa's chemical and biological weapons activities to be professionally sanctioned. However, the focus on Basson has resulted in a specific kind of attention that has meant the actions of others have faded from view. Others like…

Surgeon General Niel Knobel – As the South African Defence Force Surgeon-General from 1988 to November 1997, Knobel served as the Project Manager for Project Coast and was a member of the Coordinating Management Committee, which was notionally responsible for ensuring that the programme was run in an efficient and accountable manner.

Dr Jan Lourens – As a technical expert for Project Coast and head of some of its myriad front companies, Lourens's 1997 amnesty application regarding his role in the development of assassination weapons catalysed many investigations. This included the criminal trial of Wouter Basson in which the doctor was charged with multiple counts of murder and conspiracy to murder, drug possession and fraud. During the three years of the trial (1999–2001), over 150 witnesses, including Lourens himself, testified for the prosecution but only one testified for the defence, Basson himself. At the end of the three years, Judge Willie Hartzenberg found Dr Basson not guilty on all the charges brought against him, in addition to having thrown out charges in 1999. The former would be justified in large part by discounting testimony by individuals such as…

Johan Theron – He would claim that, as a member of the South African Defence Force, he disposed of hundreds of bodies of enemies of South Africa by sedating people and dropping them from a plane into the Atlantic Ocean. Disagreements about what counted as sufficient proof that such actions took place at all, and whether they could be linked to Project Coast, exemplify the disputes about the scope of the programme.

That no victims are named in this short list signals how those negatively affected have so often been invisible, with most remaining unnamed and unidentified. (For a list of all those we know were affected by poisons used by the security forces, please see Appendix 1.)

Chandré Gould has, over many years, investigated, written about and tried to make sense of Project Coast. This started when the amnesty application of Dr Jan Lourens landed on her desk at the TRC. For some time she firmly believed that telling 'truths' about the past offered lessons for the present – and that knowing about how things can go wrong can help to prevent us from making the same mistakes again. She is no longer so certain. Chandré, in partnership with others, has authored many of the books, chapters and articles about Project Coast and is deeply implicated in the answer to the question 'What was Project Coast?'. She and Brian conceptualised this text as they tried to make sense of the many unsolved questions about the Project and realised that a lack of resolution is perhaps inevitable – and may even be desirable.

Brian Rappert has, over a number of years, investigated secrets with particular regard to international armed conflict. While this work was initially motivated by a desire to bring to light the machinations of statecraft so that they are not repeated, he now regards the relation between seeing, knowing and acting as far more challenging. He and Chandré devised this book about Project Coast as a means of dwelling in the possibilities for social inquiry.

SITES

Although Project Coast was a secret undertaking, hidden from view in many respects, its activities were conducted in places and spaces that could not simply vanish into thin air. These sites would come to define the programme and the programme would cast a long shadow over these sites.

Roodeplaat Research Laboratories (RRL) was one of the prime, military, front companies. Its work centred on the production and development of biological weapons and, particularly, attempts to identify and develop chemical and biological substances that could be used to kill while leaving no trace.

Delta G Scientific was another central, military, front company. Among its other activities, it produced CR (dibenz(b,f)-1,4-oxazepine) tear gas, as well as tonnes of ecstasy and methaqualone.

South Africa – What counted as the legitimate scope of South Africa's reach was a matter of contestation in the 1970s and 1980s because, to maintain its internal order, the government sought to shape the external order of the southern Africa region. To this end, the South Africa Defence Forces intervened in Angola, Mozambique and Zimbabwe, and sought to secure administrative control of the territory of South-West Africa (present-day Namibia).

ORGANISATIONS

Responses to the question of 'What was Project Coast?' are inextricably linked to notions of what was outside of it: what opposition it was aimed at, as well as how it became known by outsiders. In this regard, several organisations were central in its history.

South West Africa People's Organisation (SWAPO) – In South-West

Africa (present-day Namibia), the apartheid South African state sought to counter the military and political liberation attempts of SWAPO. SWAPO has governed Namibia since it achieved independence in 1990.

African National Congress (ANC) – Prominent internal enemies of the apartheid state included members of the ANC, a movement that politically and militarily sought to end apartheid. The ANC has governed South Africa since 1994.

The Truth and Reconciliation Commission (TRC) was established in 1996 to investigate gross human rights violations and to help bridge the transition from apartheid to democracy. As part of its activities, the TRC held hearings in which victims and perpetrators testified with the intention that truth-telling would aid reconciliation. In 1998, the TRC held hearings on Project Coast.

The Health Professions Council of South Africa (HPCSA) would be the only professional body in South Africa to find one of its members guilty of misconduct – Dr Basson – because of his participation in Project Coast.

MATERIALS

Besides people, places and organisations, Project Coast involved a diverse range of materials, including documents, biological agents, equipment and physical infrastructure. As objects cannot speak for themselves, which materials should be included as part of the programme has proven thorny. So, too, has the matter of how they should be judged. For instance:

Biological agents – In the production of biological weapons, life and death are closely tied. Within Project Coast, living bacteria such as anthrax and cholera, as well as the secretions of bacteria like botulism, were used as agents of death. Or at least, this is how the situation has been portrayed since the discovery of the Verkope (Sales) list (see Appendix 2). The list appeared to link the deadly products of the programme to members of the South African Police and the South African Defence Force. Some, though, have sought to portray items on the list – such as bottles of cholera or anthrax-laced cigarettes – as agents for *preserving* life. Still others have found cause to call these devices 'murder weapons', but then have added the further qualification that this did not make them *offensive* weapons.

CR – While the malign applications of biological and chemical weapons have been central to many investigations into Project Coast, in some interpretations, this preoccupation has effectively side-lined the other activities. This includes the large-scale production of CR, a form of 'tear gas'. This production was justified as a means of crowd control, given the strife that characterised South Africa at the time – a purpose many of those in the programme regarded (and still regard) as admirable. For some, the preoccupation with weaponry has also side-lined the work done by Project Coast to develop defences against chemical weapons.

STRUCTURES OF ACCOUNTABILITY

Project Coast was not just an assemblage of many things – it was a highly organised system that established who had to justify what and to whom. Structures that were relevant in the history of the programme include:

International treaty regimes – The 1972 Biological Weapons Convention (BWC) and the 1993 Chemical Weapons Convention (CWC) place a wide-ranging ban on the possession and use of biological and chemical weapons by signatories. They also place reporting demands on states to disclose how they are adhering to the terms of the treaties, such as through so-called confidence-building measure (CBM) forms in the case of the BWC. South Africa ratified the BWC in 1975 and the CWC in 1995.

Coordinating Management Committee – A South Africa Defence Force military body that was established to oversee Project Coast; contentions about the level of its involvement in the day-to-day running of the programme resulted in disputes about who was responsible for what took place.

Apartheid, which means 'separate' in Afrikaans, was the legal, political and ideological system in South Africa designed to segment 'racial' groups in a hierarchy of worth. In this system, individuals and groups needed to account for themselves, such as justifying their conduct and beliefs to themselves, to others and the state. Much of the rationale behind Project Coast was an attempt to ensure the continuation of apartheid. A central question in thinking about the lessons that can be learnt from the past is whether an undertaking such as Project Coast required the extreme and corrosive environment that characterised apartheid.

INQUIRING

HOW SHOULD ONE WRITE about what is openly discussed but not officially acknowledged? How can justice be done to amassed documentary evidence while also acknowledging the vast amount of material that has not been made accessible? How can the legacy of previous thoughts and data be pressed into service to open novel possibilities for the future?

These and other questions have motivated *The Dis-eases of Secrecy.* A basic move in response has been to seek ways to cultivate awareness of the conditions for knowing. A primary way of doing this is through the way in which we assembled claims and arguments. In the main Chronology section, the text is broken up into numbered entries which are ordered roughly in the sequence of their occurrence. These include text quotes, analyses, diary reflections (from Chandré Gould), interview extracts and descriptions of events. The Reflection section likewise contains ordered entries; in this case, entries related to various conceptual themes. Both sections can be read from front to back in the conventional fashion. In addition, though, the entries are organised into 11 themed strands, which we call sutras. Entries 1 to 11 in the Sutras section provide the first entry for each of the themes. At the end of these entries, you are given the number of another entry (for instance, What? 480), which continues that theme's sutra. At the end of each entry you will be directed to the next entry for that theme (for instance, What? 38), and so on, until the thread finishes (What? END). As you progress through the text, at times you will find yourself circling back on entries you have already encountered, but situated in a different flow. The circularity of the thematic organisation points to the lack of resolution – the absence of a clear endpoint – which exemplifies the process of inquiry and investigation. We use the Sanskrit term 'sutra' to label the organising themes in relation to two of its meanings: (1) 'discourses' or distilled texts and (2) strings or threads that hold things together.

The inspiration for this organisation came from Sven Lindqvist's *A History of Bombing*. This technique enabled Lindqvist to produce an absorbing, detailed, yet accessible overview of the fantasies, expectations and terrors of aerial bombing. Through his thread-based entries into the 'labyrinth' of the past, he encourages his readers to sense that they are taking only 'one of many possible paths through the chaos of history'.[3]

We, too, are interested in opening options that enable a tracing of the past. Our orientation in relation to Project Coast differs somewhat from *A History of Bombing* because we are often not sure of how to characterise what took place – whether it was a labyrinth, a scheme, a network, a circus or a cycle. Our sutras are not single-track lines for getting through a complex labyrinth. Instead, by offering themes that interlink, branch off and get read in reverse order, we seek to stimulate the imagination to diagnose situations anew. This may well leave you, the reader, feeling somewhat at sea to begin with, but it is worth persevering with the disorientations and pulls because these are the disorientations experienced in attempting to make sense of a programme such as Project Coast. We also seek to place you amidst the sometimes contradictory, often confusing interpretations from multiple sources to enable you to fashion connections anew. In this way, our use of the term 'sutra' is in line with the function sutras play in Buddhism or Hinduism: we offer these texts as prompts for contemplation.

Our goal, in short, is to turn a technique for reading into a method for inquiry.

SEWN THREADS

FOR THE PURPOSES OF CONSULTATION, the numbering for each of the sutras is as follows:

1. What was done? 1, 480, 38, 184–5, 163, 193, 45, 316, 186–7, 353, 373, 221, 224, 299, 229, 492, 268, 270–1, 234, 241, 40, 259, 243, 244, 248, 250–2, 269, 249, 296, 301, 320, 354, 297–8, 41, 145, 295, 294, 389, 77

2. Total war: 2, 94–5, 115, 427–30, 432, 80, 61, 84, 88, 119, 99, 121, 133, 141, 156–7, 155, 160, 511, 262, 272, 219, 473, 396, 463–6, 546–7, 402–03, 453

3. Forgetting and remembering: 3, 14, 431, 454, 459, 178, 15, 504–06, 482, 59, 508–10, 20, 294, 389, 27, 444, 451, 30, 379, 382, 503, 19, 329, 343, 331–2, 198, 204, 374, 199, 488, 391, 512, 330, 352, 372, 359, 328, 177, 302–03, 230, 229, 267, 190, 193, 312, 163, 220, 28

4. Legacies of the past: 4, 532–4, 390, 47, 202, 48, 535, 391, 336, 338–9, 375, 360–2, 401, 363–6, 376–8, 22, 538–9, 542, 457–8, 449, 178, 433, 452, 460–2, 459, 472, 516–17, 450, 528–30, 487, 525, 337

5. Need to know: 5, 241, 150, 243, 496, 163, 228, 282–9, 306–10, 50, 497, 527, 436–7, 52–3, 494, 55, 485–6

6. Victims: 6, 483, 203–04, 153, 240, 374, 346, 304–05, 367–8, 455–6, 266, 205, 524, 242, 245, 313, 206–09, 331, 392–3, 210, 345, 125, 211–13, 146, 214–166, 486, 253, 540, 254, 394, 255–8, 147, 246–7, 548, 323, 217, 497, 515, 511, 513, 405, 347–8, 64, 446–7, 543–5

SUTRAS

WHAT WAS DONE?

2002

Dastardly in its concept and execution, Project Coast was a reflection of the inherent evil of apartheid... This book by Chandré Gould and Peter Folb makes a vital contribution to our understanding of how the apartheid regime planned the deliberate use of chemical and biological agents on people, how those involved put together a determined programme to acquire knowledge and materials to develop the means to poison people within and outside South Africa's borders and how corruption inside that programme eventually led to their downfall.[4]

'Foreword' by Archbishop Desmond Mpilo Tutu
Project Coast: Apartheid's Chemical and Biological Warfare Programme
What? 480

'The I is always in the field of the Other.'[5]

Jacques Lacan

Total war 94

3   FORGETTING AND REMEMBERING

2013

A radio interview with Wouter Basson on 18 December, by journalist John Maytham, after a judgment by the Health Professionals Council of South Africa (HPCSA) that Basson was guilty of unethical conduct:

> Every single fact that has ever been involved in this court case has been through the court system, and there is not a single pointer that I am guilty of anything. Either intentionally or unintentionally or whatever, factually and there was never any perception or any intention to damage or harm anybody. The intention of the whole project was to protect South Africa and its people and to stop people from annihilating themselves, from burning and necklacing and burning down buildings and causing endless harm and damage to themselves and other innocents... Forgetting 14

4   LEGACIES OF THE PAST

There are many things that do not add up about this chemical and biological weapons programme, and which remain unsatisfactorily answered by the documentary evidence, or by the accounts given by those who worked within the project. Legacies 532

5   NEED TO KNOW

1999

Truth and Reconciliation Commission of South Africa Report: Special Investigation into Project Coast

The Commission finds that:

- Scientists were recruited to the CBW programme from universities and research institutions in South Africa because of their 'patriotism' and loyalty to the government of the day. They were lured by generous conditions of service, facilities, working arrangements and pay packages.

- Work was conducted on a 'need to know' basis, subverting the very purpose of science. The free discourse of information and ideas that characterise scientific endeavour was subverted. Moreover, those who were appointed were intimidated and threatened, even with their lives, if they stepped out of line.[6]   To know 241

6   VICTIMS

2013
Project Officer of Project Coast, Dr Wouter Basson, interviewed by John Maytham, Cape Talk radio

John Maytham: 'I do try to understand, because you are getting a lot of support from our callers and from our smses, but you are getting even more condemnation, people unable to understand why you don't seem to understand why you did anything wrong in your work as soldier-stroke-doctor.'

Wouter Basson: 'It's very simple, they must just show me what I did wrong [voice higher pitch and speaking very rapidly]. It's easy, all they need to do is bring one single case of anybody that was either damaged and/ or hurt in this process and I'll live with it. But nobody can do that. I mean it's been 20 years that this has been going on and there is not a single scratch and/or blue mark and/or bruise on anybody that could be proven anywhere, so who did I damage and how?'[7]   Victims 483

7   INTERNATIONAL RELATIONS (IR)

2013
Interview notes
UK Foreign and Commonwealth official

Diplomacy is, in some respects, a sordid business. The strict application of principle doesn't apply. Other issues come along and become the issue of the hour, displacing earlier, less pressing issues that take on less importance.

IR 102

BEST OFFENCE

'It wasn't actually an offensive programme; it was an effort to try to find assassination weapons.'

Dr Volker Beck

Chemical and biological weapons expert

Offence 13

SILENCE AND THE FURY

1995

South Africa ratified the Biological Weapons Convention in 1975. No offensive biological research and development programme has ever been declared by South Africa under the treaty. South Africa last updated its Confidence Building Measure, Form F, in 1995. It stated: 'South Africa had no offensive biological research and development programmes in the past.'[8]

Silence 100 | Offence END

TRANSITIONAL JUSTICE

'Instead of allowing for a full reckoning with the messy business of collaboration, South Africans have allowed the secrets of the past to gain an afterlife.'[9]

Jacob Dlamini, *Askari*

Justice 163

LESSONS FROM THE PAST

1998

Truth and Reconciliation Commission of South Africa Report

[T]he past refuses to lie down quietly. It has an uncanny habit of returning to haunt one. 'Those who forget the past are doomed to repeat it' are the words emblazoned at the entrance to the museum in the former concentration camp of Dachau. They are words we would do well to keep ever in mind. However painful the experience, the wounds of the past must not be allowed to fester. They must be opened. They must be cleansed. And balm must be poured on them so they can heal. This is not to be obsessed with the past. It is to take care that the past is properly dealt with for the sake of the future.[10]

Lessons 397

REFLECTIONS

12 Before providing a detailed chronology of events, we thought it would be useful to elaborate on our orientation to some the more conceptual issues at stake in recounting an activity like Project Coast. Below we offer comments on the notions of history, secrecy, silence and discourse.

HISTORY

13 Writing history entails sticking labels onto events and individuals. These act as markers, distinguishing one thing from another – this is a way of sorting things.
Offence 65

14 Attempts to offer a history of events are often accompanied by questions: How was it assembled? What forms of evidence were drawn upon? What reliance has been placed on personal memory versus documentary evidence? Such questions direct our attention to what gets included in stories about the past.
Forgetting 431

15 The histories made today are necessarily enabled and constrained by the histories of yesterday. In other words, they are conditioned by conditions of the past.
Forgetting 504

16 In the case of Project Coast, these conditions included the failure to record the activities of statecraft, the eventual destruction of many documents, and the widespread turning of a blind eye to events.

17   For many reasons, no straightforward account can be given about who suffered through Project Coast. Stories of victimhood are not out there to collect in a simple fashion. Much depends on who is asking the questions, for what purpose, and according to what criteria and assumptions. Justice 526

18   The many unanswered questions about Project Coast suggest several secrets that have not yet been uncovered and which may even be uncoverable.   Legacies 534

19   A non-conventional way to tell a history is to provide an analysis of that which cannot be included in it. Such 'histories in the negative' deal with what has been excluded from attempts to establish official accounts of past events and examine how the partial histories fashioned at one point in time provide the basis for subsequent accounts.   Forgetting 329

20   Researching secretive programmes such as Project Coast requires not only contending with official historical records fashioned by conditions of the past, it also entails contending with a thicket of sometimes discordant memories and agreements of confidentiality.   Forgetting 294

21   In *The Dis-eases of Secrecy*, this thicket of negotiations is illustrated in the numerous and sometimes incompatible interviews, conversations, emails and other interactions in the Chronology section.

22   It is not easy to predict what you will be told when you start asking questions, and we and others have been scratching for a long time; but what does one do with information that cannot be verified? Does it mean anything at all? How much of it is misinformation, passed on to discredit those that repeat it? These are the kinds of questions confronting investigators at every turn. And the decision about what to include, what to follow up and what to ignore is based on a range of considerations: what would be believable, what is ethical, what is constructive, and what would simply fuel conspiracy theories?   Legacies 538

23   How then to contend with the challenges of providing a history of Project Coast? One way to promote a skilful relation with accounts of the past is to ask what is expected from them. Rather than presuming that history operates akin to a camera that captures the scene of the crime, another orientation places the question of 'What purpose does history serve?' at the front and centre of the inquiry.

In the case of Project Coast, attempts to assemble accounts of what took place have often been motivation by a strong sense of purpose.

24   The investigations into the South African chemical and biological warfare programme began in 1992 with a secret, internal, military inquiry into the involvement of covert military units in fomenting violence to undermine the process of transition.[11] Later, in 1997, when Basson was

found in possession of large quantities of ecstasy, the police narcotics unit started a separate investigation. Meanwhile, the Office for Serious Economic Offences was investigating allegations of fraud made by scientists involved in the programme.

Another, separate investigation was undertaken by the Transvaal Attorney-General (later the National Prosecuting Authority) into allegations of murder, torture, conspiracy and intimidation by Dr Wouter Basson and other military operators. Then, in 1997, the Truth and Reconciliation Commission (TRC) began its inquiry after having received applications for amnesty from scientists involved in the programme. Finally, a professional inquiry was held by the Health Professions Council of South Africa (HPCSA) to determine whether Basson was guilty of unprofessional and unethical conduct when, as a military doctor, he was responsible for the manufacture of street drugs and tear gas, and the provision of cyanide pills to military operators.

These investigations gave rise to a three-year criminal trial (which resulted in Basson's acquittal or a finding of not-guilty on all charges); a public hearing of the TRC and a report passing judgment; a monograph published by the United Nations Institute for Disarmament Research (UNIDIR); a three-year court battle by the South African History Archives, which ended in the creation of an archive of military and other documents about the programme, now available to the public; and a HPCSA finding in 2013 that Basson *was* guilty of unethical and unprofessional conduct.

Is this an example of a successful transitional justice and traditional justice process? Legacies 542

25 This question is important because many of the investigations were justified as enabling South Africa to move on from its fractured apartheid times. This was perhaps most explicit in the case of the TRC, where it was said that the gathering of stories of misdeeds was to provide a basis for national reconciliation.

26 As would become evident in time, the story of the chemical and biological warfare programme was not one of the narratives that would bring South Africans together. The first reason was that this was a fragmented story – and an incredulous one – which did not lend itself to easy telling or retelling. Those who held critical pieces were either dead (such the Surgeon General under whose watch the programme began), inaccessible to the TRC or they opted to maintain their secrets – like Basson. But perhaps more importantly, this was one of the few hearings held by the TRC in which the narrators were exclusively white. It was

thus a story of contested perpetration and one in which the victims had no voice and no identity, so there could be no forgiveness. Justice 168

27　Questions about the role of history for the present, and what should be left out of it, takes on an enormous complexity when posed at the level of a society. If we give up on the often-made but poorly supported assumption that the denser the details of history, then the more likelihood of future peace, the issues at stake become even more complicated.[12] Forgetting 444

28　To the extent that the TRC was conceived as a process of making private troubles into public issues, it achieved this only in a splintered manner. Forgetting went hand in hand with remembering. As a result, what kind of change was achieved and for whom should not be assumed – and these matters are still not resolved. Forgetting END

29　Examining Project Coast thus offers us a series of cautions about the expectations invested in accounts of the past.

30　One of the many reasons why writing the past does not necessarily lead to a harmonious future is that many people question whether the past should be written about at all. Even if there is accord on this matter, the issues surrounding what should be in history can lead to the resurfacing of old divisions. Forgetting 379

31　The Chronology entries that follow suggest other matters – though let us consider some of these for the moment.

32　The frequent refrain that lessons could be learnt from Project Coast has sat uncomfortably with counter claims that the past is an irrelevant aside, a distraction from current priorities, an indecipherable foreign land, etc. Lessons 498

33　Learning lessons from the past becomes highly demanding when this requires us to challenge our starting values and assumptions. As a matter such as Project Coast is thoroughly embedded in questions about national pride, personal identity and international relations, drawing lessons from it entails treading on thorny questions about who we are and what we are pursuing through the histories we assemble. Lessons 420

34　The novel format of this book is intended to underscore these considerations.

The need for such an engagement with history is evident today.

35　Around the world, people who are, and have been, engaged with memory work and formal transitional justice processes are grappling with a range of troubling issues, and a disturbing sense that no measures to reckon with the past can offer the satisfaction or resolution that is sought. Certainly, in dealing with the case of the chemical and biological warfare programme, the lofty ideals of the TRC – to prevent a recurrence of abuses, to develop a shared sense of nationhood, to acknowledge harms and to provide a complete picture of violations leading to healing – were far from met.

In 2013 and 2014, the Nelson Mandela Foundation and the Global Leadership Academy of the German Development Agency brought together memory-work practitioners from 10 countries. Some of the insights from this process included the recognition that, 'What is regarded as important to remember, and what is not, is shaped by today's interests and powerful groups within societies.' This raises the following questions: How does one determine what needs to be remembered to facilitate healing? What should be forgotten? Is there a healthy forgetting; equally, is there an unhealthy remembering? The report from these dialogues includes the observations that:

> Every society emerging from oppressive rule or conflict to a stable democracy is faced with the difficult task of fulfilling the needs of justice and healing. We also face the task of recording and representing the past in ways that fulfil the need for social justice. Yet, very often how the past is represented and dealt with is influenced, if not controlled by those holding political power, and/or past elites. We are troubled by the fear that the way in which we do memory work makes us complicit in the creation and reinforcement of a master narrative.
>
> Any public process also produces new silences and exclusions. Cross-societal dialogue is often missing, and archives can be slow to link to civil society memory work. How do you diversify the voices represented and draw attention to marginal voices?
>
> While many practitioners feel called to this work, they were also aware of their own limitations and power in many situations. Who gives the right or licence to represent the past in a particular way?
>
> They noticed that in many contexts, when governments own and create dominant narratives about the past that are supported by capital and international donors, the result does not always favour a resolution of injustice, support inclusivity or result in a reduction of hatred between former enemies.[13]

Justice 36

36 The timing of revelation and concealment is critical to what can be said and what cannot be said because it is impossible to separate individual and personal interests from national or even international processes. Much thought is now going into the timing of truth and reconciliation processes, asking whether there is or can be an ideal time for these kinds

of reckonings of the past to take place. As in the film *The Act of Killing*, the distance of time allowed for alternative representations of the history to be told. So, too, with generational change comes a distance that allows for a different type of dealing with the past – it may close certain avenues of investigation while opening others. Justice END

37   Through the innovative format and disjointed content of *The Dis-eases of Secrecy*, we have tried to provoke imaginations, interpretations and innovations related to knowing the past, while recognising the closures that necessarily accompany such moves.

SECRECY

As suggested by the previous points about history, investigations of Project Coast have been undertaken in demanding situations in which access to information has been thwarted by fraught secrets and silences.

38   What was done under Project Coast? What biological and chemical warfare capabilities were produced? To grapple with these questions is to grapple with the import of secrecy. Intentional concealment was not only central to how the programme was justified, conducted and covered up in the 1980s and early 1990s, it also continues to be central to how it is milled, dismissed and mystified today.

Scholars that examine secrets in social life often refer to them as 'paradoxical'– paradoxical in the sense that 'it is in the very nature of secrets that they get told'.[14]

At one level this quote signals the way in which discussing secrets necessarily entails discussing what is not completely hidden.

At another level though, the sharing of secrets is paradoxical because the act of sharing what is meant to be secret goes against the notion that it should not be disclosed. Thus, anyone discussing secrets must account for why it is appropriate to talk about them. As a result, the telling of secrets is often accompanied by explicit or implicit instructions that what was just told should not be repeated (further), as well as justifications for why this specific telling was legitimate. From schoolroom gossip, to the rites and rituals of initiations, to off-camera media briefings by government officials, these instructions mean that knowing how secrets are kept is a matter of knowing how they are shared. In this sense, to study secrets is to study acts of *telling*.

The intertwining of concealment and disclosure are evident in the associated word of 'secrete'. Secrete refers to acts of releasing and hiding.[15]

The bringing together of opposites is also evident in the linked term, 'transparency'. Making something transparent can refer both to making it see-through, as well as making it apparent.

Because keeping and sharing often come packaged together in secrecy, the potential for betrayal is never far away. Telling secrets becomes illegitimate when they are told to the wrong person or in the wrong situation. Yet, what counts as 'wrong' is often disputed or uncertain.

In relation to Project Coast, information about what took place was shared within a coterie and yet it could never be fully contained. The outputs of the programme – documents, samples, chemicals, equipment, weapons, experienced technicians and researchers – were subject to many suppressing efforts, but again and again they proved unruly.   What? 184

39 Consider one aspect of the demands of secrecy.

40 To keep the materials, equipment and even animal experimentation from being widely known, Project Coast operated through commercial front companies; this, in turn, meant that keeping the secrets of the project required keeping certain aspects of the programme visible to the trade.

What? 259

41 In part because of the way in which telling and sharing, concealment and revelation often come packaged, examining secrets purely in relation to their content can be very limiting. What is also needed is an appreciation of the processes and performances of secrecy. The Latin root for the English word 'secret', *secretus,* meant 'to separate' or 'set apart'. The potential to set apart is not simply or even necessarily determined by the content of what is restricted. To understand this potential, we must consider the attachments and commitments associated with being 'in the know' (or not) and 'having access' (or not). The reputational advantages of being set apart, for instance, can result in state officials limiting access to what might otherwise be regarded as trivial or mundane details.[16]   What? 145

42 A tension-ridden dynamic of secrecy, identified by scholars, is the way in which secrets are, as Johnson put it,

> perched on a fence between their conservation and their exposure. Without a desiring group, an audience of have-nots or haves, secrets would cease to exist. Their magic lies in the constant prospect of their revelation which is ultimately inevitable.[17]

This quote refers to how secret-keepers have a certain power – yet this status is temporary because it cannot be granted in perpetuity. In changing situations, the secret-keeper must be seen as holding something in reserve to be set apart. One example of this is the way in which state officials regularly refer in public to what is known only to themselves to bolster their legitimacy and diminish that of others.

As a result, the existence of secrecy (if not the content of secrets) is often paraded. To put the point differently, the hiding is often known even if the hidden is not.

The suggestion by Johnson that the revelation of secrets is 'ultimately inevitable', while overstated, speaks to the ways in which secrets are most powerful when they become known. As such, the temptation to reveal them is ever alluring.[18]

In the case of the members of Project Coast, post-apartheid secrets were often treated as forms of 'security' – waiting for a moment of revelation would protect the holder of the secret from persecution by revealing the complicity of those with higher rank.

From the points above, two observations can be made. Secrecy can be directional: it is constituted by how attention gets drawn along certain lines, thereby distracting the focus from elsewhere. Secrecy is relational too: who is seen as in the know, depends on who else knows what, when and where.[19]

Thus, to understand secrecy as practice, it is necessary to attend to how it entails both a holding on and a letting go. To know 188

43 The consequences of secret-keeping and secret-telling signal that they should be understood as transformative acts. They are bound up with the formation of individual and collective identities.[20] Some people get labelled as members of a group, others get excluded. These labels can then get marshalled as part of the wider stories about the nature of the state, etc.

To know 439

44 In addition to these general points about how we conceive of secrets and secrecy, the affective dimensions of secrecy are highly relevant for this book.

45 Talk of secrets is typically charged. Secrecy is often associated with deception, conspiracy and scandal. When it is conceived as a form of intentional concealment, secrecy acts to block access and understanding.

As a result, in relation to allegations about the excesses of statecraft, secrecy is often seen as something to be countered: this requires opening closed boxes and exposing shadowy corners. What? 316

46 As we have experienced, those investigating the past can get pulled along by the promise of exposing.

47 The hint of a secret, of untold stories and unfinished business, and the possibility that one is on the verge of answers is what often draws an

investigator into an investigation and holds them there. It is a belief that the view will change spectacularly around the next corner – that a truth hitherto uncovered will emerge. And yet, in practice, an investigation into a troubled past is often a slow collection of fragments that together create a somewhat blurry image than stumbling upon the answers.   Legacies 202

48 Through this book, we intend to take you on the trail with us, let you feel for a time – we hope, the lure of what could be revealed if one dug just a little deeper into the fragments. Some of these fragments are drawn from investigative diaries, some from the TRC hearings; while others are drawn from statements and affidavits, from documents and the testimony from the criminal trial of Wouter Basson, which led to his acquittal.   Legacies 535

4 9   SILENCE

A discussion of secrecy invites a discussion of silence. Secrecy is typically seen as maintained through acts of silence, and a state of silence can foster suspicions that deliberate concealment is afoot.

However, while we suggested the need to treat secrecy as a complex phenomenon, the same applies to silence.

50 Silence is often defined as an absence: the lack of sound or speech. In the most commonplace usage, 'to silence' is to produce an absence – a muteness or omission. What cannot be said, what is marginalised and what is made too costly to pronounce are all forms of silence.

And yet, silences are poorly understood as simply being holes, lacks or devoid spaces. Instead, however, they can be highly generative in fostering certain kinds of relations.   To know 497 | Silence 500

51 In *The Dis-eases of Secrecy*, we are interested in how silence is formed by and pervades the practices of diplomacy, politics and scientific research.[21] As part of this endeavour, in moving silence beyond a notion of lack, we explore its varieties. Along these lines consider the following points:

52 What counts as a silence is variable and the significance of what is defined under this label is patterned across cultures and situations. Thus, the question, 'What is being silenced?' needs to give way to more sociologically aware questions like, 'Silent for whom?', 'When?' and 'In what manner?'.   Silence 409 | To know 53

53 For gaps to be noted as silences in the first place requires meaning to be imparted to them. For instance, governments can fail to speak about certain policy matters for years. To turn this situation into a recognised instance of non-speaking can require considerable effort.[22] This is another

way of saying that silences are normatively accountable departures from expectations.[23] Formulated in this way, audiences to silences should be understood as playing a role in their enactment. To know 494

54 Once the importance of audiences is acknowledged, some points follow on.

55 Silences can have a diversity of meanings. To be silent can be intended or interpreted as a way of demonstrating deference or defiance, giving or avoiding giving offence, as well as displaying or suppressing emotion. It can also be a defence against an expected retaliation or unwanted consequence. In this way, silence is pregnant with possibility. In terms of function in relation to social knowledge, silences can both frustrate and facilitate intersubjective agreement, act as a mark of expertise or of ignorance; as well as stifle the exchange of ideas or proliferate meanings.

Silence 407 | To know 485

56 How can inquiry be made into silences? How is it possible to come to terms with topics that raise awkward questions – at least for some – of complacency or complicity? How can engagement be made with the factors that delimit understanding?

One way to do this is to attend to one's objectives. Rather than seeking to describe the world 'as is', inquiry can adopt the goal of trying to positively transform silences. What is needed for this is not just a good explanation or theory, but the development of practical knowledge that speaks to the conditions in which individuals find themselves. To achieve this development demands an approach that is open to experimentation, one that can learn what is needed. It is also likely to require multiple cycles of planning, action, observation and reflection that seek to improve situations.

This general orientation to research is at least indirectly promoted in many social science funding agencies in recent times with their growing emphasis on 'impact'. As noted by the leading funder of social research in the United Kingdom, the Economic and Social Research Council (ESRC), impact is vital because:

> In recent years, the government has placed increasing emphasis on the need for evidence of economic and social returns from its investment in research. By ensuring that ESRC-funded research makes the biggest possible impact on policy and practice, and improving how we measure and capture this, we are better able to support the case for research funding. Impact helps to demonstrate that social science is important – that it is worth investing in and worth using.[24]

But given that diplomat policy and practice is often both slow to develop and is often hidden from public view, impact may often be difficult to discern. Silence 410

57 It may be regarded as fine in the abstract to acknowledge that attempts to speak about silences are consequential interventions into the world, to take as a goal for research more than describing the world 'as is', and to undertake multiple cycles of observation and reflection in the promotion of transformation. Such positions though beg a question of some importance: what are the legitimate bounds for inquiry? Silence 474

58 The speculative format of this book is motivated, in part, as a technique for exploring the bounds of inquiry and the limits of knowing.

DISCOURSE

When writing history involves sticking labels on events and individuals, the words that are used matter. Words also matter when testimonials are gathered as the basis for histories.

The gravity of language, combined with the scope for dispute about it, suggests the need for careful consideration of how language is conceived. 59 In studying social life, two contrasting orientations can be adopted towards the statements made by individuals.[25]

First, they can be taken as (more-or-less believable) accounts that serve as a resource for building arguments about what really happened. The reasoning offered by science professionals about why they did what they did, for instance, could be taken as accurate or inaccurate, sufficient or insufficient representations of their motivations. In this process, other evidence could be collected to triangulate conclusions about what really unfolded. These arguments could be marshalled to build concepts, frameworks and theories.

Second, instead of orientating to statements as representations of the world, they can be approached as a consequential form of action. In what is often referred to as a 'discursive' orientation, depictions of the world are treated as accounts given in a specific setting that should be examined for their meaning within that setting. Here, the 'task is to see how those accounts are constructed, how and when they are produced as explanations, how they are designed and positioned with regard to alternative accounts, and in what interaction sequences they are produced'.[26] The statements given by individuals can be examined for how they help form a sense of identities and situations, rather than as representations of the world.

When examining Project Coast then, it is possible to adopt different orientations to accounts given by those involved. These can be taken as inputs for making claims about what really took place or as materials to be examined for how they are 'rhetorically organised, construct the nature of the events, assemble description and narrative, and make attributional inferences available'.[27] Forgetting 508

60   As another way of stating the distinction, in the second approach the use of language becomes the topic of focus.

The Dis-eases of Secrecy adopts both orientations to construct a history of Project Coast, but also to question how histories get constructed. One of the ways in which the 'discursive' orientation is pursued is in relation to the moral standing of chemical and biological weapons. We are interested in how the claims about weaponry and humanity are advanced.

61   How to set humanity and military necessity against each other has been fraught in modern times, as the limits of what is acceptable in a state of war have shifted along with technological developments. Total war 84

62   Why are some means of killing and injuring deemed worse than anothers? Why are some labelled as abhorrent and others as 'conventional'? Scholars of modern arms control and disarmament have often approached such moral 'why' questions by turning them into 'how' ones. How have interests, ideas and power figured within efforts to negotiate conventions and treaties? How have domestic and international groups in civil society influenced decisions? How have states and non-state groups scrutinised one another's conduct? Through examining such questions, it is possible to detail the way in which certain weapons get labelled as 'inhumane', 'abhorrent', etc. It is also possible to identify the assumptions informing evaluations and labels. IR 78

63   These assumptions can inform a stark conclusion in line with discursive approaches to language.

64   Rather than condemnations of chemical and biological weapons being based on a fixed sense of what was inherently deplorable, condemnations have depended on perceptions about the rights and wrongs of who uses what against whom and in what sort of situations.[28] IR 87 | Victims 446

65   During the undertaking and subsequent investigations into Project Coast, perhaps no labels were so charged as 'offensive' and 'defensive'. These were treated as straightforward bywords for judgments, insinuations and accusations.

In many instances, however, it was not clear what these tags were supposed to mean. Offence 66

66   The label of 'defensive' was often positioned as a protective covering

17

against reproach. For instance, this term and related notions served as rationales for the development of chemical and biological warfare capabilities – this prior to the start of Project Coast, during it and afterwards.   Offence 154

67   For some, defence served as a basis for (more-or-less qualified) moral justification for their involvement in the programme.   Offence 263

68   Doing 'defence' meant being able to readily position one's work as serving to protect from harm.

69   In contrast, 'offensive' and related labels were almost always applied as a way of signalling the perversions of what took place under apartheid South Africa.   Offence 319

70   Whatever those producing undetectable means of killing might have felt about their work in the 1980s and early 1990s, by the time formal investigations began into Project Coast in post-apartheid South Africa, there was little public space for justifying the assassinations of those fighting apartheid.

71   The choice of which label to use to describe one's activities, and the way in which labels get understood, often depend on the purposes for which these labels are offered.

72   The Biological Weapons Convention (BWC) forbids the use of biological agents and toxins for non-peaceful or non-defensive purposes.

73   As a signatory to the BWC treaty, in theory, many of the activities that took place under Project Coast should have brought prominent international condemnation to South Africa. They did not. As will be seen later in this book, part of the reason why these activities were not condemned was because of how the diplomats, civil servants and others labelled the programme.

74   Even if there had been uncontested evidence that many people had suffered and died as a result of the technologies developed as part of Project Coast, for some, this would not have implied that the programme should be deemed 'offensive'.   Offence 106

75   Appreciating the grounds for dispute about chemical and biological warfare capabilities – what they are and how this can be established – provides reasons for hesitation regarding how to proceed with the investigation of a programme such as Project Coast.

If labels are disputable, an alternative line of inquiry to figure out which is the best one, would be to examine when these labels get invoked and with what consequences.   Offence 9

76   This is one of the aims of *The Dis-eases of Secrecy*.

CHRONOLOGY

77 The 'holiest of the holy' is a phrase reserved to describe the innermost sanctuary of many ancient religious temples. As in the architecture of the Temple of Edfu in Egypt, these sanctuaries were nestled within other rooms. Access was tightly restricted to only the select few. These sanctuaries – or so the high priests assured everyone – contained the most treasured artefacts and scripts; instruments for knowing the divine.   What? END

78 Evidence of disagreement about the rights and wrongs of conflict is as old as the record of conflict. Ancient Greek and Roman civilisations debated the morality of contaminating water supplies, driving enemy troops into mosquito-infested areas and deliberately poisoning people.[29] These debates were not only about the means but also about the subjects; in other words, who was a legitimate target of attack.   IR 79

79 The limited recourse to poisons and diseases since ancient times illustrates how the means of warfare have not been unlimited in practice.

And yet, the periodic use of disease and poison also illustrates that the moral condemnation has not been absolute.[30] During the siege of the Crimean city of Caffa in 1346, Tartars loaded plague-infected cadavers onto catapults and hurled them over the city walls; an event often (but probably incorrectly) identified as leading to the spread of the Black Death throughout North Africa, the Near East and Europe in the mid-14th century.[31] Better documented, in the 18th century, Sir Jeffrey Amherst ordered one of his British generals to spread smallpox among the tribes in the Ohio–Pennsylvania region by distributing infected blankets. During the American Civil War, Confederate forces poisoned wells with the carcasses of infectious animals, etc.   IR 80

80   1868

Modern attempts to devise formal international agreements to limit the weapons of war can be traced back to the 1868 Declaration of St Petersburg in Russia.

In expressing the shared recognition of the need to consider the 'limits at which the necessities of war ought to yield to the requirements of humanity', the assembled governments concluded that exploding bullets had crossed the threshold.   Total war 61 | IR 81

81   The Declaration of St Pietersburg would prove a precedent for later legal prohibitions.[32]   IR 82

82   1899

Under the initiative of Nicholas II, the Czar of Russia, the First Hague Peace Conference was held in 1899. Twenty-six governments convened 'with the object of seeking the most effective means of ensuring to all peoples the benefits of a real and lasting peace, and, above all, of limiting the progressive development of existing armaments'.[33] A convention on land warfare was established, wherein, under Declaration II, the 'Contracting Powers' agreed to: 'abstain from the use of projectiles the object of which is the diffusion of asphyxiating or deleterious gases' – a provision ratified by all major powers save the United States.

As suggested by the term 'Contracting Powers', this declaration as well as other agreements reached were treated as contracts: this meant that they were not deemed to apply to non-contracted parties.   IR 83

83   1915

Whatever the formal contracts pre-World War I, after the first use of chlorine gas in warfare by the Germans at Ypres in Belgium, persistent, lethal and harassing chemical agents were deployed on a wide scale. While at Ypres, German troops carried thousands of cylinders to the front by hand, by the time the Great War ended, nearly 2 000 tons of chlorine, mustard gas, phosgene and other chemicals had been produced and incorporated into varied forms of delivery systems, which affected over one million individuals – leaving them blinded, burnt, scarred or dead.

Within the militaries and publics of Western Europe, much debate ensued during the war about the appropriateness of chemical weapons, in part because of their perceived indiscriminate effects on combatants and non-combatants alike. While relatively few of those exposed to chemical weapons died, at least for many, of all the methods of injury developed during the war, chemical weapons were regarded as different.[34]

84   1918

The predicaments and troubles associated with labelling certain weapons as 'inhumane' or 'abhorrent' would come to the fore after World War I in relation to how the setting apart of chemical weapons from other means of killing was reinterpreted.

As Jenkins details, post-war chemical weaponry became a site of investment – financial and symbolic. The possibilities for novel forms of weapons enabled by developments in chemistry and aeronautics – or so advocates claimed – meant the world was on the cusp of a radical transformation. This would not bring heightened levels of barbarity but the elevated prospering of humanity.[35]

The potential attached to new forms of killing was summed up in the 1921 US Chemical Warfare Service motto: 'Every development of Science that makes warfare more universal and more scientific makes for permanent peace by making warfare more intolerable.' Save for certain savages or outlaws for whom chemical warfare would need to be reserved, naturally, the promise was that war would come to an end because it *would have to* come to an end.

The idea that achieving destructiveness could serve as a basis for ensuring peace was an echo of previous contentions made about bows, artillery pieces and tanks.[36] The idea would be echoed later in the 20th century with respect to the nuclear retaliation policy of 'mutually assured destruction'.[37]

In the case of chemical weapons though, whatever the overall promise for humanity in the end, proponents were keen to awaken and advance the interests of their own nations. Scenarios of the annihilation of cities from chemical weapons dropped by German fighter bombers, flying thousands of miles over the Atlantic, were used in the United States to argue that the government needed to stay ahead in the arms race. Only by being on the cutting edge of new powers could the nightmare of total war (against the United States) become the fantasy of total control (by the United States). What was needed were domestic policies to subsidise the chemical industries at home and foreign policies to suppress competitor industries – naturally.[38]

85   Post-World War I, those countries setting to limit the recourse to chemical weapons (as well as fledging effort to develop biological weapons)[39] also set them apart from other 'conventional' weapons. In contrast with attempts to fit them into a narrative of the progress of humanity though, detractors portrayed chemical weapons as a sign of

inhumanity. Organisations such as the International Committee of the Red Cross argued that these were 'barbarous inventions'[40] likely to devastate civilian populations, which generated a deep psychological aversion. As a result of this, developments in science required forms of international control.

IR 86

86 1925

Contrasting logics for chemical and biological weapons were deliberated in forums such as the 1919 Paris Peace Conference and the Washington Naval Conference of 1921–1922.

With the signing of the 1925 Protocol for the Prohibition of the Use in War of Asphyxiating, Poisonous or other Gases, and of Bacteriological Methods of Warfare (or the 'Geneva Protocol'), those demanding additional constraints secured what amounted to a 'no-first-use' pact for chemical and biological weapons.

Although the international agreements reached were significant at the time, the nature and extent of the condemnation was open to question. Against whom the chemical weapons could be used was one of the questions. Just as the Hague Declarations did not apply to non-contracting powers, countries such as the United Kingdom and France added a similar reservation to their support for the Geneva Protocol. In effect, these qualifications introduced a split between those nations it was deemed acceptable to subject to chemical attack and those it was not.

In addition, chemical attack on certain signatories to the Geneva Protocol was not always condemned. For example, Ethiopia ratified the Protocol in 1935, but when Italian forces used chemical weapons against it in 1935–1936, only muted international condemnation followed.   IR 119

87 As scholars of chemical and biological weapons have argued, violations of, or exclusions from, international agreements should not lead to the conclusion that these agreements are irrelevant in practice. Emerging stigmas and norms between the wars affected the extent and nature of the funding of offensive programmes, the calculations of the likely military retaliations and political ramifications of their use, and the willingness of military commanders to incorporate these in their arsenals.[41]

In turn, the repeated portrayal of some weapons as 'beyond the pale', over time had wide-ranging consequences for how their use was understood.[42] For instance, the stigma attached to certain weapons has affected whether they were judged to be compatible with 'military culture'. This then affected the militaries' resource allocation for these weapons, which, in turn, affected their use in practice. In these ways, norms 'enter into, and change, the cost–benefit calculations of interests but... they also help to constitute those interests, identities and practices in the first place. Interests and international norms may coincide, but this coincidence does not render norms superfluous.'[43]   IR 88

88   1941

It is notable that even in the near 'total war' situation that characterised World War II, chemical and biological weapons were treated as distinct from other weapons. Except for the Japanese actions in China, there was general restraint in their use. Much of this was tied up with the international identity of states and what it meant at the time to be a 'civilised' nation. US President Roosevelt famously said of chemical weapons that the 'use of such weapons has been outlawed by the general opinion of civilized mankind'.[44]   Total war 119 | IR 89

89   More than this, in many countries, offensive capabilities were neglected and offensive preparations limited.[45] For instance, the United Kingdom made chemical defensive preparations only shortly before war and had only limited capabilities during it. In only two instances – in the case of the German invasion and as a retaliation for V-rocket bombings – did the British government seriously plan to use chemical weapons.[46]

To say preparations and plans were limited is not to say they were non-existent. To aid the British forces in the event of chemical war, South Africa set up two factories, in collaboration with Britain, dedicated to the production of mustard gas and phosphine.[47] After the war, the mustard gas was dumped into the sea.   IR 90

90   Crucial to understanding the importance of stigmas and norms is their relation to conceptions of state identity. When the possession and use of certain weapons is incompatible with the identity a country wishes to foster at home or abroad, this can influence conduct.   IR 91

91   1948

In the years following World War II, chemical and biological weapons occupied a fraught place in the arsenals of states as they struggled to make sense of and come to terms with their destructive potential. This was when the term 'weapons of mass destruction' was first coined. In 1948, a commission of the United Nations, tasked with reducing and regulating non-atomic weapons, defined weapons of mass destruction as:

> atomic explosive weapons, radio-active material weapons, lethal chemical and biological weapons, and any weapons developed in the future which have characteristics comparable in destructive effect to those of the atomic bomb or other weapons mentioned above.[48]

Through this labelling, both chemical and biological weapons were grouped with the most severe options available at the time. This set them apart from most of the weapons held by militaries. And yet, whatever the exhibited reluctance to use chemical and biological weapons, in the decades after World War II, the major military powers such as the United States, the United Kingdom and the Soviet Union sought offensive capabilities for chemical and biological warfare.   IR 92

92 In the 1940s, 1950s and 1960s, determinations of what and whether these capabilities should be developed were subject to the play of the perceptions of interests, threats, resources and identities of and between states. The morality of chemical and biological weapons, as well as the control measures that were justifiable, were worked out in relation to evolving local and historical circumstances.   IR 93

93 One such historical shift was the increase in the number of states that had the ability or potential to develop weapons. With the growth of scientific industries worldwide and the movement of equipment and people, chemical and biological weapons were no longer the preserve of a few states. Price has argued that as the capabilities for producing chemical weapons spread over time, the regard for them within highly industrialised states changed. While initially the development of chemical weapons was cited by some as a sign of a progressive and humane state, over time this gave way to the opposite view – that refraining from the possession of such weapons was a sign of what constituted 'being civilised'.[49] In short, preventing the 'proliferation' of these weapons became what was expected of states.   IR 97

94 1948

Symbolically, politically, economically, socially and in so many other respects, the system of apartheid was a system of marking difference. Racial groups were positioned in relation to one another and within a hierarchy. Individuals were defined not only through the racial grouping they were ascribed, but also by the ones they were not.   Total war 95

95 1948

The system of segregation in place between 1948 and 1994 relied on a simple racial classification.

Tick one: White [ ], Coloured [ ], African [ ], Indian [ ].

A label was affixed to every individual, which significantly defined their opportunities. However, because many people cannot and would not be boxed in and defined by a tidy classification, implementing apartheid entailed social engineering to create a South Africa that fitted the classification system. This meant pervasive attempts to eliminate sources of 'contamination'.

Imposing huge resource demands on the country and even greater consequences for its people, laws were policed on who could live or work next to whom, who could marry or sleep with whom, and who could urinate next to whom. Day-to-day social interactions were positioned as a front to prevent pollution. Total war 115

96 1960

South Africa's interest in chemical weapons during World War II was rekindled in 1960, when the company Mechem was established. It served as a chemical defence unit under the Department of Trade and Industry and was tasked with keeping a watching brief on chemical and biological warfare threats to the nation.[50] IR 90

97 1963

Nearly 40 years after South Africa became party to the 1925 Geneva Protocol, it still maintained reservations: the Protocol should only be binding on those states that had ratified or acceded to it, and its obligations were not binding on states and their allies that had not. These reservations would be withdrawn in 1996. IR 100

98 1966

The appointment of PW Botha as Minister of Defence in 1966 signalled a change in the understanding of the security situation, both in South Africa and in the southern African region. Instead of focusing on threats directed at South Africa, Botha espoused a broader vision of security, encompassing the global, East–West ideological conflict and South Africa's role in it. Three themes predominated in his speeches: that the West was threatened by Soviet expansionism; that South Africa was part of the West; and that the Soviet strategy was to cut Europe off from South Africa's essential raw materials.[51] Seegers says that this was not a departure from National Party thinking, but a solidification of that thinking. Since 1958, the National Party had believed that 'South Africa had an important role to play in the Cold War, both as a strategic geopolitical asset of the West (because of its position in terms of the Cape sea route), and as a provider of strategic assets such as minerals and labour. Their anti-communist theme was to remain in place well into the 1980s.'[52]

South Africa's neighbouring states were important in Botha's security thinking: they were South Africa's first line of defence against Soviet expansionism. In the late 1960s, the South African government concluded security agreements with Portugal and Rhodesia, so that Angola, Mozambique and Rhodesia became South Africa's front line. Influenced by the findings of the Potgieter Commission of Inquiry, Botha drew no distinction between the external conflict on the country's northern borders and the internal conflict. He argued that the external conflict was merely an extension of the internal war between his government and the South African liberation movements. The Potgieter Commission had concluded that: 'it is no secret that the enemies of the Republic are trying to attack in all fields',[53] and argued that South Africa was faced by a 'total onslaught' from beyond its borders, and recommended the adoption of a 'total national strategy'.[54]

99 1960s

When initially deployed during the 1960s, CS gas was justified as a way of saving lives. Commonly referred to as 'tear gas', this irritant would be employed 'only in those situations involving riot control or situations analogous to riot control'.[55] After some initial use in Vietnam by the US military, the remit for CS gas expanded to include the separation of combatants from non-combatants. As the 1960s progressed, other varied purposes were found for it. These included harassing enemy soldiers in combat, forcing Vietnamese fighters out of underground hideouts (sometimes followed by conventional bombing raids) and rendering areas uninhabitable. Between 1964 and 1970, almost 16 million pounds of CS were procured.[56]   Total war 121

100 1972

The signing of the Biological Weapons Convention (BWC) in 1972 represented a major achievement of the international community. The BWC prohibits the development, production, acquisition, transfer, retention and stockpiling of any biological and toxin-carrying weapon. The categorical nature of this ban was not only a historical precedent at the time the convention came into force in 1975, but it remains unsurpassed today as a legal agreement.

As depositaries of the BWC, the United States, United Kingdom and the United Soviet Socialist Republic (the USSR, now the Russian Federation) are entrusted with it.   IR 129 | Silence 108

101 Within the international community, whether activities are properly labelled as 'defensive' or 'offensive' can be fraught because of the unsettled debate about the exact nature of obligations under the Biological Weapons Convention.   Offence 105

102 1972

Preface and Article I of the Biological Weapons Convention

The States Parties to this Convention,
Determine to act with a view to achieving effective progress toward general and complete disarmament, including the prohibition and elimination of all types of weapons of mass destruction, and convinced that the

prohibition of the development, production and stockpiling of chemical and bacteriological (biological) weapons and their elimination, through effective measures, will facilitate the achievement of general and complete disarmament under strict and effective control...

Determined, for the sake of all mankind, to exclude completely the possibility of bacteriological (biological) agents and toxins being used as weapons,

Convinced that such use would be repugnant to the conscience of mankind and that no effort should be spared to minimize this risk, Have agreed as follows:

Article I

Each State Party to this Convention undertakes never in any circumstance to develop, produce, stockpile or otherwise acquire or retain:

Microbial or other biological agents, or toxins whatever their origin or method of production, of types and in quantities that have no justification for prophylactic, protective or other peaceful purposes;

Weapons, equipment or means of delivery designed to use such agents or toxins for hostile purposes or in armed conflict.   IR 62

103 1972

In establishing a wide-ranging prohibition against using science and technology to deliberately spread disease, the Biological Weapons Convention allows signatories to undertake steps to defend themselves against attacks. Yet the distinction between biodefence and bio-offence is not always a matter of accord.   Offence 104

104 Allegations have been raised from time to time about whether some activities named as defensive have, in fact, aided offensive ends.   Offence 128

105 Some of the deliberation around the Biological Weapons Convention (BWC) over the years has turned on 'who was the object of attack'. In the case of South Africa, since Project Coast was largely aimed at attacking the African National Congress (ANC) and its supporters, many did not see it in the same light as other state programmes. At least some of the officials perceived 'offensive', in terms of the BWC, as the use of weapons against other states.   Offence 447

106 The past provides many examples of where the classification of a chemical and biological warfare programme has been a matter of controversy.   Offence 107

Assassination has long been a tool of statecraft, albeit a contentious one.

For instance, a prominent investigation in 1975 by the US Senate Church Committee found that the assassination of foreign leaders had been an option covertly pursued by agencies of the United States.

Perhaps the most famous example of this, were the repeated attempts to kill Fidel Castro during his time as Prime Minister and President of Cuba.[57] The many and varied plots hatched included the use of pills incorporating a neurotoxic botulinum, a diving suit contaminated with the bacterium that causes tuberculosis, and a fountain pen containing a deadly toxin.   Offence 108

108   As part of the political obligations on governments to exclude the possibility of using biological agents and toxins as weapons, those party to the Biological Weapons Convention are required to complete a Confidence Building Measure, Form F, each year. This pertains to their past offensive and defensive research and development programmes.   Offence 109 | Silence 110

109   As agreed at the Second Review Conference to the Biological Weapons Convention (BWC), in 'order to prevent or reduce the occurrence of ambiguities, doubts and suspicions, and in order to improve international cooperation in the field of peaceful biological activities', parties to the BWC are required to note their offensive biological research and development activities since 1 January 1946 as part of their annual Confidence Building Measure declarations.   Offence 111

110   For many years, States Parties to the Biological Weapons Convention have argued that the Confidence Building Measures serve the purposes of enhancing transparency and building confidence in the treaty.   Silence 471

111   Should the US assassination attempts be declared under the Confidence Building Measures of the Biological Weapons Convention then?

In relation to the distinction between offensive and defensive activities, one way of considering the question, 'What is it?' is by asking 'where' the qualities of offensiveness or defensiveness are located. Does this happen by assessing individual parts of a programme or by looking at the bigger picture and the whole range of activities underway?   Offence 278

112   It is possible that the first use of chemical agents by the South African military took place in 1972, before the establishment of Project Coast. This was revealed in testimony before the 1973 United States Subcommittee on Africa in the House of Representatives. This committee considered testimony regarding the implementation of the US arms embargo against Portugal and South Africa. Testimony was given about the sale of herbicides and aircraft to South Africa and Portugal, which had

been reported in a British newspaper, the *Sunday Times*, the previous year. In this report, details were given of an operation undertaken by South African mercenaries and the Portuguese Air Force to spray defoliants over rebel-held areas in Mozambique.[58] It appears that the use of defoliants was restricted to this incident and the single use of a commercial herbicide, Hyvar X, in the Caprivi Strip, because the South African Defence Force (SADF) believed that guerrillas used the thick plant growth to hide their weapons-smuggling activities.[59]

113 The South African focus on the development of covert chemical and biological agents as assassination weapons was not unique. Indeed, thinking about such agents may have been influenced by programmes of the US Central Intelligence Agency (CIA), particularly the clandestine Operation MKNAOMI, which was initiated in 1967.[60] A Select Committee of Congress, held during 1973, found that the CIA had developed a covert programme with the following objectives:

- To provide for a covert support base to meet clandestine operational requirements.
- To stockpile severely incapacitating and lethal materials for the specific use of the TSD [Technical Services Division].
- To maintain in operational readiness special and unique items for the dissemination of biological and chemical materials.
- To provide for the required surveillance, testing, upgrading, and evaluation of materials and items in order to assure absence of defects and complete predictability of results to be expected under operational conditions.[61]

The objectives of Project Coast, as articulated in a 1990 document authored by Basson and signed by the Chief of the Defence Force, General Jannie Geldenhuys, demonstrate remarkable similarities to those presented above:

The goal of Project Coast is to, in a covert and clandestine matter, conduct research and development and to establish the production technology in the sensitive and critical areas of chemical and biological warfare to provide the South African Defence Force with a CBW capability in line with the CBW philosophy and strategy.[62]

In this document, Basson spelt out the goals of Project Coast in more detail, stating that these goals included the 'support of CBW operations (offensive and defensive) carried out by security forces'. He explained that such operations fell into two categories: 'conventional' and 'covert', the latter 'provided to MD [Managing Director] Special Forces and his organisations, CSI [Chief of Staff Intelligence] and his organisations, the SAP and National Intelligence. This service includes the preparation of equipment, training in the use thereof, the transport thereof, as well as support during use.'[63]

It is evident that the intention of Project Coast was to provide covert chemical and biological weapons for use by the intelligence services, much like the intention of the CIA's covert programme of the 1960s. This CIA programme was publicly revealed in a series of Senate Committee hearings between 1975 and 1977, which sought to determine: (1) why the CIA developed quantities of lethal biological poisons; (2) why these poisons were retained for five years after their destruction was ordered by President Nixon; and (3) why their retention had remained undetected.[64] This programme, which was associated with the Special Operations Division of the Army Biological Laboratory at Fort Detrick, had as its chief objectives the:

[M]aintenance of a stockpile of temporary incapacitating and lethal agents in readiness for operational use; assessment and maintenance of biological and chemical dissemination systems for operational use; adaptation and testing of a non-discernable microbioinoculator – a dart device for clandestine and imperceptible inoculation with biological warfare of chemical warfare agents – for use with various materials and to assure that the microbioinoculator could not be easily detected by later examination of the target; and providing technical support and consultation on request for offensive and defensive biological warfare and chemical warfare.[65]

The objectives of the CIA programme are strikingly like those of the South African chemical and biological weapons (CBW) programme. It seems likely that Basson was influenced by the nature of the US programme in conceptualising the function of the South African one. However, it is also possible that the objectives of a clandestine CBW programme for special operations are likely to be the same anywhere.

114 1974

The structural changes in the state machinery took place at a time of rising political pressures inside South Africa and in the region. The fall of the Portuguese government in April 1974, and the consequent rise to power of revolutionary governments in Angola and Mozambique, combined with the struggle for liberation in Rhodesia, 'traumatised the apartheid regime in Pretoria'.[66]

115   The setting apart, demanded under apartheid, would become seen as necessitating actions not only within South Africa's borders, but also outside of it. Ensuring internal order – what was characterised as making non-negotiable 'the principle of the right of self-determination of the white nation'[67] – necessitated ensuring a conducive external order. As the two were parts of the same challenge, the more effort was required for the former, meant the more effort required for the latter. A 1975 Defence White Paper characterised the 'economic, ideological, technological, and even social' mobilisations required as amounting to a 'total strategy'.[68]

Total war 427

PW Botha became one of the key definers of this notion and one of those responsible for turning it into official government policy. First as Minister of Defence from 1968 and then as Prime Minister from 1978, he articulated a vision of security that implicated South Africa as a key battleground in the global Cold War between East and West. In this vision, in 1973, maintaining white-dominated rule was presented as a way of avoiding the influence of Communism and its 'cohorts – leftist activists, exaggerated humanism, permissiveness, materialism and related ideologies' in South Africa and, indeed, in the 'Free World' as a whole.[69]

In this vision, South Africa's neighbours represented sites for global power struggles as well as buffers against internal Communism. With the conflicts in Angola, Mozambique and Zimbabwe – each eventually resulting in colonial independence from the mid-1970s to 1980 – the total strategy would eventually become portrayed as a *response* to a 'total onslaught'.

In turn, external conflict shaped the understanding of those closer to home. The African National Congress, the South West People's Organisation, and other such cohorts were positioned as agents for Moscow.

In response to the total onslaught, General Magnus Malan as Minister of Defence would argue in 1981 that the 'security of the Republic of South Africa must be maintained by every possible means at our disposal. Therefore the SADF must be prepared to guarantee orderly government by maintaining law and order and securing the country's borders' and even 'be prepared at all times to ensure the security of the territory of the Republic of South Africa by taking offensive pro-active steps'.[70] Total war 427

116   1975

According to the 1975 Defence White Paper, the 'total strategy' needed in response to the 'total onslaught' from beyond South Africa's borders was to include 'economic, ideological, technological, and even social matters',[71] in developing a defence against the threat. The theory of 'total strategy', originally put forward by the French general, André Beaufre, was based on his experiences in World War II and the Indochina War. Beaufre saw a role for politicians in the development of military strategy. He argued that a war could be won through the effective coordination of all elements of the state with a single purpose – to engage the enemy on all fronts: military, economic, psychological and political. Beaufre's thesis was considered so important in South Africa that it became the basis of lectures on strategy at the Joint Defence College.[72] The primary objective of 'total strategy' was to ensure the survival of a society in which 'the principle of the right of self-determination of the white nation must not be regarded as being negotiable'.[73] The South African government, its security forces and its electorate (most white South Africans) saw themselves as being at war with whoever opposed this 'right', that is, at war with the majority of South Africans and most of the world. In the preface to his 1973 Defence White Paper, Botha said:

> The Republic of South Africa is a target for international communism and its cohorts – leftist activists, exaggerated humanism, permissiveness, materialism and related ideologies. In addition, the RSA has been singled out as a special target for the by-products of their ideologies, such as black radicalism, exaggerated individual freedom, one-man-one-vote, and a host of other slogans employed against us on the basis of double standards... Because the RSA holds a position of strategic importance, these ideological attacks on the RSA are progressively being converted into more tangible action in the form of sanctions, boycotts, isolation, demonstrations and the like. This renders us – and the Free World – the more vulnerable to the indirect strategy applied by the radical powers in the form of undermining activities and limited violence, whether employed openly or dissimulated behind ideological fronts.[74]

117 The war in Mozambique began shortly after the country won independence from Portugal in 1975. The Mozambican Liberation Front, Frelimo, which had gained political control of the country, aligned itself with the Zimbabwean liberation struggle, providing Zimbabwean guerrillas with refuge. The white Rhodesian government responded by supporting the Mozambican National Resistance, which later became known as Renamo, in its fight against the Frelimo government.

118   When Zimbabwe gained independence in 1980, support for Renamo shifted from the Rhodesian to the South African military. Under the guidance of the South African Military Intelligence, Renamo became a fighting force to be reckoned with, resulting in a conflict that, despite peace talks in 1984, continued until a cease-fire was signed between Mozambique and South Africa in October 1992.[75]

119   1975

It was not until the mid-1970s that the United States ratified the 1925 Geneva Protocol. This was after it had been accused of violating the international customary norm set by it because of its use of gas, napalm and herbicides in Vietnam.[76] In contrast, the US government argued these chemicals were outside the scope of the Protocol. This claim was made despite initial agreements in the 1930s that agents such as tear gas and herbicides were included within its scope.[77] American officials also argued that such weapons might provide a more humane option in certain settings.[78] When the United States did ratify the Geneva Protocol, this was done with various provisos, which allowed the use of harassing chemical agents in defensive military actions.   IR 120 | Total war 99

120   Despite the potential importance of emerging norms to constrain or condition action, these cannot determine it in a straightforward manner. What it means to adhere to a norm, like what counts as following a rule, must always be negotiated at some level. What it means to follow or deviate from norms, as well as the likely consequences from their transgression, are matters that must be managed. In this sense, norms are not so much standards for guiding action, as resources on which to draw to account for and give meaning to actions.   IR 64

121   1976

According to prominent police and defence force leaders in South Africa at the time, efforts to build a chemical-weapon capacity in the mid-1970s were launched for two reasons: to provide defensive protection for SADF troops abroad and to provide the police force with crowd-control options at home. As the former police forensics chief, General Lothar Neethling, contended at the Truth and Reconciliation Commission: 'When the riots started in 1976, the South African Police were caught unawares. They had nothing apart from guns, shotguns, and sharp-point ammunition. Nobody wanted to use that and that's why there was a search for various techniques...'[79]

The riots in 1976 included a series of protests in the township of Soweto by high-school students against the use Afrikaans as a medium of instruction in schools, among other things. As one source recounted, during the initial protest march, students 'were met by heavily armed police who fired teargas and later live ammunition on demonstrating students. This resulted in a widespread revolt that turned into an uprising against the government.'[80]

122 A document entitled *Current Anti-riot Chemicals*,[81] written by the then head of the Council for Scientific and Industrial Research's (CSIR's) Applied Chemistry Unit in September 1976, states that o-chlorobenzylidene malononitrile (CS) was used in South Africa for anti-riot purposes and that it was available in pyrotechnic smoke munitions, grenades and cartridges, and that equipment had been developed for dispersing it in powder form from aircraft. The document states that there were four chemicals that could be used as anti-riot agents:

> Chloracetophenone, Phenacyl chloride (CN), o-Chlorobenzylidene malononitrile (CS), Diphenylamine chlorasine, (Adamsite or DM) and Dibenzoxazepine (CR), all of which are standard anti-riot agents. At the time the Chemical Defence Unit (CDU) had in stock some 150 kg of CN and 1.5 kg of DM (Adamsite). CS was manufactured at the time by AECI for the Armament Corps, and CR had been manufactured in a very small quantity by the Chemical Defence Unit.[82]

Project Coast later engaged in the large-scale production and weaponisation of dibenzoxazepine (CR). De Villiers and his team at the CSIR had begun to lay the basis for the initiation of a chemical-warfare programme, although this may not have been their intention.

By mid-1977, it seems that there was an increased interest in chemical and biological warfare in the SADF. At the time, De Villiers authored a chapter in the SADF's *Manual for the SADF Command System, Volume I: National security and total war"*[83] in which he set out the various categories of chemical-warfare agents and made a brief analysis of the Geneva Protocol of 1925. As in earlier writings, he concluded that, while there was no threat of chemical-warfare agents being used against South African troops, the use of both lethal and irritating agents may be to the SADF's advantage in certain circumstances when fighting its war against 'terrorists'. On the one hand, De Villiers pointed out that the Geneva Protocol did not forbid the use of such agents within a country and, therefore, South Africa would not be in violation of the Protocol if it used chemical agents in an internal war. On the other, he stated categorically that biological warfare was not a threat to South Africa and that no specific training in biological warfare was necessary.[84]

It is significant that three years before the initiation of Project Coast, De Villiers concluded that there was no threat of chemical weapons being used against South African soldiers, even though he recognised the usefulness of these weapons for the defence force. Similarly, he saw a limited clandestine use for biological weapons but did not consider these a threat. It is, therefore, likely that the establishment of Project Coast was less a response to a direct and specific chemical and bioloigal warfare threat, than it was a response to the general threat articulated through their 'total strategy' policy.

123 **1977**

The idea that chemical and biological weapons would have tactical utility in the apartheid government's effort to maintain white rule was established by De Villiers in 1977. At the same time, the South African government (1) faced increased international pressure to end apartheid discrimination; (2) was isolated by the imposition of a United Nations Security Council arms embargo; (3) faced increased internal resistance to apartheid; (4) as a result of the international pressure and attention focused on the activities of the security forces, had to find alternative ways of suppressing the growing internal resistance to apartheid policies; (5) experienced an increase in the escalation of conflict in Angola and assessed that chemical weapons may be used by the People's Movement for the Liberation of Angola.

124 The Rhodesian war of independence in the late 1970s may have been one of the first instances in Africa in which poisons were used as weapons of war. Fragmented information about Rhodesia's use of poison was published in at least four books,[85] but senior Rhodesian military personnel have never conceded to what the late Ken Flower, Director General of the Central Intelligence Organisation, said in a paragraph in his book, *Serving Secretly*,[86] namely that poisons were used with devastating effect.

By mid-1977, the small, conventional, multiracial, Rhodesian security forces were engaged in a war they could not win – a vicious war punctuated by acts of terrorism by all sides. The two organisations committed to liberating Rhodesia from minority white rule, the Zimbabwe African National Union (ZANU) and the Zimbabwe African Peoples Union (ZAPU, now the ruling ZANU-PF), both had military wings, which operated from Zambia and Mozambique and inside Rhodesia. ZANU's military wing was the Zimbabwe African National Liberation Army (ZANLA) and ZAPU's was the Zimbabwe African Peoples Revolutionary Army (ZIPRA). Although both liberation armies were feared by the Rhodesian forces, their greatest effort was put into attacks against ZANLA, as its operations had succeeded in clearing whites out of vast areas of the country along the border with Mozambique. ZANLA, less selective than ZIPRA about its victims, routinely committed acts of terrorism, mainly against black civilians. ZIPRA, on the other hand, except for downing two civilian aircraft, was engaged in a more conventional war.

From 1976, all normal mechanisms of justice were abandoned by the Rhodesian government. Special courts were gazetted, which allowed captured guerrillas to be tried in situ, without referral to either district courts or the Supreme Court. Defence for guerrillas was often provided by the Rhodesian security forces, using legally trained conscripts. Some executions were carried out in situ, and no records were available of who was tried or when executions were carried out. A diesel-powered crematorium was uncovered in the late 1980s in the bush near the maximum-security prison at Chikurubi (near Harare), which had the capacity to incinerate four or five bodies at a time.

By the late 1970s, the Rhodesian security forces were involved in unconventional warfare and several devices were released into the civilian community, such as booby-trapped radios. An armourer, Phil Morgan, who was later to work for Project Coast, was involved in the manufacture of these devices.[87] Rhodesia's amateurish and short foray into chemical and biological warfare made use of three substances:

1. Organophosphates, put onto clothes, especially onto parts of the fabric which would touch the soft parts of the skin, under the arms and in the groin areas.[88] Organophosphates were also put into tinned food and drink or other materials to be ingested, such as aspirin.
2. Cholera, twice released into the Ruwenya River.
3. Anthrax, deposited near Plumtree, inside the Botswana border.[89]

Documents made available by Peter Stiff record the use of poisons by the Rhodesian Police's Special Branch and the Selous Scouts. These documents indicate that the use of poisons began in 1977. Former Special Branch operatives have said that they were aware of the use of poisons as early as 1973.[90] One official document, dated 24 June 1977, records 809 deaths resulting from poisoned items distributed by the Selous Scouts. Another document lists poisoned items showing where they were distributed, including 12 sets of clothing at Gwelo, 15 at Enkeldoorn, 34 at Mount Darwin, as well as poisoned mieliemeal, tins of corned beef and sweets. A document dated August 1977 records that between 8 August and 17 August of that year, 59 sets of poisoned clothing, two sets of poisoned cigarettes, one set of medical supplies and two sets of 'assorted food and drink' resulted in three direct deaths and 19 deaths of civilians, killed by guerrillas who believed that they had been responsible for the poisonings. The last report for November 1977 records that 79 'terrorists' were killed after more contaminated food and clothing had been distributed.[91]

125   1978

In Iris Murdoch's novel *The Sea, The Sea*, the ocean figures as a reservoir of potential: the lair of a monstrous beast that symbolises human frailties, an endorsement of a journey of self-redemption, a mirror reflecting back the memory of a bad acid trip, a marker of imposed social isolation, and a space for cultivating fraternity. But most of all, perhaps, the sea is a relentless unraveller of human pretence – our projects and judgements whatever their temperament. As with time, the sea disentangles the loose ends about ourselves and others we continually and habitually seek to tie up.   Victims 211 | IR 187

126   1978

In September 1978, 12 years after being appointed Minister of Defence, PW Botha became prime minster and, shortly thereafter, elaborated on the concept of the total onslaught. The 1979 White Paper on Defence recorded 'increased political, economic and military pressure on South Africa' and expressed concern that 'the military threat against the RSA is intensifying at an alarming rate'. The idea that South Africa was 'Moscow's stepping stone to world conquest' became the departure point for security-related government policy.[92]

This view was supported by the United States. In the mid-1970s, the CIA's assessments of the situation in Angola noted that the Soviet Union had increased its material support for the MPLA's armed wing, FAPLA, in Angola and had increased the number of Soviet advisers to FAPLA.[93] A 1985 CIA assessment stated that: '[T]he continued build-up of Soviet-supplied arms in Angola will help further Moscow's long-term objective of ensuring a Soviet role in southern Africa.'[94]

127   Between 1978 and 1981, the war in Angola escalated, starting with a series of coordinated attacks on South West African People's Organisation bases in Cassinga, southern Angola.[95] A 1976 CIA assessment noted a build-up of Soviet support in Angola during 1976, which may have fuelled the escalation of conflict in the following years. According to the CIA estimate, the value of the Soviet contribution to the war effort of the MPLA government in Angola in 1976 amounted to some US$ 88 million.[96] This might explain the change in the threat analysis between 1977, when De Villiers wrote a chapter for the SADF manual, and 1981, when Project Coast began. A more cynical analysis may be that the escalation of the war in Angola merely provided an additional excuse, when increasing

internal pressure was a more important factor in the decision to initiate the programme than any conventional, external threat.

128   1980s

When Project Coast was in its initial phases in the early to mid-1980s, debate raged in the United States about the wisdom of a proposed expansion of American biodefence capabilities as part of the stepwise growth of military spending under President Ronald Reagan.

Much of the debate turned on whether the activities to be undertaken were actually offensive in character. In the years that followed, analysts would apply different labels to what was done and, in doing so, employ varied bases for making determinations.   Offence 148

129   With the tapestry of norms and agreements on chemical and biological warfare in place by the 1980s, cooperation and assistance in developing offensive capabilities was treated as a matter of significant concern – at least at times.

With respect to South Africa, the question of aiding Project Coast was particularly salient because of an arms embargo imposed in 1977 by United Nations Security Council Resolution 418.

As a result, what, if any, international cooperation – official, non-official, witting or unwitting – was offered to South Africa as part of Project Coast was a topic of some concern. It was a topic that might raise awkward questions about the international relations between the agents of the state.   IR 221

130   During the 1980s, opposition to apartheid from within South Africa increased dramatically, as did the brutal suppression of civilians by the state. In Angola, several large conventional battles were fought by the SADF against Soviet-backed MPLA forces between 1980 and 1987 during which allegations were made, but never proved, that the MPLA forces had used chemical weapons. In Mozambique, Frelimo, which had gained political control of the country, aligned itself with the Zimbabwean liberation struggle, providing Zimbabwean guerrillas with refuge. The white Rhodesian government responded by supporting the Mozambican National Resistance Movement, which later became known as Renamo, in its fight against the Frelimo government. When Zimbabwe gained independence in 1980, support for Renamo shifted from the Rhodesian to the South African military. Under the guidance of South African Military Intelligence, Renamo became a fighting force to be reckoned with, resulting in a conflict that, despite peace talks in 1984, continued until a cease-fire was signed between Mozambique and South Africa in October 1992.[97] The independence of Zimbabwe in 1980 provided additional security concerns

for the apartheid government as the country served as a safe location for South African liberation movement soldiers.

131 1981

In early 1981, the Minister of Defence, Magnus Malan, met with the Chief of the SADF, General Constand Viljoen, and members of the Defence Command Council to discuss the threat of chemical weapons being used by Cuban forces in Angola. Viljoen was convinced that there was a strong chance that the Soviet-backed forces both had access to chemical weapons and would use them. He convinced Malan, who instructed the SADF to find a solution to the problem. A young military doctor, Wouter Basson, was ordered to travel abroad to collect, covertly, information about the chemical and biological warfare programmes of the West and to use these models as the basis for developing a blueprint for a South African programme. Basson was also instructed to make contact with organisations that might provide information about the chemical and biological warfare capabilities of Eastern bloc countries.[98]

Basson joined the SADF as a medical officer in January 1979, the year after PW Botha became prime minister. He held the rank of lieutenant and worked at 1 Military Hospital until February 1981. Between 1979 and February 1981, Basson completed various courses and became a specialist in internal medicine, with a military rank of substantive commander.[99] He must have caught his commander's eye, because from March 1981 he served as a specialist adviser at defence headquarters and as Project Officer for the Special Projects of the Surgeon General. He was under the operational command of the Commanding Officer, Special Forces of the Defence Force at the time he was appointed Project Officer of Project Coast.

132 1981

The decision in late 1981 to establish Project Coast was influenced by factors that also informed the focus of the programme: crowd-control agents, covert assassination weapons and protective clothing for troops. The official documentation of Project Coast summarises the objectives of the chemical and biological warfare (CBW) programme as follows:

- To develop chemical warfare agents that could be used by security forces to control crowds.
- To do research into offensive and defensive chemical and biological warfare.
- To develop offensive chemical and biological weapons for operational use.
- To develop defensive training programmes for troops.
- To develop and manufacture protective clothing.[100]

The SADF's philosophy regarding chemical warfare included 'the right to reactively use non-lethal chemical warfare', 'the integration of chemical warfare into all conventional actions', and 'the acceptance of the use of chemical warfare on a proactive basis to ensure the survival of the state, for example, in controlling the massive violence in the current revolutionary situation'.[101] The stated objectives of the programme reveal that chemical warfare operations were envisaged, which would have included the use of chemical warfare agents inside the country and imply that external use was also considered.

Very few military documents exist in the public domain, which date to the initiation of the CBW programme, and none which provide a contemporaneous explanation of what motivated those who set it up. Such documentation as is available, together with testimony from those involved in the decision-making process, leaves little doubt that the principal motivation was the need to provide the SADF troops fighting in Angola with protection against chemical weapons. A subsidiary goal was the provision of novel crowd-control agents to the South African Police.[102] Neither of these aims, however, provides any persuasive reason for establishing the biological component of the programme.

133   Later justifications for starting chemical weapons activities in Project Coast by individuals such as Basson and Surgeon General Knobel, would make reference to the threats to South Africa from the growing proliferation of chemical weapons capabilities across the world and the chemical threat to the SADF forces fighting in countries such as Angola.

As Basson described the situation: 'The threat now lay in the existence of a large number of potentially undisciplined distributors of chemical weapons, who would make them available to anyone with money or the correct ideology – potential chemical chaos.'[103]   Total war 141

134   1981

Handwritten notes by Basson (found in trunks after his arrest in 1997), about one of his first international trips in 1981, indicated that he had a private, post-conference presentation conversation with Dr WS Augerson (then US Deputy Assistant Secretary of Defense for Health Resources and Programs) at a meeting of the Aerospace Medical Association. In 1998 Augerson would refute the claim that he offered advice, suggestions or assistance, or that he indicated anything about Soviet biological-weapons' capabilities. Augerson reported indicating that he was interested in further contact so that he could get details about adversaries to the United States and Basson's claimed knowledge of Soviet biowarfare training. Augerson reported indicating that he was interested in further contact. He also claimed to have reported the conversation to the US Military Medical Intelligence and Information Agency at Fort Detrick.[104] There seems to have been no follow-up action by the US government at the time, however.

135 In August 1981 funds were allocated by the Minister of Defence, Constand Viljoen, to complete a feasibility study for the establishment of a CBW programme in South Africa. Towards the end of that year, Viljoen officially approved the establishment of Project Coast and funds were made available for the purpose.[105] According to a retrospective report by Knobel and Basson, it was initially envisaged that the parastatal arms manufacturer, Armscor, would assist the SADF in developing the CBW programme.[106] In a meeting with the Surgeon General at the time, General NJ Nieuwoudt, Armscor officials apparently said that this would be too sensitive a task for them. It was, therefore, decided that the SADF would be solely responsible for the project. Knobel reported in his briefing to the Minister of Defence that Nieuwoudt and Basson had met with Piet Marais and Fred Bell of Armscor, who said that they would not be in a position to recruit or maintain the scientists necessary for the programme as they had too much work already.[107]

This was an incongruous position since Armscor was responsible for procurement for the nuclear programme. A senior Armscor official has stated that it was more likely that Armscor's decision not to host the CBW programme related to issues of power and control: Armscor would not have taken on the responsibility for a programme over which it did not have full control and for which it would not get full credit. It is equally unlikely that Basson and Nieuwoudt would have wanted to hand over a project they had invented, and for which they could gain the favour of the Minister of Defence and the State President.

In 1981, the Minister of Defence approved the establishment of Project Coast under the sole auspices of the SADF and, at the same time, approved the establishment of its management committee. This committee, known as the Coordinating Management Committee (CMC), included the Chief of the SADF, the Surgeon General, the Chief of Staff Finances, the Chief of Staff Intelligence and other co-opted members.[108]

When Basson returned from his information-gathering trip to the United States, England and Taiwan in 1981, he reported back to the Defence Command Council.[109] He told them that the CBW programmes elsewhere in the world used civilian, front companies to conduct all offensive research and development to the point of weaponisation. In fact, this was not the way the Russian, American or British programmes were structured. Yet, on the basis of this information, it was decided that front companies would be used as opposed to structures in the SADF. These front companies were to become an important component of the labyrinthine arrangements of Project Coast.

136 1982

In 1982, the Steyn Commission Report upheld and reinforced PW Botha's view that the Soviet Union's aim was world domination, stating that the Soviets' methods included subversion, disinformation, psychological war, espionage, diplomatic negotiations, military and economic aid programmes, terrorism and guerrilla warfare. The Steyn Commission concluded that the ANC, SWAPO, the South African Communist Party and 'other related organisations' were Soviet surrogate forces.[110] This thinking enabled Botha to present to his electorate and security forces, the view that they were at war with their fellow citizens.

The SADF drew a distinction between terrorists and guerrillas,[111] arguing that the former targeted civilians and the latter engaged unconventionally with military targets. The SADF viewed the liberation movements as terrorist organisations, which implied that every white South African was a potential target. Fear was instilled in ordinary white South Africans, reinforced by reports of ANC speeches in which members were called upon to arm themselves. Racism and appeals to whites' fear of Africans became the basis of the total strategy mentality. This created an environment in which it was possible for the scientists, who were to drive the chemical and biological warfare programme, to justify their actions to themselves as being patriotic.

137 1982

> Many research scientists may initially have moral observations [sic] about working on chemical warfare agents. But they will find chemical warfare a fascinating subject, full of intellectual stimulation and obscure by-ways and these will, like any other intellectual problem, rapidly intrigue them and seduce them from practical judgements.[112]
>
> Dr JP de Villiers
> Head of the Applied Chemistry Division of the
> South African Council for Scientific and Industrial Research

138 While the most obvious advantage of utilising front companies for the organisation of Project Coast was that they hid the military's involvement in chemical and biological warfare and prevented detection of the programme, they also offered additional advantages. Front companies were able to procure equipment and substances more easily than official military structures, an appealing feature in the light of economic sanctions against South Africa. The use of front companies also allowed the scientists access to the international scientific community[113] and scientists could be attracted by the higher salaries offered at these institutions; salaries that were far higher than could have been offered to military personnel within the strict military hierarchy.

Concealment was another consideration. The Soviet Union made use of apparently civilian companies for the conduct of their biological warfare programme for much the same reasons. The former deputy director of Biopreparat, the Soviet biological warfare research institute, argued that, '[O]sensibly operating as a civilian pharmaceutical enterprise, the agency could engage in genetic research without arousing suspicion. It could participate in international conferences, interact with the world scientific community, and obtain disease strains from foreign microbe banks – all activities which would have been impossible for a military laboratory.'[114]

Front companies had to be authorised by the Minister of Defence. In the case of Project Coast, the minister approved the formation of three companies: Delta G Scientific, the chemical-warfare facility; Roodeplaat Research Laboratories (RRL), the biological-warfare facility and evaluation and testing facility for the chemical agents produced at Delta G Scientific; and Infladel, the administrative and finance company. According to Jan Lourens, a close one-time associate of Basson, the name Infladel was an abbreviation of the Latin term *in flagrante delicto* – translated as 'caught in the act'.

Initially, Delta G Scientific and RRL were the only two facilities where research and production of chemical and biological agents was carried out. Later, the private company Protechnik would produce small amounts of agents to test protective clothing. Infladel was responsible for the technical information system,[115] operational coordination of the programme, and the security and safety systems of the other two companies. This company was used to channel funds from the SADF's Secret Defence Fund to RRL and Delta G Scientific. In 1990, Infladel ceased to exist and its tasks were assumed by Sefmed Information Services, which served as the information front of the project until 1994. The financial and administrative aspects of Infladel's work after 1990 were contracted out to D John Truter Financial Consultants,[116] and two other companies were formed to own the properties where Delta G Scientific and RRL were situated.[117]

RRL's cover story was that it was a contract research facility in the pharmacological, agricultural, biological, veterinary and medical fields.

Covert projects undertaken by the company on behalf of the military or the police were initially classified as H projects, or hard projects, a coding later changed to R. According to Schalk van Rensburg, RRL's head of laboratory services, commercial projects represented five per cent in the early stage of operations and gradually grew to about 30 per cent; he claimed that the costs of these projects did not account for more than 10 per cent of the budget.[118]

The planning of both the RRL and Delta G facilities included consideration of the need to ensure that the true nature of the companies remained secret. It was for this reason that RRL was located close to other commercial, agricultural facilities and Delta G was eventually located in the heart of the industrial chemical area in Midrand, to add credibility to their claim of being private companies. However, in both cases care had to be taken to ensure that the waste products were carefully disposed of so as not to arouse suspicion. In the case of Delta G, this referred to chemical wastes, whereas the clandestine disposal of animal carcasses was the chief concern for RRL. An incinerator was built close to the RRL animal-experimentation laboratories so that any observations (including by satellite) would not be able to detect the large number of animal carcasses which were disposed of after testing – certainly a higher number than would have been disposed of by a conventional commercial facility. At Delta G, one of the plants was originally designed as a waste-treatment facility, but according to a senior organic chemist at Delta G Scientific, this plant was seldom used[119] as ultimately the waste generated by Delta G was relatively innocuous. All wastes were dealt with by a commercial waste-disposal company, Waste-Tec. The waste-treatment plant was later turned into a production plant for Bromoxinyl, a herbicide used in sugar-cane cultivation, and one of the commercial projects taken on in order to maintain the company's cover.

139 When Wouter Basson was tasked with recruiting a scientist to establish and direct Delta G Scientific, he approached the most obvious candidate – the head of the Chemistry Department at his *alma mater*, the University of Pretoria – Professor Willie Basson.[120] According to Willie Basson, Wouter spoke 'vaguely' about the threat of chemical weapons being used against South Africans, and claimed that chemical stockpiles had been found in Mozambique and Angola.[121] The two men held several meetings, after which Wouter asked the academic to develop a proposal to establish a chemical defence facility. Soon afterwards, the Surgeon General, Dr Nico Nieuwoudt, approached the Rector of the University of Pretoria and asked his permission for Basson to conduct the work

required. Permission was granted and soon Willie Basson had three young scientists working with him to develop a model for a chemical-defence unit, and a brief to recruit more. Initially, he remained at the University of Pretoria, while some of the scientists worked from basic laboratories at Special Forces Headquarters in Pretoria, where a process was developed for the manufacture of the tear gas CR and a decontaminant. From April to September 1982, the facility moved to a house in Brooklyn near the university, whereafter offices were rented in an office block in a Pretoria suburb called Val de Grace.[122] When Lourens joined the unit in 1983, he shared a laboratory with Delta G staff. He assisted in the development of plans for an upgraded research and production facility, and oversaw its construction. In early 1985, the new facility, situated in Midrand between Pretoria and Johannesburg, was ready. A substantially larger Delta G moved into its new premises.[123]

In the early stages of Delta G's existence, Willie Basson had monthly meetings with Wouter Basson and the Surgeon General to discuss the direction and intention of research and development at the company. However, a few years into the process, Willie Basson became uncomfortable with the situation in which he found himself. He had lost contact with the Surgeon General, whom he had admired, and experienced a change of attitude in Wouter.[124] In 1985, work that Willie Basson had been conducting for a private company, Protea Chemicals, throughout his time as head of Delta G, and of which he had informed Wouter, became the basis for an apparently trumped-up allegation of fraud.[125] Willie Basson left the company and later claimed that he had had misgivings about the direction the programme was taking for some time before he left, but he did not say why.[126] Basson was replaced immediately by Philip Mijburgh, a close friend and associate of Wouter Basson and nephew of the Minister of Defence, Magnus Malan. This process was repeated at RRL in 1986, with the replacement of Dr Daan Goosen by Special Operations Unit member and Basson-associate, Dr Wynand Swanepoel. By the end of 1985, most of the Delta G staff were based at the substantial Midrand factory with its four laboratories and three production plants.

140 Sometime during 1982, Dr Daan Goosen was approached by scientists from Delta G Scientific for guidance on the use of animals for experiments with the 'household chemicals' they were manufacturing – 'like swimming-pool acid'. This was certainly a cover story. He advised them on the basics of dealing with laboratory animals. Later that year he met Wouter Basson when giving a presentation to the Surgeon General about the trauma project and how it could benefit victims of landmine

explosions. Testifying years later in the Basson trial, Goosen said that from early 1983, he and Basson frequently discussed the use of chemical substances in a war situation. They wrote reports together about the threat of chemical attack on the SADF, about biological warfare agents, and about the use of rats as landmine detectors.

Goosen and Basson talked about sensitive matters and had to trust one another implicitly.[127] So close was their relationship that, in 1983, Basson had no qualms about asking Goosen to provide him with a black mamba and its venom. Goosen claimed that Basson told him 'they' had access to a state enemy, who would be offered a few drinks while in a remote setting and would be then injected with the venom. The snake would be killed and its fangs pressed into the dead man's flesh to indicate a bite. The cause of death would be recorded as a snakebite.[128] This was the first indication that the front company, RRL, which Goosen was to establish, would be used to develop assassination weapons. Goosen established the size of a lethal dosage of mamba venom for a baboon and before dawn one morning, he, Basson and Dr James Davies (a member of Special Forces and thus not considered a security risk) injected a baboon with the venom. Within a minute the baboon was dead. Goosen gave Basson the rest of the venom and a 'huge' mamba.[129] If Goosen's version is correct, the clandestine way in which this incident took place shows that those involved were aware that what they were doing was both dangerous and illegal. It set a precedent for future activities at RRL. A few months later, Philip Mijburgh brought the snake, which had been nick-named 'Fielies', back to RRL.[130] He said that it had served its purpose and could be destroyed.

141 1984

One aspect of Project Coast included the production of a new generation of tear gas. Under the code 'FP003', CR 'tear gas' was sought as a more potent irritant than the traditional CS tear gas.

According to some, significant impetus for the development of South African CR capacity derived from the 1984/85 uprisings in the Vaal Triangle. Plans by councils in the area to raise tariffs for municipal services led to marches and school boycotts. When police opened fire on a march on 3 September 1984, the conflict between the protesters, on the one hand, and the police and township councillors, on the other, quickly escalated. By 1985, some 600 people had been killed in the national violence that ensued.

In response to these events, the CR developed as part of Project Coast was 'intended to counteract rolling mass actions led by the ANC or its surrogates'.[131] Total war 156

142 By the mid-1980s, the internal threat to the apartheid government was increasing while the conventional threat in Angola and other neighbouring states was decreasing. In 1987, the SADF largely withdrew from Angola and the focus of South African security policies was on internal security. The threat was now posed by civilians inside South Africa and the liberation movements who were operating underground. The Project Coast's focus on the production and development of crowd-control agents and chemical and biological assassination weapons can be understood to have been a response to this changed threat.

143 The replacement of Willie Basson and Daan Goosen with Philip Mijburgh and Wynand Swanepoel at Delta G Scientific and RRL, respectively, was the first of a series of changes to the structure of Project Coast made by Wouter Basson in the mid-1980s. This significant change, in which his close associates took over the management of the front companies, was followed almost immediately by the establishment of several companies, run by former Special Operation Unit members, to provide services to the chemical and biological warfare programme. None of the companies established in this way were official front companies of the military, however they relied almost solely on military contracts for their income. While the advantage to the military was that these companies did not require military management, this argument was apparently never put forward as Basson failed to consult with Knobel, Liebenberg or any other senior military officer about the broad restructuring. Had he done so, some consideration may have been given to the potential proliferation risk posed by private companies, which had both the capacity and the technical knowledge to undertake the development of chemical weapons, and which would be prepared to sell chemical weapons to individuals or countries seeking to proliferate.

144 One set of dangers associated with secrecy is the expectations, investments and longings associated with revealing secrets. This wanting and aversion can make one insensitive to the driving assumptions and dispositions. Further, what is exposed, what is sought to be exposed, or what is sought not to be exposed, can be taken as the basis for attributing the world with fixity, order or definitiveness, which is dubious. A persistent temptation with claims that hitherto unavailable information has been made available is that this information takes on the status of unshakable fact. What is (or could be) revealed – in having been revealed – appears solid and significant. What? 294

145 1985

Location: Pretoria

Event: Weekly Intelligence Briefing of the police security branch.

As a young security branch officer in the early 1980s, Johan Burger attended a top-secret meeting of security branch members at police headquarters to share weekly intelligence updates. One of the documents presented was a clipping from *The Star* newspaper, which had been published the previous day, now stamped 'Top Secret'. The absurdity of classifying a newspaper article was not raised, rather it was met with silence (though Burger was bemused). What? 295

146   1987

Vancouver Commonwealth summit, Press conference, 19 October

> A considerable number of the ANC leaders are Communists... When the ANC says that they will target British companies, this shows what a typical terrorist organisation it is. I fought terrorism all my life... I will have nothing to do with any organisation that practises violence. I have never seen anyone from ANC or the PLO or the IRA and would not do so.[132]
>
> British Prime Minister Margaret Thatcher

Victims 214

147   While at dedicated Project Coast military sites access could be strictly controlled, this was not always the case elsewhere.

When the University of the Witwatersrand proposed to build an animal experimentation laboratory to undertake work for Project Coast, this raised a thorny problem: how to ensure that what was taking place in a university setting did not become widely known?

Professor CFB Hofmeyr, head of the Veterinary Faculty of the University of Pretoria and an officer in the SADF,[133] was asked by Wits university to advise them on this matter. As the Society for the Prevention of Cruelty to Animals had filed a lawsuit to gain entry to all animal experimentation units at Wits, there was significance to figuring out what should be done. After a conversation with Surgeon General Knobel, Hofmeyr accepted.

In a 1988 'Secret Memorandum' to Wouter Basson, Hofmeyr recommended designating the proposed facility as an 'animal hospital' instead of an experimentation unit.[134] At this so-called hospital, the 'veterinarian, who will also be a researcher, as well as the nurses are all professionally bound by the discipline of the Veterinary Council... and this argument can be used effectively to stave off free access to lay persons' organisations. My real motivation is therefore to ensure that it will be impossible for enemies with secret motives to gain entry to secret experiments.'

But would the Veterinary Council, which oversees professional standards in South Africa, endorse calling an experimentation laboratory an 'animal hospital' to avoid its activities becoming public? Professor Hofmeyr expressed qualified confidence to Basson in noting:

> Dr Erasmus is the Vice-President of the Veterinary Council. I believe that he has Top Secret clearance. I expressed my fear of interference from laypersons' organisations with possible secret motives if the Veterinary Council does not accept the recommendations. He agreed to use his influence, but said that due to the fact that some members of the Council may be security risks he would not be able to use this as an argument.

Victims 246

148 Some would look to the individual components of the notionally 'biodefence' activity taking place in the United States to see if any crossed the permissible line. For instance, much of the medical biodefence work undertaken was done at the US Army Medical Research Institute of Infectious Diseases. Its one-time director, David Huxsoll, advocated a distinction between work untaken for preventive biodefence and for offensive.[135] While both might entail studying and growing organisms and researching vaccines, bio-offence would require mass production and storage activities, as well as efforts to enhance the natural pathogenicity of agents.

Others, too, focused on the characteristics of individual activities but drew alternative conclusions. Novick and Schulman contended that military efforts to produce vaccines were of dubious protective value in practice.[136] What they would provide, however, was the ability to develop offensive work capabilities quickly if it was deemed necessary.[137]   Offence 149

149 In contrast, other critics of the US efforts stressed the need to establish purpose through an assessment of all the activities taking place. Since so much could be justified under the heading of biodefence, it was necessary to move beyond examining elements in isolation. Rather, they needed to be seen together.[138]

For Milton Leitenberg, major doubts were raised by the US efforts when the different activities taking place – the building of aerosol test facilities, the investigation of pathogenicity, the creation of powdered anthrax – were put together.[139]

Likewise, in their book *Gene Wars*, Piller and Yamamoto argued that while individual projects undertaken in the United States might not be questionable on their own, taken together the fractured picture formed was worrying. The inability to see the whole picture of what was taking place due to restrictions on what details were made publicly available was itself taken as a source of concern about the purposes being pursued. As, too, was the confrontational stance of the Reagan administration in world affairs – this, Piller and Yamamoto argued, needed to be regarded as part of the bigger picture for understanding notionally defensive biological work.[140]

Offence 349

150 1989

Later investigations into the activities of Project Coast would be hampered by a 1989 decision to destroy management, technical, scientific and operational documentation associated with the programme. Wouter Basson requested this and it was approved by Knobel to free space and because it was deemed to no longer be relevant to the programme. For auditing and management purposes, only documentation related to the previous two years was retained.[141]

To know 243

151 1989

In February 1989, PW Botha suffered a mild stroke and resigned as leader of the National Party (NP). His successor as leader of the NP, FW de Klerk replaced him as president in September. Although from early in his presidency De Klerk made it clear that he would follow a reformist path, the security police and covert military units continued to operate as before – even escalating their activities as De Klerk failed to gain their support for a transition to democracy. Between 1990 and 1994, levels of political violence in South Africa were higher than ever before. A war was being fought on the streets of the townships in the Transvaal, Natal and Cape Province and in the rural areas of the eastern part of the Cape Province; cross-border raids were also still being planned and executed. In his autobiography, De Klerk commented on the escalation in the levels of political violence from 1990, stating that the number of politically motivated deaths outside Natal (where conflict between the ANC and Inkatha Freedom Party resulted in an extremely high number of deaths) stood at 124 in 1989 and had increased to 1 888 in 1990.[142]

152 One of the earliest published references to South Africa's interest in chemical and biological warfare (CBW) was made in 1989, when the Stockholm International Peace Research Institute (SIPRI) reported incidents suggesting that South Africa may have developed a military chemical and biological capability. While the author fell short of stating that a CBW capacity existed, he analysed the South African evidence and concluded:

> Although fiction heavily outweighs the facts of the case... in the psychological climate in southern Africa, reflecting a growing polarization

between black and white, there is apparently no limit as to what the South African regime is expected to do in order to preserve white supremacy.[143]

By the time this was written, the CBW programme in South Africa had been in existence for six years. Accurate about the programme, SIPRI also identified the motivation underpinning it – anything that would prop up the South African government of the day.

153   1989

Shortly before taking a trip to the United States, anti-apartheid campaigner and Secretary General of the South Africa Council of Churches, Reverend Frank Chikane, flew to Namibia, where he fell ill with acute gastritis. He returned to South Africa to convalesce for 10 days, before flying to the United States with the same suitcase, still packed from his trip to Namibia. In the States, he became intensely ill with symptoms of severe pain and respiratory difficulties. He recovered, but fell ill once again shortly after his release from hospital. This was repeated a third time, two days after being discharged. The FBI was called in to investigate the matter and took his clothes for testing, although by this time most of them had been laundered.[144]   Victims 240

154   1990

The first briefing of State President De Klerk about Project Coast was given by Dr Wouter Basson on 26 March 1990. De Klerk had been informed that the chemical warfare work focused on the production of defensive equipment for South African troops, as well as the non-prohibited 'incapacitants' and 'irritants' for riot control. The biological-warfare capacity was said to be similarly defensive in orientation – it sought to produce 'new organisms in order to develop a preventative strategy as well as a strategy for treatment'.[145]   IR 162 | Offence 67

155   1991

After many years of negotiations, in 1991 it was clear the Convention on the Prohibition of the Development, Production, Stockpiling and Use of Chemical Weapons and their Destruction (commonly known as the Chemical Weapons Convention or CWC) would soon be ready for signature. Total war 160

156   1992

Until 1992, South Africa's CR capacity had been kept secret; a secret that was threatened by the investigations of the Commission of Inquiry Regarding the Prevention of Public Violence and Intimidation led by Judge Goldstone.

This commission was tasked with determining the source of the violence that marked the negotiating period between 1991 and 1994.

It may be that the fear of losing the ability to contain crowds was prompted by President De Klerk's announcement, back in 1989, permitting protest marches, which had until then been forbidden under the State of Emergency.

De Klerk stated in his autobiography that some of his security advisers were 'strongly opposed' to the decision and were 'haunted by the spectre of the mass demonstrations that were taking place in Eastern Europe and had led to the overthrow of Communist governments in country after country'.[146]

Total war 157

157 1992

The Goldstone Commission's investigations deeply concerned the military, and particularly the Surgeon General, Niel Knobel, who feared that information about secret projects and operations would not withstand the scrutiny of this commission. However, concern about the prospect of losing access to the crowd-control agents and weapons meant that abandoning the chemical and biological warfare programme was not considered a viable option:

> [T]here are still a whole range of projects for which the technical information must be protected. Recent developments have indicated that, in public investigations such as, for example, the Goldstone Commission, the SADF and the SAP cannot withhold information any longer. So it appears now as if the Goldstone Commission is at the point of subpoenaing Swartklip Products, a Denel affiliate, to make known the nature, content and effect of all products manufactured for the South African Police. A large number of the products which are manufactured for Jota [Project Coast had been renamed Jota by that time], must in the future be used during critical unrest situations. If knowledge of these weapons should leak out now, the instigators of this unrest will already begin to make propaganda against the use of these agents and to develop effective counter measures. That the SADF is the developer and client of these products must definitely remain undercover so that the tactical high ground can be maintained.[147]

Total war 155

158 1993

In 1993, the Chemical Weapons Convention (CWC) opened for signing. The treaty forbids the development, production, acquisition, stockpiling, retention, transfer and use of chemical weapons. When it entered into force in 1997, 165 states had signed it. The CWC built on and furthered long-standing claims that chemical weapons are abhorrent and unacceptable. IR 159

With the imminent signing of the Chemical Weapons Convention, the order was given that all work on incapacitants in Project Coast should cease and the stockpiles destroyed. The coordinator for the latter was Dr Wouter Basson. The plan was to pack the chemicals into drums placed on pallets and load these onto a South African Air Force plane at Air Force Base Zwartkop. The contents would then be dumped into the sea off Cape Agulhas on 27 January 1993. While the dumping was meant to be supervised by the police, according to Basson they did not want to be involved and, instead, Commandant JG de Bruyn from Military Intelligence undertook this role. The 'Top Secret' certificate of destruction, drawn up by De Bruyn three months after the reported event, stated that the following items had been dumped into the sea (reference to code letters given in square brackets):

a. 18 blue plastic drums (weight 50 kg, contents 100 litres product M) [methaqualone]

b. 73 white metal drums (weight 12.5 kg, contents 20 litres, product BX) [ecstasy]

c. 2 white metal drums (weight 12.5 kg, contents 20 litres, product C) [cocaine]

d. 2 small white plastic containers (weight ± 500 gm, contents ± 1 litre, product P) [unknown]

e. 2 small white metal drums (weight ±6 kg, contents ±12 litres, Product C) [cocaine]

f. 11 green metal drums (weight 80 kg, contents 200 litres, Product B) [BZ]

g. 4 paper drums (weight 50 kg, contents ±200 litres, 2 containing product M and 2 containing product B) [BZ]

h. 2 cardboard boxes, air supply-type containing 60 mm and 81 mm mortars, respectively.[148]

In May, five months after the dumping, samples of the containers required by the Ministry of Defence were delivered for forensic testing. While Basson contended that De Bruyn had taken random samples,[149] De Bruyn wrote that Basson had done the sampling.[150]

On 30 March, Basson had given another three samples to De Bruyn, with assurance that they had been taken on the day of the dumping at sea.[151] By June 1993, all the samples were tested at the South African Police laboratory.

IR 125

On 14 January 1993, South Africa signed the Chemical Weapons

Convention (CWC). It prohibits the development, production, acquisition or stockpiling of chemical weapons and requires that all state parties destroy any prohibited chemical weapons in an approved manner.[152] On 31 March 1993, a meeting of Project Coast's Coordinating Management Committee (CMC) was attended by, among others, General AJ (Kat) Liebenberg (Chief of the SADF), Lieutenant General DP Knobel (Surgeon General), the Chief of Staff of the Army, the Chief of Staff of the Navy, Brigadier Wouter Basson, and Colonel BP Steyn. The CMC decided that South Africa should deny its possession of chemical weapons until the CR project had been completed.

At that stage, the Surgeon General was still in possession of six tons of CR and 10 tons of chemical intermediaries. It was decided that the research into the delivery systems for waterborne CR and the foam form should continue until the end of the 1993/94 financial year.

The management of the CR project would be the responsibility of Col Ben Steyn and was budgeted for at a cost of R2.3 million (US$ 655 500 at 1992 exchange rates).[153] Work was being done on a water cannon that could disperse a water-based formulation of CR.

In briefing the Minister of Defence in 1993, Knobel told the minister that were South Africa to declare its work on CR before the signing of the CWC, 'the groups responsible for mass action' would have an opportunity to consult their international advisers to find ways to counter the agent. This, claimed Knobel, would 'neutralise the army's most effective weapon in handling internal unrest'.

Knobel was supported by the Minister of Defence, Eugene Louw, in his proposal to keep South Africa's CR stocks a secret.[154] This was not a violation of the CWC, which required the disclosure of riot-control agents only after the entry into force of the convention in 1997. However, the CWC prohibited the use of CR in a conventional war outside the borders of the producing country. This meant that the 155 mm shells containing CR had to be destroyed after South Africa signed the CWC. This condition did not escape the attention of the CMC. In a January 1993 meeting, it was noted that if the holders were to be removed from the grenades and stored separately, they would no longer be in conflict with the CWC and this course of action was accepted.[155]   Total war 511

161 1994

According to the US Ambassador Lyman, when the ambassadors of the United States and the United Kingdom met South African State President Frederik Willem de Klerk on 11 April 1994, the foreign powers had two items high on their agenda:

1. Preventing the proliferation from Project Coast of information on chemical and biological weapons, particularly to Libya;
2. Expressing reservations about South Africa's 1993 Confidence Building Measure form submitted as part of the Biological Weapons Convention. To enhance transparency and build confidence in the BWC, states are asked to declare certain information each year, including past activities in offensive biological research and development programmes. With the lack of such a declaration by South Africa, the US and UK expressed concerns this would undermine the integrity of the BWC. As Lyman recounted, officials from South Africa retorted that that any offensive dimensions were done without authorization.[156]

The American and British officials made requests: that they be fully briefed on the details of the programme, a diplomatic and public confirmation be given of the termination of the biological-weapons activities, all abuses be fully investigated, and that Nelson Mandela be fully briefed on this.[157]

The briefing of the US and UK experts about Project Coast would be done by Dr Wouter Basson.   IR 154

162   1994

On 11 April 1994, State President De Klerk again met with officials from the United States and the United Kingdom in relation to Project Coast. According to the US ambassador, at this meeting De Klerk expressed concern about the information brought to him about the programme.[158] At a later meeting on 22 April 1994, however, De Klerk would become more assertive, arguing a defensive chemical and biological warfare programme was justified.   IR 181

163   The earliest attempt to provide a public picture of Project Coast was given in a special hearing of the TRC. The TRC was established by the Government of National Unity after the 1994 election. Tasked with investigating and documenting gross human rights violations, such as killing, abduction, torture and severe ill-treatment between 1960 and 1994, in its own words the commission 'was conceived as part of the bridge-building process designed to help lead the nation away from a deeply divided past to a future founded on the recognition of human rights and democracy'.[159]

In its hearings, the TRC functioned as a court-like body that heard evidence from both victims and perpetrators of human rights violations. With its aim of transitioning South Africa from a troubled past, the commission was set up with several distinguishing features. It could compel individuals through subpoenas to come forward and testify and it had powers of search and seizure. The hearings, which began in 1996, were held in 'the full glare of publicity' with the aim of facilitating reconciliation.[160] Another feature was the power of the TRC to grant amnesty from prosecution if perpetrators were deemed to have fully disclosed the truth.

What? 193 | To know 228 | Justice 179 | Forgetting 220

164 The TRC's mandate comprised three elements: fact finding, amnesty and determining reparations for victims. Reparation involved both the determination of a policy of monetary compensation and 'restoring the human and civil dignity of such victims by granting them an opportunity to relate their own accounts of the violations of which they are the victims'.[161] As a southern African studies scholar, Sanders, argued, this meant that victims' testimony had a dual function of truth-telling and reparation – an uneasy combination that 'the commission endeavoured to palliate by distinguishing "factual or forensic truth" from "personal or narrative truth".'[162] The testimony of victims, shared in public hearings and represented in the more than 20 000 statements gathered by the TRC's statement takers, was the essence of the TRC's work and of the narrative presented to the world and to South Africans.

Justice 165

165 Central to the TRC was the notion that truth-telling would enable reconciliation, nation-building and the prevention of the recurrence of the harms of the past. The TRC had to meet high expectations, including:

- Providing certainty of non-recurrence of similar harms in the future;
- Building a shared sense of nationhood by both those who had benefited from apartheid and those who had been disadvantaged or victimised by it;
- Offering an acknowledgement of the harms caused to victims and providing reparation for victims, their families and/or communities (either in the form of monetary compensation or through memorialisation);
- Providing a complete picture of the nature, extent and causes of human rights violations; and
- Healing through: 'rehabilitation and the restoration of the human and civil dignity of, victims of violations of human rights'.[163]

The investigation and special hearing into the chemical and biological weapons programme showed just how difficult it was for the TRC to realise such lofty expectations.

Justice 166

166 Like any social contract, the contract underpinning the TRC was subject to much negotiation and compromise. Religious bodies played a significant role in the negotiations – and believed that they had a central

place in the process of revelation and reconciliation, which was based on their authority to grant 'forgiveness'. This had an obvious impact on the nature of the bargain reached – not least in that the person appointed to chair the commission (as proposed by the Southern African Catholic Bishops Conference and others) was Archbishop Desmond Tutu. 'Forgiveness' came to play a central role in the production of truth-telling and reconciliation; a production that, at times, would come to take on the rolling organised disorder of a pantomime.   Justice 167

167 1994

Nation-building through truth-telling, reconciliation and forgiveness was also premised on the need for new narratives to replace the metanarratives of the past. The South African Council of Churches recognised the role the TRC could play in enabling these new narratives when, in 1994, they minuted a discussion in which it was said that: 'The nation may only need a few good stories that can become the possession of all people. The best of our aim is to encourage people for a few master stories.'[164]   Justice 168

168 1995

The Promotion of National Unity and Reconciliation Act,[165] by its very name made the primary purpose of the TRC patently clear – to overcome the divisions of the past and enable new nation-building. But who was to be reconciled, who was divided and how they should reconcile was not made clear. It was assumed that the parties to be reconciled were broadly 'victims' and 'perpetrators'. The underlying assumption was that revelations about the past would give recognition to the experiences of those who were harmed; that the 'truth' told by perpetrators about acts of rights violations would bring some 'closure' or healing and 'forgiveness' to enable former enemies to come together in the pursuit of national unity.   Justice 169

169 Underlying the very concept of the TRC was the notion of the duality of victim and perpetrator – conceived of as neat, simple categories. And yet, this was highly contested from the start. The negotiations that gave rise to the TRC required that anyone, regardless of their political affiliation or motive, who committed a *gross* violation of human rights, be considered a perpetrator. For members of the 'liberation' movements, the equation of rights violations committed in the course of opposing apartheid with violations committed to further the ends of apartheid was unacceptable. And despite this agreement having been reached between political parties during the negotiating process, when it came time for the Truth Commission to hand its report to President Mandela, the ANC baulked and took to the courts in a bid to stop the release of the report

because it made no distinction between perpetrators of rights abuses, who were fighting against apartheid, and those who sought to defend it.[166]

Justice 170

170 By restricting the scope of the TRC's inquiry to 'gross' violations of human rights, the narrative constructed necessarily precluded the less than 'gross' experiences of South Africans who were subject to the structural violence of a militarised, racist, authoritarian state, and whose lives were informed by this reality daily. Thus, the only victims were those victims who had experienced a clearly defined set of violations.

Justice 171

171 1995

The founding Act of the TRC, the Promotion of Nation Unity and Reconciliation Act, defined victims in the following way: 'victims' includes:

a) persons who, individually or together with one or more persons, suffered harm in the form of physical or mental injury, emotional suffering, pecuniary loss or a substantial impairment of human rights –
   (i) as a result of a gross violation of human rights; or
   (ii) as a result of an act associated with a political objective for which amnesty has been granted;
b) persons who, individually or together with one or more persons, suffered harm in the form of physical or mental injury, emotional suffering, pecuniary loss or a substantial impairment of human rights, as a result of such person intervening to assist persons contemplated in paragraph (a) who were in distress or to prevent victimization of such persons; and
c) such relatives or dependents of victims as may be prescribed.[167] Justice 172

172 The investigative work of the TRC – to determine the veracity of the accounts provided both by those who sought amnesty for human rights violations and those who shared experiences of victimisation – took place outside of the public gaze. What the public saw – the performance of the narrative – was provided by the hearings, where victims were invited to tell their stories; it was sustained in the amnesty hearings and in special themed hearings, like the one for the chemical and biological weapons programme.[168]

Justice 173

173 The investigative work of the TRC was directed and informed by victim statements and applications for amnesty. With over 20 000 statements to verify and 7 112 amnesty applications to be investigated,[169] there was very little time left for investigators to pursue the thematic investigations, which many investigators felt were needed to reveal the

modus operandi of the security forces during apartheid.[170] Justice 174

174 Security force members were reluctant to come forward to apply for amnesty – and many did so only if information about their rights violations was already in the public domain. In the end, only 32 per cent of the amnesty applications received by the TRC were made by people who had worked for the state.[171] Justice 175

175 To secure the truth from perpetrators of human rights violations, a bargain had to be made: truth in exchange for amnesty from prosecution. It was argued that offering amnesty in exchange for information would be the only way to secure the knowledge held by individuals, in the absence of documentary evidence. The offer of amnesty could, however, only act as a motivator for sharing truth, if it was accompanied by a threat of prosecution.[172] Justice 536

176 So long as the perpetrators could show a political motive for their acts, which had to have taken place between 1960 and 1993, and they were deemed to have told the whole truth, they would be eligible to be indemnified for their actions. However, for the bargain to be effective, perpetrators had to play along at the TRC – they had to actually apply for amnesty for rights violations they had committed, and of course, they also had to be aware of any rights violations committed as a result of their actions. In addition, to secure the bargain, a risk needed to be added for non-compliance – those who did not apply for amnesty could be prosecuted for their crimes. But, ironically, neither the 'carrot' of amnesty nor the 'stick' of prosecution could have effect if the perpetrators denied any wrong doing or could be certain that information about their acts was not already in the hands of the investigative teams; or, as in the case of the scientists from Project Coast, they did not know how, or against whom, the products they produced were used. Or if they could afford good lawyers who were able to manipulate the legalistic structure and format to prevent uncomfortable truths about their clients' roles in sustaining gross violations under apartheid from becoming known.[173] Justice 300

177 It would be within the investigative activities of the TRC – the hearings held and the written statements given by over 20 000 people – that its aspiration to become accountable for the future through accounting for the past would be realised or not. At stake in the recall of memories and the production of history were profound matters of acknowledgement, truth, wrongfulness and restoration. Forgetting 302

178 When the TRC set out to hear the narratives of victims and to collect the applications for amnesty, there appears to have been an implicit assumption that the harms done were of such a grave nature that they were burnt into

the memory of the tellers. And yet, as demanded by the quasi-legal nature of the hearings (both amnesty hearings and victims' hearings), evidence was required to back that memory up – to verify its truthfulness or reveal a lie.

In many of the hearings, individuals were asked to remember the details of events that took place many years before. Documentary evidence – an entry in a police occurrence book, a newspaper clipping, an inquest report, a witness's testimony – would verify or dispute a victim's account. In the case of victims, there was an underlying, unspoken assumption that the claim being made was truthful and that the documentary evidence was required merely to ensure that the victim could be deemed as such and, thus, become eligible for reparation.

In the case of perpetrators, the production of documentary evidence had a different function – it served as a basis against which to establish the lies that might be told – to trip up and uncover untruths.

In both cases, however, it remains the case that memory was fundamental to the process – not remembering was not an option.

Forgetting 15 | Legacies 433

179   1995

Moving from a past characterised by routinised human rights violations to an imagined, democratic, peaceful future was deemed by those negotiating, and those scrutinising the transition from apartheid to democracy, to require a process whereby the harms of the past would be revealed and the 'truth' of what had taken place shared by perpetrators of rights violations with their victims. Through narrative accounts, supplemented by documentary evidence, it was hoped that that which was previously hidden behind veils of secrecy would be made known to the South African public and the world.[174]

Justice 164

180   For perpetrators of human rights violations, the 'truth' was a form of currency, and telling it was a way for them to avoid prosecution through being granted amnesty.[175]

But, truth-telling offered something more to perpetrators. Since the TRC was very significantly influenced and informed, in nature and structure, by its head, Archbishop Desmond Tutu, and thus by a Christian interpretation of forgiveness and reconciliation, the process of truth-telling (particularly the public expositions of their deeds by perpetrators) was a form of penance. In other words, perpetrators found that they could obtain absolution and, thus, present themselves as 'reformed' or 'redeemed', and be welcomed into the 'new' South Africa. It was this prospect of absolution, as well as an opportunity for revenge for perceived betrayal, that led two of the scientists involved in the chemical and biological weapons programme to apply for amnesty, and willingly participate in a public hearing.[176]

Justice 192

181 1995

Several days after the elections on 27 April 1994, which brought the African National Congress to power, the United States alerted the new government to a proliferation matter that would need to be addressed urgently. In January 1995, a third démarche was issued by the United States and Britain relating to South Africa's Confidence Building Measure declaration. On 13 January 1995, officials from the United States, Britain and South Africa met again, primarily to discuss how to prevent proliferation threats.[177] At this meeting, it was decided to rehire Wouter Basson as a cardiologist in the new South African National Defence Force.

IR 406

182 1995

Question 2 of the Confidence Building Measure, Form F, for the Biological Weapons Convention asks State Parties to declare 'Past offensive biological research and development programmes'. In its 1995 declaration, and in subsequent years, the Republic of South Africa stated: 'South Africa had no offensive biological research and development programmes in the past.'[178]

IR 158

183 Before 1997, little detail was known publicly about the chemical and biological warfare programme, either in South Africa or abroad. Investigative journalists had exposed the existence of the programme and details pertaining to the privatisation of its front companies, which did the work of the project. However, little was known about the nature of the work undertaken by the programme, its intentions or products.

184 As such, in asking, 'What was done in Project Coast?', it is necessary to stay with the unfolding of the intricacies of secrecy in attempts to establish what happened.

What? 185

185 1996

As early as late 1994, South Africa newspapers had begun running reports about the activities and financial dealings of Project Coast. By 1996, investigations undertaken by the Office for Serious Economic Offences and the Parliament's Standing Committee on Public Accounts provided the basis for further stories. And yet, because of the extent of the details that remained outside of public consideration, the situation was summarised by the *Mail & Guardian* newspaper as one in which: 'Secret Chemical War Remains Secret'.[179]

What? 163

At times, the investigation into what took place in Project Coast literally took the form of opening closed containers. What? 187

187   1997

On 29 January 1997, South African Narcotics Bureau detectives set up a sting operation in a parking lot near the home of Dr Wouter Basson, long-time head of the chemical and biological weapons programme. He turned over a black plastic bag with 1 040 capsules of the street drug, ecstasy, to a business acquaintance, who then placed R60 000 on Basson's car seat. When armed officers approached, Basson fled, stumbling into a stream.

The operation eventually led the police to the home of an associate of Basson's. There, two blue sealed steel trunks were located and, subsequently, two others. When opened, they were found to contain further drugs as well as hundreds of sensitive and classified documents about Project Coast. This included files about individual projects undertaken as part of the overall programme, details about the finances of the elaborate web of front companies, and information about other collaborating companies.[180] What? 373 | IR 241

188 To the extent that it makes sense to think about the revelation of secrecy in statecraft through an analogy of opening closed boxes, it needs to be borne in mind that there is often more than just one box. Instead of simply opening one box, there may be many others nested inside.

Secrecy is often more like a set of Russian nesting dolls than a cracked security safe. Exposed secrets can easily give way to the next round of questioning about what secrecy is still in play. The need for opening and opening and opening speaks to the consequences and generative dimensions of secrecy. What? 438

189   1997

Among the documents found in sealed containers at the home of Basson's associate were ones related to the 1993 and 1994 démarches by the United States and Britain to South Africa regarding Project Coast. IR 290

190   1997

The historical truth established by the TRC was negotiated in relation to which documents its officials could access, use for investigative purposes and place in the public domain.

Until Basson's arrest in 1997 on drug charges, the TRC was reliant on the Steyn Commission's report, initiated by President FW de Klerk, which raised limited unsubstantiated allegations. After the arrest, select senior members of the TRC were given a secret briefing by Surgeon General

Knobel, the Deputy Director of the National Intelligence Agency, and the Project Officer that took over from Basson.

In many respects, the TRC was an 'outsider' to both the old fading and newly emerging political establishments in South Africa. As both state and non-state, independent but not – it occupied a fraught space. The aspect of it that was 'non-state' meant it was often regarded by the state as a threat to the investigations of other agencies.

The discovery of trunks at the home of an Basson's associate in 1997 led to an agreement between the Office for Serious Economic Offences, the National Intelligence Agency, the Office of the Gauteng Attorney-General and the TRC to share these documents, but only by physically accessing them at the offices of the National Intelligence Agency.

Forgetting 193

191 1997

At stake in the determinations of what happened in the past was not just truth or reconciliation, but also culpability. One of the ways in which the TRC attributed meaning to actions under apartheid was by attributing responsibility for identified violations. This might entail, for instance, identifying named individuals as having departed from professional standards.

These deviations were closely tied to the knowledge of misdeeds. For example, if individuals knew of dubious undertakings but did not act, or if they failed to find out about matters they should have known about, then blame might be directed at them. At least in 1997, the relation between the hearings of the TRC and possible future criminal trials was still to be determined, with the expectation that trials would follow the TRC process.

To know 276

192 There was a clear division among the professionals associated with Project Coast between those who believed they had something to confess and be indemnified for, and those who believed they had done nothing wrong, or who were, at least, unwilling to cooperate with the TRC.

Justice 193

193 1997

The TRC investigation of Project Coast was initiated by amnesty applications towards the end of the 1997 from Dr Jan Lourens and Dr Schalk van Rensburg. Lourens was trained in medical engineering and had worked for the military's Special Forces. He served as a technical expert on the programme and was the head of three of its many front companies. Reference to the construction of assassination weapons in their amnesty applications, and the subsequent debriefing of Lourens and

Van Rensburg, provided the justification for the TRC to include Project Coast in its human rights investigations. Between 8 June and 31 July 1998, the chemical and biological warfare hearing took place in Cape Town – the last hearing held by the TRC. What? 45 | Forgetting 312 | Justice 194

194 Applications for amnesty were also received from Philip Morgan, who had manufactured the poison applicators designed by Jan Lourens, and Johan Koekemoer, a chemist who had worked at Delta G Scientific and who had designed the process for the manufacture of MDMA (ecstasy).

Justice 195

195 Ultimately, none of the amnesty applications received by people associated with Project Coast were subject to amnesty hearings, because there were no victims or direct human rights violations for which amnesty was sought. Justice 196

196 Those who were unwilling to cooperate with the TRC included Dr Wynand Swanepoel and Dr Philip Mijburgh, heads of the front companies, Roodeplaat Research Laboratories and Delta G Scientific, and Dr Wouter Basson and Dr Lothar Neethling. Their reluctance to testify meant that there was an incoherence to the narrative – an absence or silence from those who, arguably, held the most power in the programme. The space left by the absence of their narrative could be filled by doubt about the veracity of the information given by those who did testify willingly – it also called into question their motives for speaking out. Justice 197

197 1998

The chemical and biological weapons hearing of the TRC was closely monitored by the world media. It was the first time that the managers, scientists and architects of any country's chemical and biological warfare programme had been called to publicly account for their actions. Media coverage of the hearing was extensive, albeit sensationalist and often inaccurate. The TRC hearings also provided the scientists with an opportunity to talk about and question their involvement in the programme. Some spoke afterwards of a tremendous sense of relief after testifying.

Until the TRC hearings, some had successfully kept the nature of their work at the warfare facilities a secret, even from their families. Ironically, it was a scientist working at Pretoria University's veterinary faculty who was challenged about his role in the programme by the university, which questioned his suitability to remain in an academic position. He and others managed to retain their positions by proving their cooperation with and commitment to the TRC process to their employers. Others found that colleagues were reluctant to work with them or to include them in research teams, despite their professional abilities. Nor did their families escape persecution. The wife of one of the cooperating scientists, a cardiologist, was shunned by her colleagues, who openly and vociferously supported Basson and saw the TRC as a witch-hunt and her cooperating husband as a traitor.[181]

Justice 481

198 Any agreed history is only part of how individuals come to understand the past. Sometimes official history matters little for collective memory. Sometimes it lays threads that are followed, but only indirectly. Forgetting 204

199 Sometimes an agreed history, even about the basic facts about whether specific acts took place, cannot be established. Forgetting 345

200 There was a significant overlap between the people involved diplomatically, politically and in the intelligence services and security forces during the transitional period (1990–1994) and for many years thereafter. Not only did each of these actors have an institutional interest in the revelations and concealment, but they also had and have a personal stake. As the TRC unfolded, strange new alliances formed and dissipated. Those from the security forces, who were seen to be open to the process and honest about their participation in human rights abuses, were welcomed and gained almost hero status in some cases, such as that of Eugene de Kock (the former head of a police hit squad). In contrast, others who were seen to be uncooperative were vilified in some quarters (such as Basson). The irony was that the stories that would have been most 'believable' were those that confirmed the meta-narrative of evil versus good. It was, therefore, in the interests of scientists who did cooperate with the TRC to present themselves as 'badly' as possible. Justice 345

201 *Chandré Gould's reflections*

In 1997 I was an investigator for the TRC based in the Western Cape. Most of the files, which filled my desk and fuelled my nightmares, contained tales of horror visited upon black families in the Western Cape. Children who had disappeared without a trace, bodies burnt beyond recognition, torture at the hands of the infamous police Security Branch and the mysterious assassination of activists by their comrades. It was not until I happened upon the unusual amnesty application of Dr Jan Lourens, towards the end of 1997, that I became aware that the apartheid government had dabbled in chemical and biological weapons.

Over the following six years (1998–2003), I conducted interviews with many of the scientists who had worked in the project, military managers who had served on the borders of the project and those who had found it repugnant. Through senior court reporter Marléne Burger's lengthy daily reports about the criminal trial of Dr Wouter Basson, I examined the emerging details of Project Coast. Each witness at the trial and every person interviewed, provided an insight into his or her life in Project Coast. The compartmentalised nature of the programme meant that few knew its full extent. These snapshots combined to present the view of a top-secret military project, which was poorly managed, achieved dubious goals and allowed its leader, Wouter Basson, an inordinate amount of freedom. None of the military leaders who were interviewed, nor the Surgeon General who was structurally responsible for the overall conduct of the programme, knew much about the details. Not even the successive heads of the defence force, who were interviewed, were able to provide a convincing explanation for why the programme was established and why it had focused on the small-scale production of bizarre assassination weapons, large amounts of tear gas and street drugs.

202   Or, at least, this was my experience of the lengthy investigation into Project Coast that held me somewhat spellbound for many years. Legacies 48

203   A considered response to the questions, 'Who were the victims of Project Coast?' and 'How did they suffer?' would need to note the scope for contestation. This derives from the varying acknowledgement given to suffering, as well as to the deliberately arcane reporting and accounting structures of secret military projects and operations.

If a victim is defined as someone who has had proven physical harm directly inflicted on them, then it is possible to identify a relatively small number of victims from the programme. Victims 204

204   The most well-known individual identified as having suffered through the actions of Project Coast is the Reverend Frank Chikane. Both at the time of the TRC and well into the 2010s, he was cited prominently in the popular media and scholarly publications. Forgetting 374 | Victims 153

205   In general, attempts to establish who was on the receiving end of Project Coast have been plagued by difficulties of attributing harm to it.

In no small part, this pertains to the secrecy that permeated the programme. Secrecy limited the ability of even those central to the project to speak to its ultimate effects. Silence and secrecy were, however, not the only factors that made it difficult to identify and verify victimisation. The existence of multiple security structures, all intent on employing 'counter revolutionary' tactics to undermine organisations, individuals and institutions that opposed apartheid, meant that it was not only the preserve of Project Coast to find ways to kill or harm opponents while leaving no trace – or at least by obscuring the motive and means employed. Victims 524

206   Secrecy also hampered later attempts to promote recognition and

recourse. At times, targeted individuals that were far less prominent than Frank Chikane or Nelson Mandela were not remembered in name. They might be referred to loosely as something like 'friend of black dissident'.[182]

At other times, those that came forward to tell about the misdeeds of Project Coast based their claims on conversations with others rather than having directly witnessed the events.[183]

Victims 207

207 After the TRC hearings, Chandré Gould had contact with several people who believed that they or their family members may have been poisoned by people associated with Project Coast, or by substances produced by the chemical and biological warfare programme. Daphne Potter (née Bailey), the widow of SADF special forces member, Garth Bailey, believed that her husband's death may have been linked to Basson. She presented Gould and physician Professor Peter Folb with her husband's medical records and post-mortem reports, but it was impossible to draw any conclusions from these. A scientist at the AECI also came forward after the TRC hearings, claiming that he had been poisoned but, again, it was not possible to draw any conclusions from the documents he was able to provide. For these and many others, including the families of the young men killed near Nietverdiend in 1987 (see list of people affected in the photographic insert), the uncertainty caused by not knowing what happened and who was responsible, frustrates the process of healing.

Victims 208

208 In many respects, the story that could be told about the victims of Project Coast is one told in the negative. That is, it is a story about what has not been told, what cannot be told or what will not be told. This is because records were not always kept or were destroyed, because no one has spoken up or appropriate questions have not been posed, few have listened, research has gone undone or unheeded, and so on.

Victims 209

209 For instance, attributing harm to the programme was frustrated because, in some cases, forums in which evidence could be heard and connections established did not exist. In other cases, those involved (such as Basson) denied that they could be held responsible for having done any harm. Also, while toxins and the means to use them might have been developed under the auspices of the programme, they could have been used by any one of the operational units of the security forces – the police, the military or the intelligence units.

Victims 331

210 But even when evidence could be heard and deaths established, linking harm to Project Coast was another matter.

Victims 345

211 For many reasons, no straightforward account can be given about who suffered through Project Coast. Stories of victimhood are not out

there to collect in a simple fashion. Much depends on who is asking, for what purpose, and according to what criteria and assumptions. Victims 212

212 One of the many issues in need of consideration along these lines is: Who counts as 'meriting' the status of victim?

A foundation of the academic field of 'Victimology' is that everyone adversely affected by violence is not necessarily conferred the status of a legitimate victim. In relation to everyday offences, the 'ideal victim' is generally someone that is regarded as weak compared to the offender (which often translates into being female, very young or elderly), blameless for what transpired, a stranger to a clearly reproachable offender and, importantly, able to elicit sufficient concern about their plight without threatening other interests.[184] Victims 213

213 Many of those who were adversely affected by Project Coast may be perceived as not meeting these 'ideal' standards for victimhood. Many who suffered or died were not strangers to the South African security apparatus, and not all were in a direct oppositional relation to the apartheid South Africa. For instance, some were soldiers from neighbouring countries who had been 'turned' to work for the SADF, others were members of the SADF itself who were seen to pose a security threat, or dissidents working abroad.

As a result, the extent to which those injured or killed were blameless and the apartheid state reproachable are matters on which not everyone might agree. Victims 146

214 A sense of the scope for contestation about who counts as a victim can be extended further. Documents released to the TRC indicated that members of the SADF were the subjects of human experimentation trials relating to the physiological effects of the sedative-hypnotic drug methaqualone. The defence force has since provided no details about who was experimented on and how this was conducted, although Surgeon General Knobel indicated that he believed the test subjects where 'volunteers' from Special Forces and 7 Medical Battalion group.[185] Victims 215

215 Others that might be considered as victims did not suffer directly from the operations of the programme, but rather from the fallout of its revelation. Victims 216

216 For instance, take the children of Project Coast's staff. Although these individuals fit many expectations typically associated with 'ideal victims', it has not been possible to identify any previous newspaper articles, reports or documentaries that addressed how they were affected. In practice, victimhood has been defined primarily in terms of those who are deliberately physically harmed, with secondary consideration given to those close to such people. Victims 486

217 Other harms have not been publicly aired but, nevertheless, borne.

Victims 497

218 The TRC investigation, which began in January 1998, resulted in a public hearing in June that year. The TRC heard testimony from scientists who worked at the front companies, from the managing directors of these companies, from the Project Officer, and from the Project Manager, General Daniel Knobel, who was the SADF Surgeon General from 1988 to November 1997. These testimonies, together with formerly top-secret military documents made available to the TRC by Knobel and documents found in the blue trunks, were made public during the hearing. The documents, which number 144, have been summarised in a relational database. Many have been translated from their original Afrikaans into English and are available on the Internet.[186]

The documents fall into the following categories:

- Minutes of meetings (of the Coordinating Management Committee [CMC] and directorates of the front companies);
- Reports to senior political leaders, including the president, about Project Coast;
- Correspondence;
- Technical research and production reports from the front companies, Roodeplaat Research Laboratories (RRL) and Delta G Scientific.

The minutes of CMC meetings are short on detail and clearly only recorded decisions and discussion that the members believed was essential to demonstrate that they retained sufficient financial control over the programme. While these minutes are not an accurate or detailed record of CMC meetings, they are an important record of what the CMC wished to record about the functioning of the body. The reports to senior political leaders about Project Coast are authored by Wouter Basson and varied only slightly, albeit significantly, in content over the years. These reports include the basis for a briefing on Project Coast for President FW De Klerk (1990), the Minister of Defence (1993) and President Nelson Mandela (1994). The documents offer an insight into the factors, presented by Basson to military leaders, in support of the argument that a chemical and biological warfare programme was necessary for South Africa's defence in the late 1970s and early 1980s. The language used in these, and other reports and correspondence, is often vague and, in some cases, ambiguous. The consistency of this tendency to obscure details in all the military documents indicates the likelihood that this was the intention of the author(s), to allow both author and recipient of the document to plausibly deny aspects of the programme were they to be revealed.

The technical research reports from RRL and Delta G Scientific provide insight into the search for incapacitating and irritating agents, the obsession of scientists at RRL with finding chemical or biological agents that could be administered covertly, and which would be untraceable post-mortem. The collection of these reports, which have been made public, is incomplete, but together they provide a strong indication of the direction of research undertaken at the front companies. In addition, the reports are supplemented by lists of research projects at RRL during 1985 and 1986.

219 In the five years immediately after 1994, South Africa entered into a honeymoon period; a time when South African leaders, particularly Nelson Mandela, presented the country as being well on the way to peace and prosperity – and exorcising the ghosts of the past.

> We are extricating ourselves from a system that insulted our common humanity by dividing us from one another on the basis of race and setting us against each other [as] oppressed and oppressor.[187]

A year later he would say: 'Together we can continue to replace the darkness of apartheid with the light of freedom, peace and development.'[188]

But the language of war was persistent – this particular ghost would not rest. As political violence gave way to criminal violence in the late 1990s. the 'black other' – the enemy of apartheid South Africa – was replaced with a 'criminal other' that threatened the new state, but the racial character of 'the other' remained consistent.   Total war 473

220 1997

The hearing into the chemical and biological warfare programme was the last hearing of the TRC, and the last day of this hearing was the last day on which the commission was legally mandated to hold public hearings. The hearing was thus vulnerable to legal challenges and delays from multiple quarters – Basson and his lawyers, the President, the NIA, the Attorney-General and the Non Proliferation Council – all of which had an interest in preventing a hearing from going ahead.

Why would the post-apartheid government not want to reveal publicly details of a chemical and biological weapons programme that targeted its own members?

Evident, but not officially acknowledged at the time, was the concern that something 'unknown'/uncontrollable would be revealed by the hearing, since the information the new state had about the programme was only that which they had been given by Basson, Knobel and others associated with it – and the extent to which that information was complete could only be guessed at. What the state itself was 'allowed' to know was limited to what was officially told. The new ANC state needed to protect the state secret that it did *not* know. What the Project Coast scientists would say when under questioning at the TRC was wholly unknown.   Forgetting 28

221   1998

When the hearings on chemical and biological weapons began on 8 June 1998, the TRC immediately faced the question of how far it should seek to open and expose. As in so many other instances of national security, the overall discussion was framed in terms of where the balance should be struck between openness and closure, secrecy and release, disclosure and concealment. The public's need to know and the state's need to restrict were set against each other – at least initially.

The hearings started with a trio of government officials making representations about the possible danger posed by airing details of Project Coast. They stressed their concern that revealing information about Project Cost could lead to the proliferation of 'weapons of mass destruction' by aiding those who wished to inflict harm through biology and chemistry. The identification of individuals, within or outside South Africa, involved with the programme could itself be a proliferation threat – on the basis that these individuals might be approached by those with nefarious intent.

If such possibilities were realised, the officials argued, South Africa would breach its international treaty commitment to avoid proliferation. That, in turn, would have serious consequences for the 'good faith'[189] being placed on the fledging post-apartheid government.[190]   What? 224 | IR 222

222   Betrayal was portrayed as ever present because tight control was not feasible. As argued by government represetatives, witnesses (or their lawyers) might want to introduce hazardous evidence to bolster their defence. Questioning and cross-examination could go any number of unanticipated directions. Seemingly innocuous documents might, in fact, give away important details. Especially as the government had no wish to interfere with the minutiae of the TRC proceedings, unpredictability was abounded.

Lest anyone miss the gravity of what was at stake, the official from the South African Council for the Non-proliferation of the Weapons of Mass Destruction noted that chemical and biological agents:

pose enormous dangers not just for soldiers or other combatants but for millions of civilians and indeed for humanity as a whole. The fact that we are concerned today about the possible proliferation of weapons of mass destruction places this matter in a special category where the international community has judged it to constitute not only a threat to international peace and security but to the very survival of life itself on our planet.[191]

Such grave warnings of secrets did not speak only to the contents of the documents. Their invocation also transformed the situation. Effectivetly, members of the TRC were put on alert that they were – as the legal official for the government put it – 'co-responsible'[192] for what would be placed before them and thereby what consequences would follow. That this notice was offered as part of the broadcasted TRC hearings meant that this line of accountability was made known to a large audience.   IR 223

223 1998

The trickiness of preventing proliferation was driven home when government officials were questioned by TRC panel members. As Nicholas Haysom from the President's office argued, 'there is serious difference of opinion between the scientists as to what constitutes proliferation. Your experts would differ from somebody else's experts.'[193] Added to this uncertainty, government representations themselves were uncertain about what details would be dangerous. As Haysom noted, 'I am not really in a position to say where and what witness and what thing would constitute a danger. All I know is that it is really like rolling the dice.'[194]   IR 224

224 1998

To thwart leakage and proliferation concerns, government officials offered a proposal: to hold the hearings 'in camera' (in private), examine the evidence presented, and then release everything fully save for that which posed proliferation dangers.

The irony of officials from the new South Africa calling for private hearings about the 'sins of the past' was not lost on participants. Far from representing this proposal as a matter of shutting down the TRC, however, officials portrayed the plan as a 'weapon'[195] that would enable the hearings to be *more* public and able to uncover *more* than any other alternatives. Since certain documents simply could not be released, without moving in camera, the hearing would be forced to curtail its questioning. As argued, under the proposal advanced, more protection would go hand in hand with greater openness – at least ultimately.

In response, a TRC staff member countered with different logic for preventing the proliferation of secrets. This included noting that:

- Some documentation had already been withdrawn because of government concerns about exchanges with foreign governments and technical details;
- Later consideration would be given to whether other documents should not be released to the media;
- Technical details were not important to the TRC hearings and many such details were already available on the Internet in any case;
- Witnesses were free to spread secrets outside of the hearings at any time if they so wished; and,
- In reality, the work undertaken on chemical and biological weapons was of such dubious quality, it was not clear what dangers its release would pose.

Instead of going into private session, the logic here was that holding the hearings in public would counter the secrecy that can breed proliferation and, through this, aid non-proliferation. In contrast, limiting the population's direct access to the unfolding discoveries of the TRC would raise concerns about what was still concealed.

At stake in debates about how the TRC hearings should proceed were assessments about the potential for betrayal and control. Could the assemblage of memories, documentations, names, formulas and technologies be trusted to align with one another so as not to jeopardise international security? What means of control provided the most freedom? Would the secret-telling, made possible by the hearings, satisfy the image of the new South Africa for both the international community and the communities within its own borders?

In the end the TRC decided to hear the testimony in public and to debate which documents should not be referred to or circulated.

What? 299 | IR 225

225 The TRC did not hear any evidence to suggest that other governments had offered official support to Project Coast.   IR 226

226 1998

Given the proliferation sensitivities about chemical and biological programme in general, and particularly the sensitivities surrounding militarily aiding apartheid South Africa, concern was expressed about how easy it was under Project Coast to obtain information about other states' programmes.

At the TRC hearing, those heading Project Coast would varyingly speak of the ease of obtaining information about the activities of other states. For instance, at the start of the programme, Surgeon General

Knobel said he sent Basson on 'a world tour, he penetrated many different countries' programmes and came back with that information ... that this country concentrates on that particular group of chemical weapons and this one on that...'[196] In particular, to combat their surrogate forces in neighbouring countries, South Africa sought to:

> find out what the philosophy was in the USSR, what substances they were studying and developing and weaponizing and creating delivery systems for and what information could we obtain from them. And I want to say this, it is not so easy to get that type of information, it is not available in the everyday press or in the scientific journals, you have to penetrate those organisations and actually find out what they are working on.[197]

And while it took some time, such an incursion was achieved.

In relation to getting 'state secrets' from Western sources, Basson played down the need for any demanding penetration. As recounted:

> in all the information-gathering attempts, I always took a direct approach, I did not waste time, if I wanted to ask someone something and they answered me, I continued with that. It was my experience at that stage, it's like if you want an answer, ask the person directly, and in this way I received very direct answers from a lot of people. What their motives were, I do not know.[198]

Motives were spoken to later when Basson suggested that in Europe and the United States, individuals were interested in the capabilities of the Russian, Cuban and East Germans,

> so that they often asked me to convey information to them with regards to the information we gathered in [South Africa's] neighboring states and it is so that this information was exchanged with me I think on the basis of the fact that they also wanted the information, and that's why I had good access to senior government officials and people at that time.[199]

That Basson was a representative of an apartheid state though, was not seen as affecting his interactions with foreign officials.   IR 227

227 The identities of the officials that provided information about the chemical and biological weapons programme of their own government or others to Basson were left largely unnamed at the time. After the TRC process, some names were given.   IR 134

228 'Need to know' would be a repetitive theme in the investigations of South Africa's chemical and biological warfare programme. As a secret military undertaking, which used an elaborate array of front companies to camouflage its activities, researchers, managers and others often made reference to the 'need to know' in describing the day-to-day constraints about who spoke to whom about what. The formal procedures of secrecy included security clearances, the Official Secrets Act agreements, requirements for use of locks and keys, bars on discussions with fellow employees, and the extensive use of code names. Secrecy was also evident in the absence of collective discussion about the direction and goals of the programme.   To know 282

229 1998

Concealment was a frequent theme of the TRC special hearing into the chemical and biological weapons programme.

The 11 witnesses associated with the programme testified, but some senior figures did so reluctantly. Panel members sought to question witnesses about complicated financial, managerial and technical matters, but armed with only the limited documentary evidence that had been saved from destruction. Witnesses struggled to remember events of years past, but also with making sense of documents and activities about which they reported not knowing. Military restrictions on the 'need to know' and individual's personal wariness of questioning about Project Coast were repeatedly evoked as limiting what could be understood about it in 1998. Military personnel also feared the consequences of violating the Official Secrets Act if they spoke out.

In so many ways, such concealment spoken to at the hearings signalled the vast terrain of what was not spoken about.

What? 492 | To know 231 | Forgetting 267 | Justice 451

230 1998

While some scientists in Project Coast were willing to participate in the TRC process, many others declined to speak with investigators. Participation from members of the SADF was even more limited.   Forgetting 229

231 Determining what had taken place in the past was a practical problem which members of the TRC had to work through with the limited evidence and means of questioning at their disposal. What the TRC could understand, and what it could not, would be the outcome of interrogations of witnesses about what they knew and what they did not know.

For instance, in the testimony by Dr Jan Lourens, the TRC panel members posed many 'what' questions about the nature of Project Coast – questions that Lourens repeatedly indicated ran up against the limits of what he understood.

What did Lourens know about efforts to develop an anti-fertility vaccine for use against black women? Not 'a great deal' since he was only 'responsible for the manufacture of a stimulator that is used to stimulate and draw sperm from the male animal' needed for this work and the project was never discussed formally in any detail. What did Lourens know about where experiments with biological agents were conducted? '[A]bsolutely no idea' since he just designed the filter system to contain and decontaminate experiments. What were the screwdrivers used for that Lourens helped to develop? He 'was never told', merely given the technical specifications, although it was 'quite obvious' too. What about when Lourens handed over one of the screwdrivers and two vials containing chemicals to an unknown person in the United Kingdom, did he know what was in them? No, but speculatively he thought it was a poison.[200]

To know 232

232 Accounts of 'what' was accomplished in Project Coast were sometimes followed by questions of 'why?'. The TRC panel members would express varying degrees of belief in witnesses' arguments. To know 233 | Justice 265

233 1998

Why had Lourens not questioned his involvement in handing over a suspected poison? He responded that 'at that point in time, I mean, it was this closed project, we were fighting this great enemy, it was this absolute total secret, super-secret project and we worked on such a strict need to know basis that we questioned practically nothing. I didn't question it at that stage.'[201]

Since the TRC was meant to understand the perspectives of those involved in human rights violations, could Lourens try to speak to how someone trained as a scientist could become part of such dubious activity? Well, he indicated:

[U]nfortunately I think it's a character of individuals as scientists to often not think about the application or the consequence. That's the first part. I mean that's the easy part. The second part is that why don't we question, why didn't I question? Unless you've been in that system you wouldn't know, and the manner in which we operated, within that system, you know we have this term which we call the need to know basis, and it was an excuse utilised by the system to not tell you. And you become used to it. You simply just live in this environment. I lived in that environment for four, five, six years where I knew quite well, being an intelligent individual, that I was seeing a small segment of a big picture, and I believed that the people that knew what was good for me, and thus would expose me to the right things at the right time. It's a naive, it's a practically stupid approach. But that was the way it went. And it doesn't happen overnight.

To his response, TRC panel questioner Dr Wendy Orr indicated, 'It is a difficult question to answer, you have gone some way. Thank you.'[202]

To know 265

234 1998

The development of the means of killing and incapacitating under Project Coast could only be done with an array of supporting technologies and capabilities. This included, for instance, experimental testing apparatuses. Dr Lourens testified to producing a stimulator to draw sperm from baboons, a perspex chair for strapping them down, and a polycarbonate see-through gas chamber for exposing animals to 'whatever substance you wanted to'.[203]

What? 241

235 While the 'need to know' controls might have produced an environment conducive to certain kinds of morality that encouraged individuals to not ask searching questions about the downstream implications of their actions, this also had the effect of undermining the achievement of goals pursued. Ignorance of information about the individual characteristics of targets, such as their weight, meant that the substances produced might not be effective.

And yet, in the context of a highly securitised, authoritarian state, as South Africa was at the time, fear of the consequence of 'knowing' led to wilful denial – because the consequence of knowing was potentially harmful. It was simply easier and safer not to ask, not to know. To know 236

236 For the many ways in which the 'need to know' principle was said to constrain individual's understanding, the organisation of Project Coast could be said to produce ignorance as much as knowledge.[204] The strategic concealment of information manufactured a state of unknowing, which provided a basis for undertaking (and sometimes justifying) weapons-related research and development.[205] In this sense, the 'need to know' was generative as well as stifling.

Another way of speaking to these issues is to say that ethical and other silences in the undertaking of Project Coast were 'constructed'. Later investigations into the project sought to impart meaning to the silences; to suggest how they were or were not departures from professional expectations. With the pervasiveness of secret keeping in Project Coast, judgements about the appropriateness of the 'need to know' measures in operation would invariably impinge on judgements about the programme overall. To know 237

237 1998

As much as there were controls over information, Project Coast employees also spoke to the limits on the 'limits of information'. Through informal banter in tearooms, day-to-day interactions or individual reasoning, staff had some sense of what was going on outside of their immediate laboratory environment. To know 495

238 1998

Knowledge of what was happening in Project Coast was varyingly reported as having been distributed in a complex fashion, which mixed formal rules, informal actions, curiosity and individual reasoning. This distribution was also said to have taken place according to organisational hierarchies.

Dr Schalk van Rensburg (one time Director of Laboratory Services, Director of the Animal Centre and Scientific Adviser at RRL) testified at the TRC about how the need-to-know principle was applied more strictly at lower levels:

> Directors, for example, leaked a little bit more information to one another. Those were for two reasons, because you had to … for management purposes, know what was going on. And then secondly, we were a small group. There were many meetings, almost every day and the Directors and the management got together at some or other stage.[206]

At these meetings, many things were said that need not have been said, including, as Van Rensburg alleged, requests by Basson for an agent to cause a disease that would not be easily traceable.

What was recorded, and thus what remains as documentary evidence, would only have been that which was intended to have been told – thus one can only infer what is missing from the testimony of those 'in the know' and their own recollection of the motives, conversations and events. To know 239

239 The moral economy of covert warfare programmes can be complex and changing. Within such clandestine activities, individuals might make calculating moves to manage their sense of identity. For instance, they could use their understanding of what was taking place as a basis for reasoning about what would count as appropriate action, which would, in turn, set the basis for making later determinations about what should be done.[207] To know 270

240 1998

In testifying before the TRC regarding his various positions at Roodeplaat

Research Laboratories (RRL), Dr Schalk van Rensburg spoke about the attempt to murder Frank Chikane:

[W]hen I read about the poisoning about Frank Chikane in the newspapers, I said to him, I said 'André [Immelman, Head of Research at RRL], what the hell are you doing to Frank Chikane?' So he told me, 'hell it's a real mess'. And he told me exactly what had happened, the mistakes they'd made, and he told me that General Verster was furious that the attempt to kill Frank Chikane had failed, and that he wouldn't – he'd ensure that it wouldn't fail next time.

Dr Immelman was meant to train the operatives on how to use the substances. This practice was started after failures like the attempt on Frank Chikane's life. They made a lot of mistakes there. They did simple silly things like instead of spreading the toxin, which should be absorbed through the skin over a fairly large area to promote absorption, the operative put it on a tiny little spot, then he laced five pairs of underpants instead of only one, so Frank Chikane got sick repeatedly, it immediately showed it was poisoning. The intelligence said he was going to Namibia and he went to America. They were counting on very little forensic capability in Namibia. These are the things he told me, so I know that he has contact with them.[208]

Victims 374

241 Project Coast entailed a messy assemblage of people, equipment, know-how, chemicals, documents, bio-agents, formulas, samples, and much besides. Successfully developing chemical and biological weapon capacities meant keeping these together in some sort of working relationship, despite all the events and frustrations that might arise.

Successfully keeping the programme hidden meant suppressing the whole of this assemblage.

What? 40 | To know 150 | IR 243

242 1998

Concealment was a prominent theme in the capabilities developed as part of Project Coast. Witnesses at the TRC recounted how they were asked to supply means that would enable undetectable killing and injuring.

How to kill without detection? As elaborated by Dr Jan Lourens and Dr Mike Odendaal, with weapons that did not look like weapons and poisons that could not be determined to be poisons. This included a bizarre range of items: spring-loaded screwdrivers, bicycle pumps and umbrellas that released chemicals of choice. A walking stick was developed to shoot a polycarbonate ball into individuals, which would be almost undetectable by X-rays. Finger-rings with hidden poison compartments were manufactured. Clothing and roll-on deodorant impregnated with organophosphates were other achievements. The herbicide paraquat was put into whisky bottles via a dentist drill – death from widespread organ damage would follow only weeks later and possibly be confused with poisoning from common agricultural pesticides. By combining the right 'applicators' with the right 'substances', the possibilities were almost endless: chocolates laced with botulinum toxin (which cause paralysis), anthrax-contaminated envelope glue, etc.

The targets for such weapons were merely vague speculations on the part of Dr Lourens and Dr Odendaal. What? 492 | To know 229 | Victims 245

243 Successfully preventing the proliferation of chemical and biological weapons capabilities in the years following the shutdown of the programme would have required the policing of the many elements of the assemblage.

What? 244 | To know 496 | IR 384

244 1998

Preventing breaches of covertness would be highly demanding, if not impossible, because remnants of the past might be unburied – figuratively and literally. After resigning from his last job associated with the project, Dr Lourens buried screwdrivers and explosives on his farm in Northern Transvaal. These were later excavated and, in 1998, the screwdrivers were displayed before members of the TRC investigation, but the decomposing explosives were destroyed on site. What? 248

245 (Note: this document is not dated but it is signed by Dr James Davies of Roodeplaat Research Laboratories. It was established at the TRC hearing that this report is the result of a test on a modified screwdriver manufactured by Philip Morgan at the request of Jan Lourens. It was intended to be a murder weapon.)

REPORT

Screwdriver

1. There were some problems with the screwdriver:
1.1 The plunger clinches/latches over on the back and then gets stuck in the cylinder due to the impact on the aluminium plunger.
1.2 Only 2 to 2.5 ml of the 5 ml, which is the full cylinder measurement, is expelled.
2. There is not much noise because it is inside a locked room, it is acceptable.

RECOMMENDATION

1. The cylinder should be made of a much harder metal, e.g. stainless steel.

2. The cylinder volume to be decreased to 2.5 ml for all of the substance to be expelled at the same time.

Signed by:

J Davies

(translated from the original Afrikaans)

Victims 313

246 A label like 'victim' is contentious because if it is defined simply in terms of who suffered adverse consequences, those who might well be thought of as 'offenders' could be deemed victims.[209]

In the case of Project Coast, such consequences have been brought up in public forums. Victims 247

247 1998

As part of coming forward to the TRC, Jan Lourens recounted an instance when he almost succumbed to the tools of his devising. In a trip to the United Kingdom in the late 1980s, he delivered a screwdriver-type applicator with two ampoules of poison to a Civil Cooperation Bureau agent, Trevor Floyd, who later claimed that these tools were to be used against two ANC members in exile, Ronnie Kasrils and Pallo Jordan.[210] Lourens testified that he and Trevor

> went to a cottage that belonged, or that was rented by Dr Basson, just outside Ascot, that little place called Warfield. I drove him there, and at the cottage I demonstrated to him how the mechanism worked. I opened the vial, one of the vials, sucked the substance into the unit, locked it into its – it had a safety-lock mechanism. I somewhere spilled some of the substance on my hand and I don't know how it happened, but I wiped my mouth and I lost consciousness very quickly. There was a bathroom; I recall going into the bathroom, and I recall there being a bottle of Dettol, which I drank. Again, in hindsight, I have absolutely no idea why I drank the Dettol. At that stage, I to a large extent lost sight, and of course the Dettol induced a lot of vomiting etc, etc, and I woke up a period later.[211]

Victims 548

248 1998

While remnants of the past might literally or figuratively be uncovered to an audience of observers, this does not mean that the question, 'What was done?' can be definitively resolved. While some elements of the diverse assemblage of people, equipment, know-how, chemicals, documents, bio-agents, formulas, sample, etc. that made up Project Coast might become widely known, the fact that these were only some of the elements meant that determinations of what was done could be challenged. By connecting the dots presented in the hearing to other dots (such as objects, people and intentions), radically different pictures could be advanced.

The situation was made especially vexing in relation to Project Coast because of the overlap between many of the activities that needed to be done to *prevent* injury or death through chemistry and biology, and those that needed to be done to *inflict* them.

What? 250 | Offence 493

249 1998

The possibility of deriving assessments of what was done was complicated, not only because of the way in which knowing how to kill could serve knowing how to protect, but also because many of the concerns raised about Project Coast related to covert assassination.

As has been argued in relation to other disputes about chemical and biological weapon programmes, while some similarities exist between developing preventive countermeasures and offensive weapons, differences can also be noted. Offensive programmes require mass production and storage facilities, as well as extensive training of personnel.[212] At hearings such as the TRC, all these could be marshalled as part of the attempts to settle what was done.

Not so, however, if the capability sought is to develop the 'dirty tricks' of assassination.

What? 296 | Offence 250

250 1998

Contests over the meaning of activities undertaken as part of Project Coast were perhaps most pronounced in relation to the Verkope (or Sales) list. This document was uncovered in sealed trunks, found shortly after the arrest of Dr Basson in 1997. Compiled in 1989 by the head of research at Roodeplaat Research Laboratories, Dr André Immelman, the list includes a table with columns for delivery dates, items, quantities and prices. The list comprised chemicals, sometimes with their 'applicators': the pesticide aldicarb in chocolate and orange juice; beer laced with the insecticide thallium acetate; the herbicide Paraquat put in whisky; and multiple bottles of cholera. Handwritten on the document, next to some of the items, were letters. Dr Immelman claimed that these were the initials of members of the military and police that were given the items for use.

What? 251 | Offence 269 | To know 252

251 1998

He further claimed that Dr Basson personally instructed him to produce many of these substances, with assurances of approval from the State Security Council.

What? 252

The Verkope list figured prominently in the TRC hearings, being heralded as a 'Rosetta Stone'.[213] What? 269 | To know 282

253 Perhaps the category that indicates the most scope for negotiation over the category of victim is that of non-human animals.

Surviving documentation indicates that a range of animals were used for testing purposes as part of the chemical and biological warfare programmes. To name but some instances of experimentation: beagle dogs and baboons were administered the pesticide paraoxen in varying dosages and chemical mixtures. Subsequent autopsies enabled researchers to determine when and how death resulted. Some of the baboons used were captured at Kruger National Park. Other organophosphates were tested on primates too. Rats were given poisons; baboons were given rat poisons. Tests on one species led to confirmation tests being done on others – pigs, rabbits, horses and primates were all studied. Victims 540

254 1998

In some respects, the animals experimented on were recognised as victims of Project Coast. Not least because of the lack of named and confirmed human targets, concerns about animal welfare were some of the most long-standing and revisited issues raised in popular media coverage. Indeed, public controversy about animal experimentation conducted at Roodeplaat Research Laboratories predated the knowledge of its links to biological warfare. Victims 394

255 Non-human animals fit many of the characteristics associated with ideal victims: weak in relation to their experimenters, strangers to their motivations, and blameless for harms inflicted on them. And yet, their suffering was not particularly interesting or relevant to any of the formal hearings that related to the chemical and biological warfare programme.

As for the experimenters themselves, they did not fit a stereotypical mould of 'criminals'. Senior figures in Project Coast were respected members of their professions and many came from established teaching positions within universities.

During his time as the managing director of Roodeplaat Research Laboratories (RRL), Dan Goosen was President of the South African Association of Laboratory Animal Scientists, a member of the American Society for Primatologists and the International Primatological Society, a committee member of the National Laboratory Animals Committee, and on the Evaluation Committee of the Glaxo Institute for Pharmacology. André Immelman, research and development director at RRL, was Chair of the Medicines Committee of the South Africa Veterinary Council, eventually a full member of its council, and member of the Medicines Control Council.[214]

Some of those in Project Coast would eventually speak with apprehension about the treatment of animals. At the TRC, it was noted that RRL established a Laboratory Animal Ethics Committee to screen each study. The committee would reduce the number of animals tested when deemed appropriate. It required other modifications to the proposals, such as replacing experimentation with subclinical microscope work. Although Dr Schalk van Rensburg complained that, as the Chairman of the Ethics Committee, his access to experiments in the basement of RRL was limited, but he was able to offer the reassurance at the TRC that, through the scrutiny given, 'animals were killed, many died, many were put out, but they were not large numbers, no'.[215]   Victims 256

256 Not only was the welfare of animals deemed worthy of attention, but the paper trail, which could be assembled from recovered Project Coast documentation, also provided the basis for a historical record – albeit a highly fragmented one.

From this there could be little doubt that in many cases the researchers deliberately set out to kill their subjects. Records, for instance, indicated that tests were being done with chemicals 'to determine the toxic dosage in dogs'.[216] The time from exposure to convulsions, paralysis and death were precisely recorded and analysed. LD_{50} (lethal doses for 50 per cent of the test population) of test chemicals were sought and catalogued.   Victims 257

257 And yet, while at times the plight of animals was regarded as 'of concern' and records chronicling harms were produced, in many other respects their status as victims was not recognised. Even if they had not been poisoned to death, the animals of Project Coast could not speak for themselves.

The nearest thing to first-hand accounts that exist are the research-laboratory reports. In these recovered documents, on occasion at least, the scientists went on at some length about the consequences of their experimentation.

In detailing the effects of Brodifacoum®, the active ingredient in some rat poisons that works by preventing blood clotting, one laboratory report noted the following effects on groups of baboons:

Two baboons per group received dosages of 500 mg/kg as a single dosage. Another group received the same dosage, but after 24 hours received another 500 mg/kg. The last group received a single dosage of 1 000 mg/kg.

After 96 hours, the first symptoms of blood in the defecation were observed in some of the animals and these were not connected to dosages.

Real symptoms of bleeding were only detected after 6 days. The mucous membranes were also bleeding. The first death occurred 8 days after application. The post-mortem showed bleeding of all the mucous membranes, muscles and subcutane. Some of the animals were killed in the terminal stages. Post-mortems showed the same wounds and no changes were observed as a result of the different applied dosages. It can be concluded that all of these dosages were toxic and that the dosage had no effect on the length of the latent period, the chronology of the symptoms or the post-mortem results. The one important aspect was, that the animals were very ill for 48 hours before they eventually died. Death is not acute and in no cases could bleeding on the brain be determined.[217]

In what ways, though, could such descriptions be understood as providing recognition of suffering? While some indication is given of the effects of Brodifacoum®, this is done through an objectifying and passive language, which promotes distance and detachment. No space is given to how the baboons responded to what was happening to their bodies – internal bleeding and brain haemorrhage until death. No potential is given to the individuality of the baboons other than that associated with their measured reactions to the chemical. No suggestion is made in this report (or any of the others found) of moral qualms or hesitations about what was taking place. No human is even identified as taking action; no explicit reference is made to the animals as victims; and no suggestions are given to what might be done in the future to reduce suffering (there was, after all, a Laboratory Animal Ethics Committee looking into this). Nor, of course, was there any consideration of the suffering that could be expected in a human victim given these substances.

However much simultaneously presenting and not presenting suffering, these reports are the only remaining records of what took place in these experiments.[218] To what extent these reports represent the total record of animal experiments will remain unknown.   Victims 258

258   While some individuals were directly exposed to animal experiments, these activities were sequestered away out of sight. This has frustrated attempts to account for the suffering of animals both during and after Project Coast.

For instance, although Dr Jan Lourens designed many of the experimental apparatuses, he witnessed only one test at Roodeplaat Research Laboratories.

Others that might offer a radically different interpretation of what took place were barred from knowing about – let along entering – Project Coast facilities. This indicates the importance of moving beyond who said what to the political conditions that structured what got said. Victims 147

259 How did the researchers get chimpanzees into South Africa to experiment on them as part of the chemical and biological warfare programme? One method was to use 'zoo-to-zoo' transfers. Chimps imported from a British zoo to the Johannesburg Zoo would raise few eyebrows. From there they could then be 'donated' to Roodeplaat Research Laboratories.[219]

The chimps were not asked for their views on such movements.

What? 243

260 Labels of defensive and offensive served as a basis for what individuals should and could be held to account for. Offence 261

261 1998

When Dr Jan Lourens was asked at the TRC what he had told Surgeon General Knobel regarding his concerns about the offensive dimensions of Project Coast, this exchange followed:

> Mr Lourens: 'It was late '92, early '93.'
>
> Mr Vally: 'And his response was it wasn't his project.'
>
> Mr Lourens: 'It wasn't his project. Offensive stuff was not his project and he didn't know about it and he quite frankly didn't want to know about it.'[220]
>
> Offence 69

262 1998

When the former head of research at Delta G Scientific, Dr Johan Koekemoer, appeared before the TRC in 1998, he was asked, 'who in your eyes was the enemy ... that this was going to defend whoever against?' To this, Koekemoer rejected the suggestion that the chemical arsenal produced under Project Coast was aimed at South Africans. 'The enemy' included Angolans fighting against South Africans, their Cuban supporters, and 'whoever started chucking stuff against us'. This group, however, did not include the African National Congress or similar 'others' in the country.

To this contention, the exchange followed with Dr Fazel Randera (the Deputy Chairperson of the TRC's Human Rights Violations Committee):

> Dr Randera: 'Professor, I find this very difficult to understand, accept. I mean you referred several times to reading in newspapers, we're talking about 1986 to 1990, 1992 period, we're not talking about a peaceful time for South Africa. We're talking about a time when the country

was almost burning. We'd had in that period that we're talking about, in 1986 to 1990 period, we'd had two States of Emergencies declared already, so who was the enemy for you professor, I mean people were throwing things inside the country?'

Dr Koekemoer: 'Ja, I never considered that the army would ever utilise any of its CBW programme aspects internally against its own people. Let me put that quite clear, it never entered my mind.'[221]   Total war 272

263   1998

When Dr Johan Koekemoer, one-time head of research at Delta G Scientific, was asked at the hearings of the TRC, where the ethics was in his work, he responded:

My moral stance in this was that if you go in for CBW [chemical and biological warfare] work, the idea here and I was told right from the start that we were doing work in a defensive capacity, in other words, the idea was that if you had an enemy that would chuck chemicals on you, you could chuck it back on them, and that's the stance that I took with this, so I never saw my CBW work as an offensive thing that you would take this and [use it] on an unsuspecting enemy who hasn't got the capability of using CBW, going and chuck it on them [sic].[222]   Offence 292

264   Why a perpetrator did what they did can be as important to victims as knowing what was done. But, like answers to questions of *what* was done, the answers to questions of *why* were as frustratingly difficult to resolve.   Justice 232

265   1998

At times, panel members expressed incredulity about the absence of self-querying by witnesses regarding the nature of their involvement in Project Coast.

When the one-time head of research at Delta G Scientific, Dr Johan Koekemoer, testified, he spoke of the 'need to know' conventions as delimiting the horizons of his understanding. Did Koekemoer know the mission of Delta G? He replied, 'a lot of us at Delta G have never been informed to the full extent of Project Coast and what the objectives were'. Did Koekemoer have an appreciation of the delivery systems for the incapacitants his company developed? 'We were never given that brief at all,' he replied. Did Koekemoer know what happened to the 912 kilograms of ecstasy he delivered? 'No.'

Such replies led Dr Fazel Randera, Deputy Chairperson of the Truth

Commission's Human Rights Violations Committee, to lament:

> As a scientist, where scientists have the ability to investigate research, they don't really want to have obstacles in their way and yet it appears to me that when you take on this issue of need-to-know basis, you're almost becoming like an agent. You're deciding, or somebody's deciding for you, that this is the area that you can research and no further can you go and I want to follow that up by – so I want your comment on that, and then just to say to you, my perception, having listened to you, is that here you were, yes you were at one stage the head of this research department at this company, but even within your company you didn't know who was doing what research and what other areas of work was being done. Within your company, you were producing almost a thousand kilograms of ecstasy and you didn't know where that was going to. You were producing CS gas, you say to us, yes that it hadn't been used by the army, but clearly – well when we look at that other report that was shown to you earlier on, it may well have been used. Now it seems to me that you were part of a machinery, you produced substances but you didn't really know where those substances ended up or what they were used for. So, my first – I would like you to comment on this question of scientists versus need-to-know basis and, secondly, whether you actually knew where the products that you were researching and eventually making, whether you actually knew where that was going. Repeatedly you've said that you wouldn't believe that this could have happened, but clearly these things were taking place and you didn't know about it.

Further questions followed. In the absence of an identified enemy against whom weaponised ecstasy would be used, had Koekemoer suspected that his facilities might be being used for alternative agendas? That it was serving chemical and biological warfare? That illegal activities might be taking place? Did he have suspicions? At least?[223]   To know 235 | Justice 451 266 1998

Veterinarian, Dr Schalk van Rensburg at the TRC hearing:

> There is no doubt that most of the scientists working at the biological and chemical warfare facilities were, at least tacitly, supportive of the government of the day. This is not true of all the scientists, but all were able to justify their activities in terms of the need to respond to the war that most white South Africans believed themselves to be engaged in. It is impossible to fully understand their motivation without accepting this understanding was prevalent amongst white South Africans.[224]   Victims 205

Dr Randera: 'Can you tell me what, once [Roodeplaat Research Laboratories] closed down, what actually happened to all these products and experiments that were taking place?'

Dr van Rensburg: 'There was furious humming of the shredding machines and stoking of the incinerators and as I said, some of the stuff was dumped in the bathroom, cantharadines, this is one of the destructive products they used; they would go to a meeting of the End Conscription Campaign, youngsters, and dish out tissues with slogans on them, but in the meantime, they had been laced with this stuff. They are highly irritant but they are also very nephrotoxic, toxic to the kidneys. I was exposed to this stuff and when it happened I confronted André Immelman and he said no he was getting rid of a lot of stuff down the drain and the fumes were absorbed by the toilet paper. It's a very, very irritant substance, I can vouch for that.' Forgetting 190

268 1998

Some work undertaken as part of Project Coast suggested a desire to respond to threats to the apartheid state even before they emerged. Dr Schalk van Rensburg and Dr Daan Goosen, for instance, spoke to attempts to develop an anti-fertility vaccine. What? 270

269 1998

When asked to speak to the Verkope list, witnesses offered varied interpretations that made, and refused to make, connections to other evidence. For some its meaning was fixed and unambiguous. When asked whether it served some scientific purpose or constituted a list of murder weapons, Dr van Rensburg responded: it was '[u]ndoubtedly a list of murder weapons, no value for research whatsoever'.[225] He recounted knowing that substances were being issued to members of the security forces – even if he had not directly seen this taking place. What? 249 | Offence 275

270 1998

The anti-fertility vaccine work was carried out under a cover story, even internally. Project Coast researchers were told that the research was intended to aid one of South Africa's allies: UNITA troops fighting in Angola needed a way to prevent their female troops from getting pregnant.

For his part, Dr van Rensburg told the TRC that he found this justification highly dubious. As cover stories were common and not to be questioned, the ridiculousness of spending significant time and resources on this matter signalled ulterior purposes were afoot. Since he believed that the development of a vaccine was much needed to control the world's populations anyway, and the effects could be easily detectable and often reversible, he was not concerned about whether the vaccine would be mass administered covertly in South Africa. Indeed, as this work 'occupied at least 30 per cent of our research capability [at later stages in RRL] that was 30 per cent less time and effort and money to spend on developing covert ways to kill people'.[226]

What? 271 | To know 321

271 1998

Against such optimism, former managing director of Roodeplaat Research Laboratories, Dr Goosen, would later testify that he, Dr Basson and the Surgeon General, Dr Niel Knobel, had considered how to make 'a drug effective against pigmented people only'.[227]

Whereas for Dr van Rensburg, the absurdity of the justification offered for this fertility work signalled that ulterior motivations lay behind it, Dr Basson offered a different reasoning at the TRC: namely, that such work would never have been proposed by him because it was absurd. There was no cover up to be uncovered. Dr van Rensburg and Dr Goosen were making up allegations as a way of serving their own agendas. What? 234

272 1998

When asked how he could be involved in efforts to develop a vaccine intended to curtail the birth rate of the black population, Dr Daan Goosen, the first managing director of Roodeplaat Research Laboratories, pointed to the prevailing climate in the 1980s. This environment fostered the belief that:

> we had the right to decide what was good for other people. You ask me, do I think I am a racist? No, of course not. I am not a racist. I have many black friends. I grew up on the farm, I played with the black people, everything. It wasn't a thing which was directed against hating blacks or whatever. But that was the environment, that was the climate that was created around us by the propaganda of the politicians and everyone of the day…
>
> But what grieves me is that the people that created this climate is [sic] now denying it. Like if you listen to a person like Minister Pik Botha, you would have sworn he was born an ANC member. He never said total onslaught, Communism – that's the enemy. Never! He denies. And this is what grieves me Mr Chairman, that they are ducking their responsibility for what they did. Because I have no doubt in my mind that those are the responsible people that created the climate. And they supplied the money, Mr Chairman, to do this. Total war 219

273 Against the importance attached to labels, at times the possibility of separating out 'offensive' from 'defensive' in any neat way was questioned.

Offence 274

274 1998

Testifying before the TRC, former managing director of Roodeplaat Research Laboratories, Dr Dan Goosen commented that:

> Now Mr Chairman, defensive and offensive, the whole argument, if I may elaborate one second. Defensive and offensive was not really a topic of discussion. We were in a war situation and a weapon is a weapon. A weapon can be used offensively or defensively. So I have a bit of a problem with all this big discussion around was it a defensive capability or was it an offensive capability? It was a capability. The applications of the weapons was [sic] not supposed to be our problem. But in discussions I've had and already outlined to you, there was no doubt in my mind, and there was no doubt in anybody's mind, that it was offensive, intended to be used offensively.[228]

Offence 280

275 1998

Prominent media reports at the time of TRC gave a sense that the evidence presented provided the basis for making definitive assessments about the nature of capabilities and motivating purposes behind the efforts of Project Coast. The hearings were portrayed as lifting the lid on the 'military's box of horrors' and getting a 'peek behind the doors of apartheid's laboratory of death'.[229]

The day-to-day reporting retold the most dramatic headlines of witnesses, sometimes taking labels like 'murder weapons' for granted. Sometimes it was noted that these labels were only what witnesses had themselves claimed.[230] Sometimes the weapons were deemed 'mass-destruction techniques'.[231] Sometimes the activities testified about were presented as farcical, sometimes as deadly serious, sometimes as bizarre; but they were repeatedly portrayed in definite terms.[232]

Offence 296

276 Testimony given to the TRC, though, was not always simply evidence that could be used to build arguments about the past. On occasions, witnesses explicitly reflected on how the accounts being given of Project Coast helped constitute a highly contingent understanding of what was under discussion. Within this, the meaning ascribed to notions like 'expertise', 'ignorance' and 'responsibility' became topics for joint investigation between participants. Terms and expressions were queried for how they were being understood in this setting and the implications within such settings.

To know 277

When the South African Defence Force Surgeon General, Dr Niel Knobel, testified before the TRC, high on the agenda of panel members were questions about what he knew of the undertakings of Project Coast. From March 1988 until its end, as Surgeon General he played the role of project manager. In this capacity, he was also a member of the Coordinating Management Committee, a body set up to provide oversight of the programme. But, he was at pains to point out that he had 'inherited' responsibility for the programme from his predecessor, who had died by the time the TRC hearings were held. There were, thus, bounds to the scope of his responsibility.

Much of the fifth day of the hearings into the chemical and biological warfare programme consisted of attempts to determine what Knobel had approved in his role as project manager and which activities he deemed to be legitimate. Three blocks of questioning during that day returned to these themes. In the unfolding discussion, the theme of ignorance would figure prominently.

When initially probed in the morning about what he and others on the Coordinating Management Committee knew about developments under Project Coast, Knobel indicated:

> The detail made available at the Coordinating Management Committee was in terms of the achievement of objectives that had been formulated and approved by the Coordinating Management Committee and it would be very broad guidelines. The members of that committee did not have either the scientific knowledge or background to be able to deal with the absolute detail of projects at grassroots level, if you will accept that term, but in broad terms the type of reporting that would be done is: we have now completed our investigations into all irritating agents or into all the classical chemical weapons or into this particular category of the classical chemical weapon.
>
> There was never an opportunity to really discuss in detail what particular experiments were carried out about the very vast numbers of chemicals that had to be studied or... [intervention]

As expressed here, not only was the Coordinating Management Committee not briefed about the 'absolute detail of projects at grassroots level', but there was also no opportunity to do so. Even if there had been, its members would not have the capacity to make sense of such 'vast' information. Knobel treated this state of affairs as unavoidable and clearly felt it required little justification.

Such statements stood as implicit refutations to suggestions that the Coordinating Management Committee should have monitored the detailed undertaking of Project Coast: simply put, its members were not in a position to do so, even if this had been deemed desirable. Instead, Knobel indicated that members of the committee were informed in far less detail, such as:

> We have now embarked on studying the classical biological weapon groups, all the organisms as well as all the toxins that are normally considered to be classical biological weapons.

Simultaneously, the statement of ignorance on the part of Knobel accounted for the limited way in which he – as someone sitting before a group of questioners at the TRC – could answer specific questions they might pose.

Various questions then followed about whether Knobel knew of work into *Vibrio cholerae*, *Salmonella*, *Brucella*, paraoxon and monensin. Knobel said that such studies were defensive in nature. Had Knobel known of the quantities produced? 'No.' Did he know of the effects of toxins such as monensin, which made it deadly but difficult to detect? 'No.' Who kept this from him?

> Well I think by Doctor Basson but I must say at the same time, I did not expect to have that kind of detail. I was satisfied that the parameters in which the research was being carried out was against the background of the mandate of the project.

Many of the same themes were revisited later in the questioning that day in relation to Knobel's knowledge of the discovered Project Coast's Verkope/Sales list.   To know 250

278   1998

During the examination of the Verkope list at the TRC, different lines of reasoning were pursued. At times discussion focused on the acceptability of individual items. What could be the justification for putting pesticide in chocolate, lacing beer with insecticide or developing antibiotic-resistant anthrax? At other times, though, the topic of concern was not so much an individual entry as the whole list, or even the list against what else was known about Project Coast.   Offence 279

279   1998

Surgeon General Knobel claimed not to know about the Verkope list at the time it was compiled. While noting that many of the poisons on the list could be legitimate to study for defensive purposes, he also conceded in relation to antibiotic-resistant anthrax, 'that given the face value of this, and the fact that it appears on such a list and there are quantities named and a price attached to it, that is highly suspicious of either abuse or planned abuse'.[233] For him though, the lack of information about quantities, and his own limitations regarding the quantities of substances needed for murder, constrained his ability to speak definitively.   Offence 103

280   1998

As part of making a case at the TRC that the development of a defensive capability had been 'totally achieved', General Surgeon Knobel suggested that:

> It must be understood that a defensive capability does not exclude the possibility of going over into the offensive when you have to ensure that enemy troops may be using chemical weapons against you and, therefore, forcing you into your defensive equipment and, therefore, giving you a major disadvantage on the battlefield, must also in turn be forced to go into a similar situation where they are also in their defensive equipment and, therefore, then again equalising the battlefields.

In other words, at least at the time of Project Coast, a defensive capability could have a legitimate offensive component. In the case of South Africa, this strike-back, retaliation capability took the form of 'non-lethal' irritating agents (CR) or incapacitating agents (such as ecstasy). Knobel added: 'I can declare quite emphatically to you that at no time were classical chemical, or for that matter, biological weapons developed, weaponised with delivery systems and there was no intent ever to use any of those weapons on the battlefield.' As he explained, once South Africa became a signatory to the 1993 Chemical Weapons Convention, though, this treaty precluded the possibility of retaliation strike capabilities altogether.[234]   Offence 281

281   What might be done in the light of the disagreement about what label – if any – should be applied to Project Coast? Rather than seeking to answer the question, 'What was it, really?', another orientation would be to step back and pose the more basic one: 'How can one know what it was?' Considering this question might rapidly give away to another: 'What would be the stumbling blocks in trying to settle the matter?'   Offence 387

282   1998

In the TRC hearing, Knobel was asked whether the items on the Verkope list could be deemed to be in the category of classical chemical or biological weapons, and thus, proper matters for study in terms of the defensive mandate he said was in place for Project Coast.

Knobel said that the list of chemicals and biological agents needed to be investigated to determine their legitimacy as topics of study. Taking names of items from the Verkope list, the TRC began questioning him about each of them. What about phencyclidene (PCP)? What about…?

In cutting off this progression, Knobel offered the reasoning:

> I'm not a chemist and I'm certainly not, I haven't got the chemical background to be able to analyse each and every one of these and then say: 'This falls into that category and this falls into that category.' I'm saying, if you look at this list in the broadest possible way and you examine it against the list of scheduled chemicals and you have a chemical expert that can analyse it for you and tell you, then you will find that many of these substances fall within the classical list of chemical weapons.[235]

As such, the implication was that going through the substances and agents on the list in the context of the TRC hearing would be somewhat futile.

What expertise did the Coordinating Management Committee rely on then to make determination about what was a matter of proper study? As Knobel indicated, that expert relied on by the Coordinating Management Committee was one Dr Wouter Basson – a medical doctor with a Master's in Chemistry. To know 283

283 The question of whether the items on the Verkope list fell within the legitimate parameters of the programme was discussed with Knobel elsewhere in the hearings.

To aid such determinations, in this instance Knobel distributed a table from a book of classical, chemical-warfare agents to the TRC members. He also noted that:

> I don't have a sufficient chemistry background to make the fine distinction, but it wasn't necessary to do so because this sort of thing was never at the level of the Coordinating Management Committee.[236]

Phencyclidine (PCP) was the first item on the list. Was this then allowable? A discussion about its use as an incapacitant ensued when a TRC member, Dr Wendy Orr, interjected:

Orr: 'Sorry may I interrupt, I don't see phencyclidine on Table 1 of Chemical Warfare agents unless it's called by a different name.'

Knobel: 'But that's exactly the point I am trying to make Dr Orr. It would take a person with chemical background to look at the list of the accepted incapacitating agents that have been used or are potentially being used as chemical weapons.'

Orr: 'Well could we perhaps ask Professor Folb to do that check for us.'

Knobel: 'That is what I am trying to say, that is what you would need.'

Orr: 'Peter could you look at Table 1 and see if phencyclidine is on that list.'

Vally: 'Professor Folb is not a witness; are you asking him just to do background checking for you and tell you and you can raise it and he'll advise you off the record. Thank you Dr Orr.'[237]

In this exchange, the ability of the panel to understand what is being discussed is called into question. In this instance, a medically trained panel member reports not being able to discern the proper classification of a chemical.

Knobel offers the interpretation that this exemplifies the very dynamics associated with the Coordinating Management Committee: specialised expertise was required to give sense to the activities being undertaken, despite whatever competencies existed among the appointed committee members. They – like the TRC panel itself – could not be expected to know.

Peter Folb, Professor of Pharmacology at the University of Cape Town and expert adviser to the TRC, was identified as one possible specialist who might be able to understand what was being queried. Within the formalities of a hearing with official questioners and witnesses though, he could not participate in the interrogation process. Thus, the questioning had to continue without a shared certainty about what was being discussed.

The production of ignorance created in the exchange also called into question the authority that could be invested in the TRC questioning process for this topic. How well could it grasp the technical matters at hand? In this way, the exchange did not simply imply the need to call into doubt the answers given, but the basis for the questioning that generated responses.

The questioning of Knobel about items on the list continued. Phencyclidine? Well it could be a psychotropic incapacitant. Thallium?

The question of what counted as appropriate ignorance was tested in an exchange between Knobel and the TRC's national legal officer, Hanif Vally:

Vally: 'Are you aware of a case where a youth was allegedly poisoned in detention and it was thereafter, after forensic research by Professor Francis Ames, determined that thallium was the cause of the poisoning?'

Knobel: 'When you say I am aware, I might have read about it, but I simply cannot recall it.'

Vally: 'Why I am registering surprise is I would have thought, as number one, the Surgeon-General or someone very close to him, and number two, someone looking into chemical and biological warfare, that you would be very interested in any poisoning of this kind allegedly in police custody.'

Knobel: 'I totally disagree with you Mr Vally. I had no idea that there was any possibility that this programme could be abused for that purpose.'[238]

Expectations of knowledge in this exchange were informed by and implicated a sense of what the Surgeon General would, or should, have known, as well as what Project Coast was about. Hanif Vally attempts to bring into the range of expected awareness, an activity that would, at least, associate the programme with knowledge of questionable activities.

The listing and the questioning continued, with Knobel acknowledging varying ability to speak to the legitimacy of the chemicals and agents mentioned. In the questioning of Knobel, the appropriateness of the list, the adequacy of his ability to speak to it, the sufficiency of oversight, and the ultimate legitimacy of Project Coast were at stake. To know 284

284 1998
What Knobel sought to find out about Project Coast was also examined by the TRC. He was asked whether, when the Verkope list was made known to him in February 1997, he had enquired about it. He indicated that he had raised concerns with Basson previously in the light of emerging intelligence and was given reassurances that all work undertaken was in the mandate of the programme. No abuses had taken place.

But a TRC member asked Knobel whether it was wise that he had 'still relied on Dr Basson's reassurance that he had not exceeded his mandate, because surely the events that gave rise to your confrontation should have actually put you in a position to question the validity of what he was telling you?'[239] To know 285

285 As a claimed state of awareness, ignorance is a 'fickle' one – fickle because it can easily switch from being a shielding excuse to a basis for chastisement, depending on how the matters at hand are defined and framed.[240] To know 286

Expertise became a shared topic for investigation between participants in an intervention by Dr Wendy Orr, which followed on from her earlier one about what was included in the proper mandate for a defence programme:

> Orr: 'I'd just like to place on the record that in fact phencyclidine is not on Table 1 of Chemical Warfare agents and neither are any other psychotropic agents, and I think our interchange over this substance highlights for me one of my deepest concerns. I didn't know whether phencyclidine was on the list, you didn't, we had to call in an expert, but on your Coordinating Committee there were no such experts, and you were taking decisions about substances which, to me, it seems you were not fully informed about.'
>
> Knobel: 'No, I am sorry Dr Orr you are not correct. There was such an expert on the Coordinating Committee and that expert was Dr Basson.'
>
> Orr: 'I think it has been proven that reliance on such an expert eventually led to severe problems.'
>
> Knobel: 'Dr Orr, at the time there was no concern about the reliance on him. It is only now, with the wisdom of hindsight, that you can come to that conclusion. He was a – he had a Master's degree in Chemistry and all the members of the Coordinating Committee, including those that are now outside the Defence Force and in political positions, have confirmed that up to quite recently.'[241]

Herein the initial attempt is made by Orr not to treat the shared ignorance of Knobel and the TRC panel as grounds for his absolution, or for the Coordinating Committee's prior limits in oversight. Rather, it is grounds for criticism. That criticism was initially based on the lack of expertise, but then is reframed in terms of the reliance on one specific expert. The exchange continued, with Orr asking whether it would have been more appropriate to have had a group of independent people to provide advice. This leads Knobel to ask whether Orr is suggesting 'that I should have been an expert myself to be able to make that decision?' In shifting the conversation back to individual expertise, Knobel positions the issues at stake along lines that he has already countered.

Instead of ascribing this to an individual failing, Orr responds by turning the issues to one relevant to the goals of the TRC:

> Orr: 'No, I am not saying you should have been an expert yourself. My concern, and this goes to the fact that the Truth Commission has to

make recommendations as to how to prevent future violations and abuses, is how could we structure coordinating, managing, controlling bodies in order to ensure that this kind of thing does not happen again? If my suggestion is invalid or impractical, I would appreciate your suggestions about this.'[242]

As the questioning continued, Knobel agreed that having a group of experts would have been preferable, but argued that it could not have been done because chemical and biological weapons experts were 'few and far between' in South Africa.

Again, the TRC panel returned to the reliance on Basson as 'the expert'. When it was put to Knobel that, 'but even when you questioned him about excesses in terms of this programme, you had no way of establishing, except for his word, as to whether or not he had exceeded that.' He replied, 'That's correct.'[243]   To know 287

287 1999

During the criminal trial of Basson, Knobel would go on to contend that the planning and technical consideration of the work undertaken as part of Project Coast were supposed to be done by the Technical Working Group. Owing to the need to limit knowledge of what was taking place, membership of the group varied from meeting to meeting.[244] Basson was the only person who was always a member when the group convened – an event that appeared to happen seldom.   To know 288

288 While claiming to know what others do not can confer a heightened status and credibility, it would be an overgeneralisation to imagine that people always try to represent themselves as the possessors of knowledge. Whether it is desirable to be in the know depends on the specifics of a situation. Doubt, uncertainty or outright ignorance might be professed by some on occasion. For instance, in situations where knowledge would imply responsibility, not knowing is clearly advantageous. And yet, while ignorance might be sought at times, professing ignorance all (or most of) the time would undermine an individual's authority.

In practice, mixing claims of knowing with claims of ignorance can require nifty footwork.   To know 289

289 1998

On many occasions when Basson testified before the TRC, he portrayed his expertise and awareness as limited. When asked why he thought he was originally deemed appropriate for a role in chemical and biological warfare – whether it was, for instance, his Master's degree in Physiology and Chemistry or his MD in Medicine – Basson indicated that he 'had no qualifications which made me capable of doing it, but the potential lay in the fact I had the background to understand the military science, as well as the medical science, and I could combine them, and to combine them tactically.'

Under repeated questioning about what he knew about Project Coast during its operation, he downplayed any grasp of what had taken place or his own agency. In response to the suggestion that Basson had a free hand to determine its activities, he retorted:

> That is not correct, I did not have a free hand, and I repeat what I've said before, it was my task to receive the guidelines from the committee, to process them and to go back to the coordinating control committee with specific goals, and some of these goals had sub-goals, and the control committee had to approve these goals, and according to that, a budget was brought into life and I received further guidelines from them and I also received authorisation from them to act in this regard.[245]

He went on to refute being the person that determined what experiments were performed. Staff might have reported their specialised scientific results to him, but only for the purposes of managing the research. He indicated that he did not even know about all of the South African Defence Force projects undertaken.

The documents found in sealed containers at the home of one of Basson's associates would form part of a set of documents available to the TRC but not publicly circulated. South African officials argued that, while these exposed no technical details that might pose proliferation threats, if their details did emerge this could severely compromise relations between the countries.

In varying ways, however, the content of the démarches by the United States and the United Kingdom became a topic of deliberation, as in the exchange between Hanif Vally (the TRC's national legal officer) and Surgeon General Knobel:

> Vally: 'In terms of evidence presented to this hearing, because the context is, you said in 1994, after the démarche by the Americans and the British, that you got concerned [about the activities taking place under Project Coast].'
> Knobel: 'That's correct.'
> Vally: 'And by the way, and I don't think this is proliferation, but that

démarche wasn't to say this is a terrible immoral thing you people are doing, this démarche was to say hey, make sure that the ANC don't get their hands on these items.'

Knobel: 'That's correct, that's exactly the information I gave Mr Mandela.'

Vally: 'Fine.'[246] IR 291

291 Although the South African government had expressed grave concern about releasing the documents pertaining to the démarches by the United States and Britain to South Africa regarding Project Coast, and the effects these might have on South Africa's relations with these countries, the same kind of concern did not appear to trouble officials elsewhere. The US Ambassador to South Africa at the time, Princeton Lyman, wrote candidly about the démarches in his book, *Partner to History*, published in 2002. IR 161

292 1998

The TRC hearings would return many times to the themes of what lessons might be learnt from the past, particularly with regard to why the scientists, veterinarians and engineers that participated in Project Coast did so. This did not always lead to much insight. Offence 293

293 1998

When Philip Mijburgh, Managing Director of Delta G Scientific, testified before the TRC, he was asked whether he was left with any questions about why he, as managing director, was not able to answer questions about his company. He was asked, 'in retrospect and in looking at the questions that have been posed to you today, are there question marks in your own mind as to what was happening in your company?' To this he responded:

> In terms of my own involvement in the chemical warfare programme and seen in the light of the time and the period in which it took place, it was for me as a member of SAMS and later as a member of Delta G, the front company, I was brought under the impression that there was a specific threat against the country and more specifically against some of the members of the defence force in terms of chemical warfare. So, in that respect, I understood it as that we were rendering a service to the defence force.
>
> And as I said to Dr Orr just now, I didn't have a moral problem with what we were doing at Delta G in a sense that I felt that although it was quite normal, there was a major and emotional outcry regarding chemical and biological warfare, those aspects which we dealt with at Delta made

possible more humane warfare in terms of incapacitants and crowd control measures, etc. I hope that answers the question about my own involvement.

Yes, I am surely responsible in the sense that we developed certain substances. I always believed and I never had any reason to doubt that it was a well-thought-out plan of action by the defence force. My contact with the defence, whether in my capacity as managing director of Delta G or otherwise, I never thought that we were actually engaged in anything underhand or immoral.

And then yes, as far as the third question is concerned, yes there are certain questions in our minds today. We are living in a different era and I would be very glad if these questions could be laid to rest at some time or another. You do have questions but I unfortunately don't have the answers.[247]

Offence 260 | Lessons 507

294 1998

In considering how secrecy infused the understanding of Project Coast, it important to consider the investments made into believing that secrets existed and that they could be uncovered.

As part of the winding-down phase of the programme, the management committee decided that the technical documentation produced should be saved electronically on CD-ROM, while the physical versions would be destroyed. Especially after the sealed, steel trunks found in 1997 at the home of Basson's associate, after Basson's arrest on drugs charges, the question of what had happened to the physical and electronic versions of the documents became a matter of importance. At the TRC hearings, various questions were put to witnesses:

Who undertook the electronic capturing of the documents? (A front company headed by Philip Mijburgh, the managing director of Delta G Scientific.)

Who of any technical standing had gone through the electronic recording? (No one, not even Basson.)

Were the disks secure? On this question at the hearings, the Surgeon General Niel Knobel spoke in some detail about the elaborate provisions made to keep this information secure:

After the technical information was transferred from documents onto the discs, the discs were brought to me by Colonel Ben Steyn in a safe. I established that the discs were inside the safe, and as far as I remember, there's also an additional floppy along with it, which is the access mechanism, access coding that you require to be able to access the information on the discs.

102

It was then put into a very large wall safe attached to my office and my headquarters, and only Colonel Steyn and I had control, joint control over the small safe, smaller safe, the portable safe. After the démarche, and particularly after the Americans and the British expressed concern about the safety of the information on the discs, I went to see [President] de Klerk and I followed it up with a letter and that letter, I can give you a copy of. It was in April 1994.

At that stage, we changed the joint control in such a way that all three of us, the President, Mr de Klerk, Colonel Steyn and myself had to be present in order to access or to be able to open the small safe. The position was then changed; it was then changed to a safe in a different part of my headquarters, a huge safe with two keys and a combination and the small safe with its two keys was put into the bigger safe.

And in that joint control, we gave the President one of the keys of the big safe as well as the combination of the big safe. I kept the key of the big safe and one of the keys of the small safe. Colonel Steyn had the combination of the big safe and the other key of the small safe, and that was how that situation was maintained.[248]

When the new government come to power in 1994, the key and combination given to President de Klerk was passed over to Deputy President Thabo Mbeki.

In openly discussing the existence and whereabouts of the disks, the discussion at the time in the TRC and in the press posited that there was something in the disks – something that needed to be hidden away because of its profound importance.[249] What? 389 | Forgetting 389

295 Here the function of secrecy was to confer significance. This incident was also reflective of how, when secrecy is pervasive, those responsible for secret-keeping can no longer easily distinguish between what is secret and what is not, as well as what needs to be secret and what does not. In a situation of war, it might well feel as though everything should be secret.

What? 294

296 1998

For most who testified at the TRC, what the Verkope list amounted to was presented as a matter of conjecture. The Managing Director of Roodeplaat Research Laboratories at the time the list was compiled, Wynand Swanepoel, claimed not to have seen the sales document before and refused to speculate on its meaning at the hearing. When pressed by a TRC panel member, Jerome Chaskalson, to 'explain the purpose of putting poison in whisky in terms of a defensive programme', the following exchange took place:

Mr Swanepoel: 'I can possibly refer back to what I previously said, to determine how it would work in whisky, whether you could identify it in whisky, or whether you could provide that information to your client. Perhaps it was his need to know whether all these agents or substances could be traced in whisky. That is my interpretation.'

Mr Chaskalson: 'Will you not concede that this list is possibly a list of abuses?'

Mr Swanepoel: 'The application I can't speculate about.'[250]

What? 301 | Offence 301

297 Thus, attempts to provide meaning to the Verkope list, and other items brought forward for examination, amounted to trials of strength wherein individuals marshalled objects and arguments to support an understanding of the named items. What? 298

298 The list functioned as the Rosetta Stone, not so much in the commonplace notion of the slate acting as a simple decoder that unlocked meaning, but rather as a resource that facilitated the arduous and painstaking process of sense-making. What? 41

299 1998

Prior to his testimony at the TRC, Surgeon General Knobel freely distributed 'Top Secret' documents associated with Project Coast to the media. These were later recalled. What? 229

300 1998

The special hearing of the TRC convened for the final time on 31 July. The Human Rights Commission's mandate to hold hearings was to expire at midnight. The first few hours of the hearing were consumed by legal bantering between Basson's advocate, Jaap Cilliers, the TRC's legal representative, Hanif Vally, and the state's legal representative, Neville Arendse.

Mr Arendse: 'Now, the offer of the hearings being held in camera was made and was tabled here on the 8th or the 9th of June when the application was made for Dr Basson not to testify. At that stage, Dr Basson and his lawyers had an opportunity to make this application that they're now making. It is clear that this is another attempt at trying to delay these proceedings.

The government is opposed to the application. Given the limited time constraints that we have, there is absolutely no need, that we can see, why he should proliferate or why he should endanger or potentially endanger our foreign relations with other countries.

I can just think of a couple of examples. Allegations have been made

Reverend Frank Chikane, a prominent victim of poisons produced by Project
Coast. Copyright: Nelson Mandela Foundation.

Skeleton Coast, Namibia: South African Defence Force member, Johan Theron, would testify during the trial of Wouter Basson that he disposed of hundreds of bodies of SWAPO members by dropping them from a plane into the Atlantic Ocean after they were sedated with muscle relaxants. Copyright: Constructed image. Video still (out-take) from documentary film *The Man Who Knows Too Much* (dir. Liza Key, 2002). Courtesy of Liza Key & University of Cape Town Jagger Library Special Collections.

Work at Roodeplaat Research Laboratories included the development of chemical and biological substances, which could be used to kill while leaving no trace. Copyright: Liza Key & University of Cape Town Jagger Library Special Collections.

Applicators, murder weapons, or life savers? Reconstructed items from the Verkope List on display at the *Poisoned Pasts* exhibition. Copyright: Brian Rappert.

Door of incinerator for animals at the site of the former Roodeplaat Research Laboratories in 2014. Copyright: Kathryn Smith. Reproduced with permission under CC-BY-NC-ND licence.

Incinerator for animals at the former site of Roodeplaat Research Laboratories in 2014. When questioned at the Truth and Reconciliation Commission hearing, Dr Schalk van Rensburg (one-time chairman of the Laboratory Animal Ethics Committee) offered the reassurance 'animals were killed, many died, many were put out, but they were not large numbers, no'. Copyright: Kathryn Smith. Reproduced with permission under CC-BY-NC-ND licence.

Abandoned gorilla cage at the site of the former Roodeplaat Research Laboratories in 2014. Copyright: Kathryn Smith. Reproduced with permission under CC-BY-NC-ND licence.

To-scale reconstructed chair for experimenting on baboons backgrounded with animal cages from the Agricultural Research Council housed at the site of Roodeplaat Research Laboratories. Scene from *Poisoned Pasts* exhibition. Copyright: Nelson Mandela Foundation.

Spring-loaded poisoned screwdrivers buried by Dr Jan Lourens at his farm in Northern Transvaal and later excavated for the Truth and Reconciliation Commission hearings (photographed at Freedom Park in 2015). Copyright: Alexis Fotiadis and Kathryn Smith. Reproduced with permission under CC-BY-NC-ND licence.

Jan Lourens, late 1980s, Scotland. Lourens was viewing the demonstration of a simulated nuclear explosion by Brook Pyrotechnics in Scotland. Copyright: Liza Key & University of Cape Town Jagger Library Special Collections.

Silhouettes hanging from the ceiling in the *Poisoned Pasts* exhibition were used to create affect and demonstrate practically how many people were affected by these secret programmes. One visitor to the exhibition said that it felt as though she were walking under their souls. Copyright: Nelson Mandela Foundation.

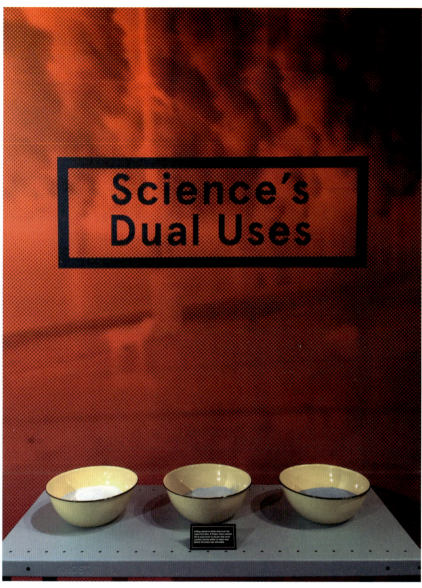

Display at the *Poisoned Pasts* exhibition. Explanation card reads: 'Adding cyanide to mielie meal turns the staple food blue. A Project Coast scientist did an experiment to see just how much cyanide could be added to mielie meal before the colour was noticeable.' Copyright: Kathryn Smith. Reproduced with permission under CC-BY-NC-ND licence.

Families of the young men killed in the incident referred to as the 'Nietverdient Ten' at the launch of *Poisoned Pasts*. Copyright: Nelson Mandela Foundation.

that toxins were made, poisons were made, at this Roodeplaats, this factory of death, by people who actually made them on his instructions. We know that toxins and poisons were put into cigarettes and into whisky and all kinds of things, people were killed, cholera was used to put into the water of certain – these are allegations that he needs to answer, they have got nothing to do with proliferation, they have got nothing to do with our foreign relations, and given the time constraints that we have today, those are the, I would have thought, the kind of direct questions that Mr Vally should be putting to Dr Basson today. So for that reason alone, and because it concerns my client directly, the leg of proliferation should fall away immediately, because the government is now saying that these hearings should go ahead and focus on the gross human rights violations…'

Mr Cilliers: 'With respect, I would like to answer his argument. He says "people were killed". I can't remember that one witness made such an allegation, not one allegation was made where one person was killed by Dr Basson or through this project. I take strong exception by this misleading and manipulation of the facts.'   Justice 324

301 **1998**

Under many lines of questioning, Basson presented a picture wherein alleged murder weapons became means of protection. Why put cyanide in peppermint chocolate? This type of thing was done to demonstrate to members of the South African security forces what Russian-trained ANC members could do with simple chemical substances. Why place anthrax on cigarettes? To test if this delivery system could harm people (tests showed it could not). Why produce bottles of cholera? To test inoculation processes and advise about how to deal with potential outbreaks in Namibia and elsewhere.

Since the quantities produced were so small, Basson argued that mass murder or sometimes even single murders would not be possible.

Besides, if they were, indeed, murder weapons, then why were there no bodies? Such evidence was absent from the assemblages that others were attempting to build to cast Project Coast in a negative light and implicate Basson in murder. In the case of cholera specifically, he contended that the origins of outbreaks were traceable and, yet again, none had been traced back to Project Coast.

To the charges made by Dr Immelman that Dr Basson had instructed him to manufacture the substances on the Verkope list for murder, on the approval of the State Security Council, the latter denied any such acts. Indeed, what the list presented was said to be far from certain. The following response was elicited to the question of whether the Verkope list was a delivery list:

> Dr Basson: 'I do not know at all, Advocate Potgieter, I did not draw up this list; it's not my list, it's not my work, I was confronted with this the first time in February '97, so I cannot explain to you this list. I've already said that I do recognise some of these products and I do recognise some of the combinations, but it's not my list.'
>
> Advocate Potgieter: 'But does it seem as if it's a record of products or substances which were delivered to people who are not really identified in these documents?'
>
> Dr Basson: 'It looks to me like a list of products and mixtures, whether it's a delivery list, I do not know. It might as well have been a production list, I do not know.'
>
> Advocate Potgieter: 'And those names, do they look like code names to you?'
>
> Dr Basson: 'I don't see any names, I only see letters; I don't understand what the names or the letters mean, I did not write them there, I really do not know.'[251]   What? 320 | Offence 354

302 1998

During the testimony of Dr Basson, questioners repeatedly asked him to offer an account of documentary evidence collected by the TRC. Attempting to tie him to what was written provided a potential basis for establishing what had taken place and, through this, the appropriateness of the conduct of Basson and Project Coast overall.

In his responses to questioning, Basson reported varying abilities of recall. When shown the Verkope (Sales) list, which Dr Immelman had claimed in a TRC affidavit constituted a list of chemical compositions intended as murder weapons, Basson categorically refuted any knowledge of the list prior to the proceedings against him, begun in 1997.

When questioning then turned to another TRC document with the heading 'Payments of Coast Projects Fund Flow' (TRC 26),[252] there was the following exchange:

> Mr Basson: 'I can't, according to my memory, no, I haven't seen this.'
>
> Mr Vally: 'Well, you were the Project Officer of Project Coast, weren't you?'
>
> Mr Basson: 'Chairperson, in this process, 100 000 or more documents

came, I had to look at all of them, so I cannot say that I have seen this document before.'

Mr Vally: 'Well, you may say you are not sure; are you saying you are not sure or are you saying you did not see it?'

Mr Basson: 'Can I repeat this slowly? I said I cannot say with certainty if I have ever seen this document before.'

In these exchanges, much is at stake in exactly what is said. While Basson's initial response above indicates, 'no, I haven't seen this', this is also done with a preface that he is relying on his memory when answering. Then Hanif Vally cites Basson's role as project manager to imply that he *should have* seen the document. To counter this, Basson makes reference to the sheer number of documents to which he would have been exposed in Project Coast as grounds for why it might be difficult for him to establish any familiarity with this particular document. Vally then refers to Basson's prior prefaced statement to question more exactly what he is claiming. After further exchanges between Basson, his advocate and Vally, Basson states: 'I do not recognise this document *per se*, but I do recognise some of the objectives which during the initial formulating of Project Coast, was [sic] put into place.'

This general but not specific recognition of TRC 26 would later enable Basson to speak, in a qualified manner, to what elements of the document meant. When Vally asked him what the designators in TRC 26 7/01 Chancellor, 7/02 Chris, 7/03 Koos, 7/04 Mealies, 7/05 Hekkies, 7/06 Barries, 7/07 Conventional, 7/08 Other meant in relation to chemical and biological warfare operations, Basson indicated, 'As far as I can remember, these are the different areas for which we gave code-names so that the operational teams can distinguish between the different areas.'

What Basson would claim or not about his ability to recall about the document would become subsequently relevant as Vally would seek to make a connection between the Verkope list and TRC 26. Regarding the former, Dr Immelman wrote in his affidavit that the security force members given items from the list included 'Chris' and 'Koos'. Was it the case, Vally posed, that the '7/02 Chris' and '7/03 Koos' in TRC 26 were the same as those in the Verkope list?

To this Basson responded:

Mr Basson: 'Chairperson, I have a problem in the sense that I am being asked to look at an undated document, TRC 26, which was probably drawn up in the early 1980s. If I must remind myself of how it happened, because later in time as the programme became more sophisticated, these objectives changed.

Dr Immelman's affidavit with regard to a specific period in time, I think it is 1989, I didn't even read it, but these two connections, I cannot make them, and I must tell you that if there are any resemblances between Koos and Chris, then I want to know where is Mealie, Hekkies, Barries, Conventional and all the others?

I am of the opinion that these two are not related, it is pure coincidence. The dates of these documents are not known to me so I cannot bring them together.'[253]

In this Basson reports back an inability to draw connections between TRC 26 and the Verkope list because of the dates in question and the lack of dates given. It is not a refutation of any possible link, but the inability to know, based on the written evidence put before him. This inability stands as counter to all claims that might be directed against him. What he reports to be able to do is to offer an opinion, and an opinion only.   Forgetting 303

303 1998

An account of history was not just something that was produced through the work of the TRC, at times it was central to its proceedings and, thereby, what history could eventually be written.

On several occasions during the testimony of Basson, he was asked, and refused to comment, on matters beyond those presented to him. For instance:

Mr Vally: '[T]he fact is that you make an allegation that possibly President Mandela is alive because of your work or, on the contrary, the possibility also exists that President Mandela is alive because there was no such plan by the ANC to murder him. Is that a possibility?'

Dr Basson: 'I cannot comment on anything except that which I've seen in writing.'[254]

The practical consequence of such moves was to bound the scope for questioning.   Forgetting 230

304 1998

One strand of activities under Project Coast, which became widely discussed through the TRC, was a plan in the mid-1980s to poison Nelson Mandela while he was imprisoned.

At the time of the TRC, the ANC cited this plan as proof that:

[I]t is clear that the chemical and biological weapons project was clearly for offensive purposes and part of an ongoing dirty tricks campaign to murder anti-apartheid activists and black people indiscriminately... It is our hope that the current TRC hearing will shed light on all these programmes and the entire chain of command involved in deciding upon these inhumane programmes as well as those involved in their implementation. What is clear is that leading scientists engaged in these inhumane experiments in the same way as those that served the Nazi regime in Germany. If ever there was a programme that truly typified the genocidal programmes of the apartheid regime, this was it.[255]

When referred to a Secretariat of the State Security Council document from March 1986, which included an option of poisoning Mandela, Dr Basson denied knowledge of this specific document at the TRC. He had, though, been able to offer an example of how his work had been part of efforts to *save* Mandela. As recounted at the TRC hearing, in the mid 1980s the Minister of Defence asked Basson to put in place a protection plan in response to intelligence reports that some disenfranchised members of the ANC were trying to assassinate Mandela. To ensure he stayed 'alive at all costs',[256] Basson used a standard red force–blue force method:

[To] the blue-force scientists, I would give an instruction to investigate all ways of killing Mandela in jail and I would leave them with that. They would do a theoretical research; they could do what they want [sic]. I would say to the red force: 'Kill Mr Mandela'. The blue forces, because blue forces were always friendly in military terms: 'Develop all techniques to save and to defend Mr Mandela and make sure that nothing happens to him in jail.'

After months of research and instruction giving, the red force comes with a plan to kill Mr Mandela and the blue force comes with a plan to protect Mr Mandela; in other words, [a] security measure which has to be put into place. So I take those two plans and I integrate them into one plan.[257]

In contrast to the way such plans to kill Mandela had been reported in the media prior to the TRC,[258] and rather than such work being a source of concern, Basson contented that: 'The fact that Mandela is still alive today can be ascribed to the fact and the way in which the political leaders of that time saved his life in order to ensure the future of this country.'[259] Victims 305 305 This was not the only time that Basson would frame the chemical and biological warfare programme as having protected lives. Nor was he the only one to do so. Victims 367

Against the dubious activities reported to the TRC, Basson as Project Officer for Project Coast faced at least two types of potential charges. To the extent that he was aware of its activities, he could be deemed culpable for his complicity; but to the extent that he was unaware, he could be deemed culpable for his failure to supervise.

Basson steered a different course. As he conveyed under questioning, while he expected to be briefed on important results, scientists in the programme also initiated their own research – and rightly without his knowledge. If the results were important, he would be briefed, but otherwise not.

In relation to the allegations made by Dr van Rensburg and Dr Goosen at the TRC, that attempts were made to develop an anti-fertility vaccine which could be used on black women, for instance, Basson argued that no such work had been part of the programme. Or at least, importantly, not 'on instruction by the South African Defence Force in any case. What Doctor van Rensburg did on his own, I cannot vouch for that.'[260]

Against documents distributed at the TRC relating to the work on fertility undertaken by Doctor Riana Borman, Basson spoke to what might be labelled 'scientific freedom' within the context of the programme:

> Each researcher had the right within his own field of interest, his or her own field of interest to a certain degree [to] do research so that they could do other work besides the work for the Defence Force. They were scientists, they had to publish, to write publications and tell other scientists what they were doing.
>
> This specific project was within the field of interest of certain scientists and their field of interest was not the control of the fertility of people. That had to do with the identification of certain sperms… but there was never ever the intention to control the fertility of any people. This is an outright lie.[261]

Through numerous similar evocations of such freedom to conduct individual research, a space was created for activities about which Basson could legitimately say he was unaware, but which were still done under the appropriate oversight controls of the programme. Since through publications other scientists would have known about the work, this provided the possibility of an additional community-based form of oversight. To know 307

307 This space for individual research activities, of which Basson could legitimately say he was unaware, also provided a justification for not being able to speak to the documents placed before him at the TRC. As in

the case of the fertility research, when asked about his knowledge of one record, he indicated:

> I don't have any knowledge of this document. It seems to me like an internal Roodeplaat document. I have no knowledge of this.[262]

Such statements cut off this questioning about the programme. As relatively little documentary evidence was at the disposal of the TRC, and its staff members were highly reliant on what was in their possession to provide a basis for engaging witnesses, claims of not knowing effectively cut off whole lines of examination.   To know 308

308 1998

Part of Basson's refutation of allegations made against Project Coast was an appeal to clear facts that were said to be undoubtable.

For instance, against the claims made by Dr van Rensburg that Basson ordered anti-fertility work to be done to prevent female UNITA troops, fighting in Angola, from becoming pregnant, he responded:

> Mr Chairman, I deny that strongly. Professor Folb is there and he will know the scientific absurdity of this proposal. There are enough substances available.[263]

In this instance, absurdity is evoked and reference is made to a technical adviser to the TRC. That this person is not able to participate in the questioning is noted in the exchange that followed:

> Vally: 'This is about the fourth time that you've referred me to Professor Folb. I would appreciate it if you answered questions. Professor Folb is not a witness here. Professor Folb, for the purposes of this inquiry, is a member of our team.'
>
> Basson: 'Mr Chairman, I apologise that I involve Professor Folb but he and Doctor Randera and Doctor Orr are the members in this hearing who will understand what I'm saying, who originally would have had the knowledge to say this was absurd. The facts of the matter are, if I had female soldiers, there are very good techniques, for example, progesterone injections could solve this fertility problem and also the menstrual problems.'[264]

In his elaboration, Basson highlights the absurdity by pointing to what the members of the commission should already know – while appearing to defer to their knowledge, he is questioning this knowledge by making a case for the absurdity of asking certain questions. To know 309

309 In interrogating Basson, the TRC panel members would act to problematise appeals to expertise.

When asked to explain why Dr Odendaal had commented on the 26 10 ml bottles of the cholera culture he had prepared, as follows:

> …the idea stuck in my mind, that in the first case it was to be used for testing purpose and in the second one, you know, there were hints that this could be used in the war situation in Angola and it never crossed my mind for one moment, that it could be used internally in our own country, because to use organisms or to spread organisms in your own country, is a very risky thing and it doesn't go along with the Convention of Biological Warfare, that you do not produce these things to use on your own territory.[265]

Basson responded:

> I understand Dr Odendaal's statement completely and his answer is correct. It is possible that you can cause epidemics with these things, in very rare circumstances. I would like to tell you to create an epidemic by using something like cholera, is almost impossible.[266]

Basson would directly challenge the ability of the TRC national legal officer, Hanif Vally, to understand the facts of the matter given his lack of scientific expertise.

When eventually asked why the 'large quantity' of bottled cholera culture would not be questionable, Basson argued that the volume, without an indication of the concentration, would not enable him to judge how much was produced. When told that Dr Odendaal 'did in fact say that it was enough cholera to cause a major epidemic', Basson retorted with a refutation of Odendaal's ability as an expert to make that determination in arguing: 'I don't think, with permission, that Dr Odendaal had the knowledge, the experience or the insight of cholera epidemics, to know how many organisms are needed to create an epidemic.'[267] To know 310

310 The same questions raised in the TRC, about who should have known and who should have done what as a result, should be asked of other professionals who did not participate in the TRC process. What should they have made known about the activities undertaken? What were the responsibilities of other professionals to discuss what took place – to redress it? To know 50

The optical disks containing files from Project Coast would again become a topic of consideration within the TRC. A line of questioning related to Basson's contribution went as follows:

> Mr Vally: 'We are talking about the decision to put all the information relevant to the CBW Programme onto optical discs. Coupled with that, the destruction of all other documents relating to the programme once the documents had been put onto disk. Are you aware of that instruction?'
>
> Dr Basson: 'I am aware that the documentation was destroyed but I was not responsible for that. I did not give an assurance or undertaking to anybody that all documentation was destroyed.'

In this exchange, Basson proves a clear refute of any responsibility for the destruction or the assurance of the destruction of Project Coast documentation.

> Mr Vally: 'Are you aware that there was a report-back to the Coordinating Committee that the documents had in fact been destroyed after the documents were put on optical disc?'
>
> Dr Basson: 'Can you give me the date of the report-back please?'
>
> Mr Vally: 'We can. It was in 1994 and I believe it was in March.'
>
> Dr Basson: 'In March 1994, I was not a member of the South African Defence Force anymore and I had no contact with the Coordinating Management Committee anymore.'

Although Vally's question about the report-back makes no direct reference to Basson, the latter interprets the words as relating to himself. As he argues, the established date of the report-back demarks a definitive line against which Basson's involvement can be gauged. The discussion continues with Hanif Vally saying:

> Mr Vally: 'You had absolutely no contact with them?'
>
> Dr Basson: 'None that I attended formal meetings, not as far as I can remember.'

In the unfolding exchange, Vally's question could be interpreted as curious. Although Basson had offered no qualifications or hesitations regarding his contact with the Coordinating Management Committee, Vally queries him again. The effect of the question–answer format is, arguably, to up the stakes of what gets spoken about next. If Basson continues to maintain the position of no contact, then that position firmly settles his stance (though with a yet-unstated relevance to what will follow). If he changes his mind, it would undermine his reliability as a witness. Basson opts for neither extreme but, instead, qualifies the argument as pertaining to formal meetings and relying on his memory.

The reasoning behind this line of questioning becomes clearer as Vally responses with:

> Mr Vally: 'Weren't you involved in a number of meetings where you had to report on what happened to all the money, which disappeared in Croatia?'
>
> Dr Basson: 'I'm not going to comment on the money which disappeared in Croatia…' [Intervention.]
>
> Mr Vally: 'I'm not asking you about the money, I'm asking about your presence at the Meeting of the Coordinating Committee.'
>
> Dr Basson: 'Periodically I reported back on the request of individuals in the CCC.'
>
> Mr Vally: 'Exactly, so don't say you were not at Coordinating Committee meetings in 1994.'

Here Vally attempts to use records of the past regarding Basson's report-backs on other matters to conclude that he has not spoken accurately. In reply, Basson returns to one of the qualifications he introduced:

> Dr Basson: 'I've attended no Committee meetings in a formal capacity, not as far as I can remember.'
>
> Mr Vally: 'And you may have attended in an informal capacity?'
>
> Dr Basson: 'I can't remember that.'
>
> Mr Vally: 'Well I put it to you that you did.'
>
> Dr Basson: 'It is possible, I can't remember.'
>
> Chairperson: 'Well it is not really being contested Mr Vally. He says he was no longer a member of the Defence Force but there were occasions when he had to attend, and I think there is a qualification. It is not a total denial of contact with the relevant authorities. Could we get onto something else?'

Vally then gets on to something else by bringing in what was said to have taken place as part of the report-backs.

Mr Vally: 'You see General Knobel testified to us, he said that you reported to him and he was satisfied with your report because he reported to the Coordinating Committee that all the documentation had been destroyed. When I put to him –

"The fact is that we know that Brigadier Basson advised you that he had destroyed all the technical documents."

I'll read out to you what he said:

"Absolutely, he also does at a Coordinating Management Committee meeting. And the fact we know he lied…"

This is referring to you. And General Knobel's response was:

"Yes, that's true."'

Here, Vally draws on the record to implicate Basson in a lie. After a side exchange, the line of questioning continues with:

Mr Vally: 'Doctor Basson, I go on to say:

"So he may have lied about lots of other things?"

and General Knobel says:

"That's also true."

Now there are Management Committee meetings in terms of which reports are made that these documentations have been destroyed. We have under oath, evidence from General Knobel wherein he said that you had advised him the documents had been destroyed. By virtue of the fact that these documents still exist, he confirmed that you must have lied to him. Would you like to comment on this?'

In this turn, Vally draws on evidence established as part of the TRC, which implicates Basson in deceit. An implication that leads to the objection:

Mr Cilliers: 'May I just enquire, what is the relevance of this specific question? You've been trying to ask the question for about five minutes. I don't even really know what the question is, but what is the relevance of this aspect regarding the investigation you are busy with at the moment? On that basis I object to this question.

Mr Vally: 'Mr Chair, to enlighten my learned friend, the relevance of the question is simply to determine to what extent was General Knobel kept informed, and honestly informed, of various incidents, to what extent was the Coordinating Committee kept informed, and honesty informed, of various incidents and if General Knobel, who was the Project Manager says that his Project Officer, Doctor Basson, lied to him about the destruction of documents, the question is what else is Doctor Basson alleged to have lied about? I want to determine whether General Knobel's statement that Doctor Basson lied to him about the destruction of documents, what Doctor Basson's comment on that is.'

Mr Cilliers: 'I can understand if you're asking him in which way did you mislead Knobel and why. Just ask a question which we can understand and which can be answered and will not take an hour to get to the question.'

Chairperson: 'I take your point Mr Cilliers. Mr Vally, if you could put questions that are more pointed to the witness.'

After an objection from Basson's advocate regarding the lack of clarity and the relevance of the question for the investigation at hand, Mr Vally offers a regloss:

Mr Vally: 'The question is very simply, General Knobel said that he understood it was your responsibility to ensure that the documents were destroyed, that you reported back to him that the documents were destroyed and, by virtue of the fact that the documents were not destroyed, just in terms of the documents we have here, that you in fact lied to him. What's your comment on that.'

To which Basson eventually responded with:

Dr Basson: 'The fact of the matter is, it was never my instruction to destroy these documents. It's an Intelligence responsibility. It was never my instruction to report back that all documentation had been destroyed. That instruction, and I can tell you that Military Intelligence still has documentation regarding this project right to the end. I had no control over that. I could not destroy that. All I did was, between the Defence Force and the contractor who put these documents, the data on the CD-ROM, I was the intermediator and I assured them that the documentation was captured on CD-ROM. I never gave anybody the assurance that everything was destroyed. It was not my task and it was not my responsibility.

Having tried to show that Basson had lied through the proceeding of the TRC, Vally then changes the direction of potential culpability to again force an establishment of lying:

Mr Vally: 'So Doctor Knobel misled us when he advised us of this?'

Mr Cilliers: 'That is not the witness's function to decide who did not speak the truth, it is your function.'

Chairperson: 'I think it's legitimate for him to say. "No, no, I think that's a legitimate question. He's not asking for his opinion, he's asking if in his view – because I mean it's either he is lying or the General [Knobel] is lying.'

The chairperson in this interjection not only allows the question but also supports the presumption underlying Vally's question: namely, that the record of the TRC supports the notion that a definite misrepresentation is being offered by someone. This is highly consequential within the exchange. Rather than being a matter open for interpretation or a matter where claims to truth might be valid, the questioning trades on an unchallenged notion that irreconcilable claims are being forwarded.

Mr Cilliers: 'But he has given his answer, General Knobel has given his answer. Why should the witness now say that Knobel told a lie?'

Chairperson: 'We ask that question every day in tribunals, which are even more strict on how we should tender the evidence.'

Mr Cilliers: 'With the greatest respect, he was not here when General Knobel said that.'

Chairperson: 'He was represented.'

Mr Cilliers: 'No, I was not present when General Knobel said that.'

Chairperson: 'Well that was your loss, you should have been here or at least somebody should have been here.'

Mr Cilliers: 'Well there wasn't, but the fact is… [Intervention.]'

Chairperson: 'Well it is being put – no, no, Mr Cilliers, no, I rule you out of order. The question is quite legitimate. It can be put to him and the witness can say: "I don't understand that because I was not here," but you can't really object to the question being illegitimate.'

Advocate Cilliers's intervention seeks to prevent Basson from being placed in a position of directing attributions of lying at his former colleague or implicating himself in lying. This is done by first suggesting there is no need for the question to be answered, then by proposing that the absence of Basson or his representatives during Surgeon General Knobel's statement means that there should not be a response to the question. The exchange continues with further objections to the question of whether Knobel mislead the TRC:

Mr Cilliers: 'But he's telling you, with respect: "I did not say that to General Knobel because it was not my task" and the question had been answered.'

Chairperson: 'No, it has not been. The one that he answered has not been.'

Mr Cilliers: 'With respect, it is my submission to you that you cannot expect from a witness, the witness is here to give you the facts and not to say which of them are speaking the truth.'

Chairperson: 'You are wasting more time Mr Cilliers, with respect. The question is allowed by me to be put to the witness. It is not prejudicial, it is legitimate. Let the witness reply to the question.'

Faced with a question that tries to make him direct a definite lie, or requires him to question what kind of truth is being debated, Basson opts for neither:

Dr Basson: 'I have no comment on what General Knobel said. I cannot speculate. I was not present when he said that. I stand by what I've said.'

Chairperson: 'Your client is much more intelligent that you allow him for.'

The consequence of Basson referring to his inability to speculate on a matter raised when he was not present is to end this long line of questioning without resolution.

312   The 'truth' of Project Coast, as constructed through the chemical and biological warfare hearings, and reported on in the media, was shaped and constrained by the TRC's mandate: to investigate and report on 'gross human rights abuses'. Despite the Verkope list – and detailed research reports about animal experiments conducted at Roodepoort Research Laboratories, apparently in pursuit of chemical and biological agents that would be untraceable post-mortem – it was not immediately apparent that anyone had, in fact, been harmed by these substances.

Statements from scientists about the development of assassination weapons and the anti-fertility programme convinced the TRC commissioners to (arguably reluctantly) allow a public hearing. Forgetting 163

313   Seeking means to kill individuals, while leaving no trace post-mortem, was the clear objective of much of the research carried out at Roodeplaat Research Laboratories. Victims 206

314   As part of many of the investigations into South Africa's chemical and biological warfare, commentators have forwarded conclusions about what lessons could be gleamed from this episode in time. Many

of these have been definite and have pointed a way forward to a better tomorrow.   Lessons 315

315 1998

Truth and Reconciliation Commission of South Africa Report: Special Investigation into Project Coast

> The investigation began with a single amnesty application, a small number of confiscated technical documents relating to the programme and documentation from the Commission's Research Department. It expanded into a comprehensive exposé, based on more than 150 documents, affidavits, amnesty applications and interviews. The results provide a basis for further investigation of the individuals involved and their apparently unprofessional and criminal activities. They also ensure that such aberrations in national policy and individual behaviour are chronicled and prevented from happening again. In this regard, there may also be lessons for the international community.[268]   Lessons 381

316 1998

In many ways, the TRC presented itself as uncovering and exposing as much as possible about the abuses of statecraft. As suggested in its final report:

> [One] of the main tasks of the Commission was to uncover as much as possible of the truth about past gross violations of human rights – a difficult and often very unpleasant task. The Commission was founded, however, in the belief that this task was necessary for the promotion of reconciliation and national unity. In other words, the telling of the truth about past gross human rights violations, as viewed from different perspectives, facilitates the process of understanding our divided pasts, whilst the public acknowledgement of [untold suffering and injustice] helps to restore the dignity of victims and afford perpetrators the opportunity to come to terms with their own past.[269]   What? 186

317 1998

In seeking to set out what was done in Project Coast, in its final report the TRC concluded that:

> Cholera, botulism, anthrax, chemical poisoning and the large-scale manufacture of drugs of abuse, allegedly for purposes of crowd control, were amongst the projects of the programme. Moreover, chemicals, poisons

and lethal micro-organisms were produced for use against individuals, and 'applicators' (murder weapons) developed for their administration.[270]

What? 318

318 1998

It further went on:

> Inevitably, the CBW programme achieved little of value or of common good. Enveloped as it was by secrecy, threats and fear, opportunism, financial mismanagement, incompetence, self-aggrandisement, together with a breakdown in the normal methods of scientific discourse, the results were paltry. Tens, even hundreds, of millions of rands were squandered on ideas that had no scientific validity. At best, the programme succeeded in producing for manufacture analogues of CR and BZ incapacitants, and in making local arrangements for protective clothing for troops against mass chemical and biological attack. At worst, the programme had criminal intent.[271]

What? 325

319 1998

While not directly seeking to establish whether Project Coast was offensive in nature, the final report of the TRC implicitly did speak to this point. Against the noted repeated suggestion by some witnesses 'that the intention was not, and never had been, to develop an offensive capacity', the report noted that:

> In strict military terms, such a defensive programme would need to be managed in accordance with each of a number of criteria. These would include careful compliance with the criteria of defensive capability, sound and disciplined leadership, careful auditing of financial dealings, compliance with international conventions determining the conduct of such military business and reliable and comprehensive systems of accountability. The Commission's hearings showed that the programme failed to meet each and every one of these criteria. In fact, there was consistent evidence of serious departures from these standards.[272]

Offence 273

320 1998

In its final report, the TRC concluded that the Verkope list combined with the affidavit from Dr Immelman made the case that the items indicated were 'clearly murder weapons'.[273]

What? 354

The control and concealment of information to construct ignorance was identified by the TRC as constituting negligence, at least on behalf of the managers of the Project Coast. The TRC found that in relation to the chemical and biological warfare programme:

- The military command, and pre-eminently the surgeon general, Dr DP Knobel, were grossly negligent in approving programmes and allocating large sums of money for activities of which they had no understanding, and which they made no effort to understand.

The TRC concluded that the Surgeon General could not hide behind feigned ignorance, finding that he:

- knew of the production of murder weapons but refused to address the concerns that were raised with him, on the grounds that they did not fall under his authority. He was nevertheless fully aware that these activities happened in facilities under his direct control and were perpetrated by staff under his chain of command.
- did not understand, by his own admission, the medical, chemical and technical aspects and implications of a programme that cost tens, if not hundreds of millions of rands. Made no effort to come to grips with these technical and medical issues, notwithstanding the fact that he was the highest-ranking medical professional in the military and that others in the military were wholly dependent on his judgement and discretion. To know 191

322 1998

When the head of the commission, Archbishop Desmond Tutu handed the final TRC report to President Nelson Mandela, he was quoted in the media as having said that the Truth Commission was 'a beacon of hope for those places like Northern Ireland, Bosnia and Rwanda, so different from Sierra Leone where just last week they executed 24 people by firing squad'.[274] The implication here being that South Africa was not the only country to have benefited from the process – indeed, the South African TRC was a model for transitional justice elsewhere in the world. Justice 404

323 Who actually fell victim to the substances tested at Roodepoort Research Laboratories will largely remain a mystery, but the spectre of unsolved murders – the ghosts of possible victims – will not rest. After the TRC hearing, *The Guardian* newspaper in Britain reported that MI5 had requested the police to investigate 'the deaths of at least six people who apparently had strokes or heart attacks but might have been victims

of a covert germ warfare programmes by the apartheid regime in South Africa'.[275] One of the men whose mysterious death was mentioned was Peter Martin, a 'former director of Special Training Services, a company based in Mayfair offering advice on counter-terrorism and supplying bodyguards'.[276] The other was a South African soldier, Garth Bailey who died when he was only 29. Both men's intimate partners believed that they had been killed – and suspected Project Coast was behind their deaths. Both cases remain unresolved.   Victims 217

324 1999

Amnesty could be granted by the TRC Amnesty Committee only on the basis of consideration of applications backed up by investigative reports and documentary evidence. Despite this, in 1999, during the criminal trial of Dr Wouter Basson, Basson's lawyer, Jaap Cilliers, claimed that Basson had been offered amnesty by senior members of the commission in exchange for details about the chemical and biological warfare programme. This claim was made while Deputy Head of the National Intelligence Service, Michael Kennedy, was on the witness stand – recounted in this trial diary entry:

> Cilliers put it to Kennedy that high-level TRC members had contacted and then met with Basson and had offered him amnesty without having to go through a public hearing, if he provided them in secret with full details of the CBW programme. The TRC also undertook to keep such details secret, says Cilliers. Cilliers claims that Basson turned down the offer of amnesty since he did not believe that he had done anything wrong.
>
> Kennedy said he had set up a TRC briefing by Knobel and Steyn about Project Coast and had arranged two meetings between a TRC official, Basson 'and others' the TRC wanted to interview. He was aware that the TRC also offered to obtain from the SA Medical and Dental Council a written undertaking that no disciplinary or professional steps would be taken against Basson or any other medical practitioners involved in Coast, provided Basson made full disclosure, but according to Kennedy, no final discussions on the subject took place with the SAMDC [South African Medical and Dental Council].
>
> Cilliers put it to Kennedy that all of the documents found in the trunks had been used by the TRC during its 1998 hearings on CBW, which were open to the public and the media, and that the documents had been available to the media.
>
> Kennedy denied this, saying there had been general access to only certain documents, approved prior to the hearings, and that many had

not been used at all. (The second set of trunks, handed over in Penzhorn's office, contained some 1 000 files, Kennedy says.)

Some documents were, by agreement, to be seen only by TRC commissioners and the various legal teams at the hearings, and were not supposed to be released publicly or to the media, but 'somehow, this did happen'.

Yes, said Cilliers, somehow it did.[278]

Whether the TRC members had offered Basson amnesty or not – which would have been a contravention of their authority – is not known.

Justice 180

325 1999

The TRC not only entailed a complex marshalling of a diverse assemblage of people, documents, technologies, substances and much more besides, through its proceedings, it also produced a considerable repository of items. While the gathering and interrogation of these items were often portrayed as opening and exposing abuses of the past, the public status of the items gathered can never be fixed and given. Rather it is always a matter of negotiation. How much of an opening was secured depended on how readily the records could be shared.

In 1999, 34 boxes of documents – including ones related to Project Coast – were removed from the TRC offices and placed under the control of the Ministry of Justice. The reason given was that the sensitivity of the material demanded this shift in custody. The detailed reasoning supporting this evaluation, though, was not clear. A Freedom of Information request by the South African History Archive for the list of the files that had been removed indicated that many had already been openly released. In addition, the great majority of those that might be 'sensitive' were already held by the Department of Justice and the National Intelligence Agency, since both entities had access to the contents of the trunks that were confiscated when Basson was arrested.

Legal battles ensued between the South African History Archive and the ministries of Justice and Intelligence, each ministry at times denying knowledge of the boxes or shifting the blame to the other regarding who should be able to account for them. At each turn claims about the danger of revealing the contents of the boxes were repeated. In the end, they were found to have been in the possession of the National Intelligence Agency. Ultimately the South African History Archive won their case and, through the Promotion of Access to Information Act, secured the release of many of the documents from those boxes.

Through such acts of literally setting apart, state agencies controlled access. More than this, the repeated claims about the content of the boxes created a mystique, symbolically setting them apart. What? 442

326 1999

In *Plague Wars*, Mangold and Goldberg provide an overview of the Japanese, Rhodesian, Soviet, South African and Iraqi chemical and biological warfare programmes. While the information presented about the Soviet and Iraqi programmes may be accurate, Mangold and Goldberg made numerous errors with respect to the South African programme. For example, they claim that Project Coast scientists worked on 'Hepatitis A, HIV, and the terrible Ebola and Marburg viruses'.[279] This is not correct. There were no scientists at Roodeplaat Research Laboratories who were sufficiently qualified to undertake research on viruses. All the scientists I [Gould] interviewed were emphatic that no work was done at RRL on viruses and none of the available documents show research projects of this nature. Other errors include the statement that Project Coast was the 'world's second largest offensive biological warfare programme',[280] whereas both the Soviet and Japanese programmes were significantly larger than the South African one.[281] Mangold and Goldberg also incorrectly record the names of the front companies and the programme itself, indicating that the information presented was inadequately checked. Do these errors disqualify *Plague* Wars from being a reliable source of information?

327 1999

Despite the Soviet Union having signed the Biological Weapons Convention, Dr Ken Alibek and others, who were involved in the Russian biological warfare programme, revealed in the early 1990s that the Soviet offensive biological warfare programme continued to develop and expand well after it had signed the agreement.

The Soviet biological warfare programme differed markedly from the South African programme, both in nature and intent. There is no evidence to suggest that the apartheid government sought to develop biological weapons for large-scale application, whereas the Soviet programme did.[282] However, there are important similarities between the two, both in terms of the way in which the programme was structured to avoid detection and in the way in which the scientists involved in it related to the work they were doing. Alibek states that the bioweapons facility he worked in was 'ostensibly operating as a civilian pharmaceutical enterprise' and as a result 'the agency could engage in genetic research without arousing suspicions'. This also meant that the scientists could 'participate in international conferences, interact with the world scientific community, and obtain disease strains from foreign microbe banks – all activities which would have been impossible for a military laboratory'.[283] These were the same reasons given by Basson for establishing the front companies Roodeplaat Research Laboratories and Delta G Scientific as the operating facilities for the South African chemical and biological warfare programme.

328 In coming to terms with how South Africa has dealt with the gross human rights violations of apartheid in the years that followed transition, many commentators have positioned the work of the Truth and Reconciliation Commission as occupying the only sensible middle ground.

Basically, the TRC had avoided two extremes. The first was the 'Nuremberg' option of pursuing prosecutions against those suspected of gross human rights violations. This was presented as unviable because the South African criminal justice system was not up to scratch; the costs, time and other demands would have been too prohibitive; and the extent of concealment meant that prosecutions would have faltered.[284] The other extreme was simply forgetting what had taken place and moving on. Instead, and in its own words, the TRC pursued 'another kind of justice – a restorative justice which is concerned not so much with punishment as with correcting imbalances, restoring broken relationships – with healing, harmony and reconciliation'.[285]

This calls for placing the past squarely in sight rather than pushing it aside. As argued:

> In our [the South African] case, dealing with the past means knowing what happened. Who ordered that this person should be killed? Why did this gross violation of human rights take place? We also need to know about the past so that we can renew our resolve and commitment that never again will such violations take place. We need to know about the past in order to establish a culture of respect for human rights. It is only by accounting for the past that we can become accountable for the future.[286] Forgetting 177

329 1999

In October 1999, one of the longest trials in South Africa history commenced. Dr Wouter Basson faced 67 fraud, murder and drug charges directly or indirectly related to his time as head of Project Coast. By the time Judge Willie Hartenberg delivered his verdict in April 2002, acquitting Basson on all remaining charges, what had taken place as part of the programme had been the subject of considerable efforts to mobilise documents and memory in aid of remembering and forgetting.

What? 330 | Forgetting 343 | Justice 36

330 1999

Just how much was 'concealed' versus 'disclosed' by the Basson criminal trial was somewhat fraught. Most of the trial was inaccessible for those who did not speak or read Afrikaans, except for some news reports in other languages and the daily trial reports in English produced by Marléne Burger and Chandré Gould. Even for those fluent in Afrikaans, the extent and duration of the trial was testing. Lasting over 30 months, involving 153 witnesses and relying on thousands of pages of documents, the sheer quantity of (contradictory) information produced impediments to comprehending what had happened.   What? 341 | Forgetting 352

331 1999

At the start of the High Court trial of Wouter Basson, Judge Hartzenberg dropped six of the 67 charges. A 1989 proclamation, only revealed because of the trial, granted amnesty to all South African Defence Force personnel and others for crimes committed in Namibia prior to its first democratic elections in 1989. Citing this amnesty, the judge threw out charges against Basson related to the murder of some 200 SWAPO fighters, plans to poison the water supply of a SWAPO refugee camp with cholera, and the murder of an official.

The other charges related to conspiracy to murder in Swaziland and Mozambique through the supply of poisons. As these had taken place outside of South Africa, even if they were planned within it, Judge Hartzenberg ruled that they could not be prosecuted in the country.

Forgetting 332 | Victims 392

332 1999

From the start, the case against the accused was plagued by difficulties with evidence because the only witnesses to many of the murders and chemical interrogations in which Basson was alleged to have played an active role, were those operatives that had carried them out. Their motives for testifying before the court called their credibility as witnesses into question. When allegations centred on the supply of assassination weapons, documentary evidence was even more difficult. Many of those associated with the SADF either refused to testify or did so reluctantly. Even if the names of many of the victims had been known at the time, they were lost from memory by the time of the trial. 'An ANC member', 'a foreign operative', etc. might be their only identifying mark for linking a victim to an offender. The SADF files that might have existed previously (such as those related to acts again SWAPO in Namibia) were not turned over or could not be found. Forgetting 198

333 1999

Basson's relationship and dealings with Swiss Intelligence Unit Chief, Peter Regli, and the arms dealer Jurg Jacomet was raised during the TRC hearings. It became the subject of two Swiss parliamentary inquiries – one in 1999 and another in 2001. Basson would argue that during the Cold War, the South African military had access to intelligence about Soviet and Cuban weaponry and operations in Angola, which was considered of value by Western powers. This provided him with bargaining power and access to Swiss intelligence. But the Swiss government was quick to deny that their Intelligence Chief had given Basson any information that could have aided the South African chemical and biological warfare programme.

> With regard to the significance of contacts with South Africa, General Regli [Chief of the Swiss Intelligence Unit] pointed out … that an intelligence service needs information from different sources (including, therefore, from counterparts in other services) in order to be able to provide its own military and political authorities with reliable and corroborated analyses. During the Cold War, the Soviet Union and the Warsaw Pact countries represented the main threat for Switzerland. Any information on these countries was of great importance. At this time, South Africa … was engaged in a war in Angola against communist forces equipped with Soviet *matériel.* Any information gleaned from this war was of vital importance for the Swiss intelligence service. None of Switzerland's neighbours in Europe had a comparable experience from which it could benefit. Furthermore, the communist secret services were also very active in the African continent. For this reason, too, the Swiss intelligence service was very interested in maintaining contacts with the South African secret services. It should be stressed, however, that it was the Swiss intelligence service which benefited from South Africa, rather than vice versa.[287]

After Basson testified in court that he had been assisted by Regli and Jacomet to acquire 500 kilograms of methaqualone from Croatia in a complex and opaque deal, which involved forged Vatican bearer bonds, and allegations that the Swiss had used the deal to procure nuclear material, the Swiss government reopened their investigation.

By this time in 2001, Regli had been discharged from the Swiss Intelligence Unit. He denied ever having known about the South African chemical and biological weapons programme, telling a Swiss news service that 'The Swiss intelligence service – and the director of the intelligence service – was not aware of the secret programme of South Africa, because it was secret, part one, and part two, the Swiss intelligence service had nothing to do with this intelligence service, and neither had its director.'[288] He told Swiss media that Basson's allegations were 'unsubstantiated slander' and a 'sweeping defence by a criminal'.[289]

IR 334

334 It was not only the Swiss who were implicated in relations with Project Coast. Tom Mangold claimed that scientists from the UK chemical and biological research establishment, Porton Down, reportedly visited South Africa to advise on Project Coast and that Basson had met with scientists from Porton Down.[290]

IR 335

335 1999

During Basson's criminal trial, many references were made to his contacts with intelligence agents and other officials, both by the defence and the prosecution. The nature of these links, though, was often a matter of dispute or uncertainty. The defence cited Basson's close relationship with a Libyan intelligence agent, Yusaf Murgham, though others refuted this suggestion.

Basson had travelled to Libya between 1993 and 1995 for various business-related reasons, such as working as a consultant on a railway line in Tripoli and the construction of hospitals in the country. Basson, Mijburgh and another colleague also set up a company in Libya. Such engagements would come to the attention of the United States and United Kingdom who – fearing that Basson posed a proliferation threat – successfully called for him to be re-employed by the South Africa military in 1995 after Project Coast had been terminated.

IR 189

336 *Chandré Gould's reflections*

As I worked through my archive of documents about Project Coast, and the now, equally voluminous documentation associated with my investigations thereof, I begin to remind myself of the rather unflattering character at the centre of Ester Peeren's article: 'Lumumba's ghosts'.[291] In this article, Peeren grapples with the value of the immaterial that necessarily accompanies – or lies behind – the material documentary evidence that informs historical accounts. She proposes a greater respect and attention to immateriality.

The character she speaks of is Jacques Brassinne de la Buissière, a Belgian colonial officer who made it his life's work to prove that Belgium was not behind the assassination of Patrice Lumumba. Like this rather unpleasant character – whose archive is described by Peeren as 'ever expanding', I find myself attached to the bits of paper that record sometimes tantalising leads, little pieces of secrets that hint at answers and conspiracies. I tend to grasp these, as if the meaning they hold is something precious, something that needs to be preserved for someone else to use and make more sense of. I like to console myself with the belief that, unlike the portrayal of De la Buissière, my desire for the preservation of the material is not premised on a belief in its essential truth, or its ability to reveal a single 'correct' answer, but rather because the questions themselves – whose answers cannot and will not be teased from the tightly typed lines or the handwritten scrawl – feel like they should be found by someone else looking with different eyes. Legacies 338

337 Any narrative or account is shaped as much by what is and can be said as it is by what cannot or is not said. To appropriate a narrative structure, to create a story that can be followed by readers, is to set aside, discard and 'make absent' the bits that do not fit. While one might point to questions that still need to be answered, things that still need to be understood, it is far more difficult to show a reader the messiness of a subject such as Project Coast through any account of the programme – which inevitably will be the result of a process of extracting, discarding bits of information that upset the narrative structure – or are irrelevant to the story being told. What that story is and how it is told are informed both by convention (what is expected by readers and the community for whom the text is intended) and by what is appropriate to tell – for example, personal details or snippets of information about a character in the story, which could be told over a glass of wine but would not be suitable for inclusion in an academic text. The policing of what is said, and what is not, is both external and internal to the author.

Perhaps the author wishes to present themselves as an 'objective,' rational, fair narrator – which means that only that which can be verified, substantiated by more than one account or by documentary evidence can be included in the text. And yet, as Peeren argues so convincingly, we ignore immateriality at our peril. Legacies END

338 2000

Chandré Gould's diary, 8 January

I have been prompted by my mentors, Western experts in chemical and biological weapons, to find reference to the military doctrine that informs the chemical and biological warfare programme. This doctrine will provide a foundation leading us to a correct interpretation of the intention of the programme – or so we hope. I interview a military officer who served as the personal staff officer to the Chief of the Army and Special Forces Commander, General Kat Liebenberg (deceased), and he tells me very little, saying only: 'Liebenberg protected people who needed to know' and 'CW [chemical weapons] were never part of the doctrine'. Legacies 339

339 Over the years, as I interviewed more and more soldiers and developed trusting relationships with the scientists, who I saw and spoke with repeatedly, I was told about the characters of high-ranking military officials and how their characters had influenced the way in which the programme was run.

To some of the chemical and biological weapons experts from the United States and United Kingdom, who mentored me at the start of my investigations, it was inconceivable that the military was not run according to strict lines of reporting and accounting, but it seems that the strictures of military hierarchy and rules did not apply equally to all. Some could and did operate outside of the rules – at least when their actions benefited or appeared to benefit the state.

Ironically, in the end, it was this that protected Basson against conviction. Legacies 375

340 2000

On 2 March, Dr Larry Ford, an American gynaecologist, killed himself at his home in Irvine, California. The investigation that followed and the criminal trial of Basson indicated a complex, but still unresolved, link with Project Coast. Ford had travelled to South Africa three times between 1987 and 2000 and had served as a consultant to the programme. His relationship with Project Coast included:

- holding a training day seminar for Project Coast scientists on how to impregnate everyday items with toxins;
- the establishment by Basson at Delta G Scientific of the 'Ford Hair' project to cure male baldness, based on a toxin it produced;
- allegations by self-claimed FBI informers that a South African trade attaché secured biological weapons for South Africa with the aid of Ford and others;
- the drawing up, by Basson, of details for a six-month project into a peptide treatment for HIV-positive patients in which Ford would serve as a consultant, as well as a source of literature on chemical and biological weapons.

According to Surgeon General Niel Knobel, Ford had also supplied antitoxins to South African forces stationed in Israel during the 1991 Persian Gulf War.

After Ford's suicide, searches through buried canisters, hidden compartments and elsewhere in his house, revealed illegal weapons, military explosives, potassium cyanide, jars of suspected toxins, and the biological agents – *Vibrio cholerae*, *Clostridium* and *Salmonella typhi*. Investigators, who were trying to establish whether Ford had conspired to kill a business associate, found evidence that he had conducted unauthorised experiments on patients and fraudulently claimed scientific achievements.

IR 333

341 2000

The Basson trial provided an opportunity to revisit and extend the claims made in the TRC that Project Coast sought to develop means of covert assassination. Daan Goosen, former Managing Director of Roodeplaat Research Laboratories (RRL), testified to providing Basson with a 'huge' black mamba snake and its venom. The untraceability (at least back to Project Coast) of organophosphates as poisons post-mortem was another such capability spoken to at the trial. André Immelman, Research and Development Director at RRL, testified to how paraoxon was incorporated into toiletries like lip balm, shampoo and roll-on deodorant, as well as consumables like alcohol and tobacco.

What? 342

342 2000

Just as the traceability of materials to Project Coast was said to be an issue during operations, so, too, was this an issue during the trial. A former member of the secret Civil Cooperation Bureau testified that he had been given vials of cholera and yellow fever, with instructions to contaminate the water supply to refugee camps, just before Namibia's pre-independence election. This apparently proved ineffectual because the water supply was chlorinated. However, the trial judge ruled that the link between the use of these infectious agents and Basson had not been established. Thirty-one other bottles of cholera, listed in a Project Coast document, remained unaccounted for within the hearing.

What? 343

343 2000

Because the Basson trial was an undertaking to consider criminal charges against the accused, it was not set up to hear – let alone resolve – disputes about activities raised in previous investigations which were not connected to the fraud, murder or drug charges. As a result, activities such as the authorisation and development of an anti-fertility vaccine were not examined in detail.

What? 344 | Forgetting 331

344 2000

Allegations of drug trading made against Basson put the work involving drugs in Project Coast into a prominent position during the trial. Whereas the boundary between offensive/defensive purposes was so often disputed in relation to the activities of Project Coast, in relation to drugs, the boundary between the weapons programme and outright criminality was also at stake.

Incapacitants were sought, and some of these involved popular street drugs or their related chemical analogues. The sedative-hypnotic chemical, methaqualone – widely used in South Africa as a recreational drug (Mandrax) – was researched with the intent to produce projectiles, including hand grenades, 81-millimetre mortar bombs and 155-millimetre projectiles. Eighty kilograms of cocaine was purchased through a Peruvian contact and shipped to South Africa in a consignment of bananas, although it was later found to be inappropriate as an incapacitant. Over 900 kilograms of MDMA (more widely known by its street name, ecstasy) was produced at Delta G Scientific for crowd-control purposes. Seemingly incompatible with crowd control, in the order of one million capsules of ecstasy were produced, as were methaqualone and LSD, also in capsules. Five-thousand kilograms of the psychoactive agent BZ was purchased though General Peter Regli, then head of Swiss Intelligence, in 1992. At the trial, Basson claimed that 1 000 kilograms of it was produced in South Africa for hand grenades, mortar bombs and projectiles, although this was not substantiated. What? 42

345 2000

Testifying during the Basson criminal trial because of a said rebirth in God, former South African Defence Force member Johan Theron told the court about his involvement in the deaths of 'hundreds' of those deemed 'enemies of South Africa'. These individuals were sedated and then Theron dropped their bodies into the ocean. He contended that the muscle relaxants, anaesthetics and sleeping pills used to incapacitate (or more likely kill) individuals were supplied by Wouter Basson. However, because Basson held multiple positions in the military, it remains far from clear that, even if he had provided the muscle relaxants, this action was in any way related to his role as head of Project Coast.

The flights of Operation Dual were only one part of wider clandestine operations by the forerunner of the Civil Cooperation Bureau (CCB), a unit known as Barnacle. It sought to gather information and eliminate (sometimes through 'chemical operations') those deemed – for one reason or another – opponents of the apartheid government.[292]

Theron spoke about the meticulous attention given to how the killings were conducted. By learning about tidal currents, he could determine that drops should take place 100 nautical miles out to sea to prevent their bodies washing up on shore. By sedating individuals rather than killing them, there was no chance that the recovered bodies could be linked back to the SADF through tracing injuries. Falsifying flight records provided a further level of protection. For more than 20 years, the activities of Operation Dual were not known to anyone who was not directly involved.

Theron, however, paid much less care to who was killed. Although he participated in the killings between 1979 and 1987, he was unable to supply the court with the names of those killed, let alone their background stories. While the Harms Commission (1990) heard testimony from members of the CCB about its activities, nothing emerged during this commission about its predecessor, Operation Dual. As a result, what can be said about the victims and perpetrators of Operation Dual is extremely limited.

Those that perished included not only Namibian SWAPO fighters, but also members of the SADF, who were judged to pose a threat to the concealment of its activities.

After his early retirement in 1990, Theron went to work for Basson as a counterintelligence officer in a Project Coast front company. In 2000, he and others testified about Basson's supplier role in the elimination of apartheid enemies.

In relation to Operation Dual, Judge Hartzenberg deemed that the evidence heard by the court reliably established that murders took place under this operation, as well as the complicity of those testifying, but not the involvement of Basson.[293] The judge justified this determination, in part, by attributing self-serving motives to Theron for implicating Basson. Since the TRC had exposed Theron's deeds, Judge Hartzenberg reasoned, he and others were motivated to implicate Basson to protect themselves.

In this, it seems to have mattered little to the court ruling that the TRC had not heard any evidence in relation to Operation Dual, nor had the TRC heard evidence from Theron himself.   Forgetting 488 | Justice 17 | Victims 125

346 2000

Does being a victim require having suffered adverse consequences?

On 4 May 2000, Johan Theron testified during the criminal trial of Wouter Basson. Summary notes of this indicate that Theron contended 'in 1992, he and Basson discussed a plan to distribute toxic beer at taxi ranks in the Eastern Cape, where violence was rife. The idea was to observe what effect, if any, the beer contaminated with flocculant[s] would have. The operation was not carried out because the operative chosen to conduct the experiment, Civil Cooperation Bureau counter-intelligence head, Danie Phaal, failed to collect the contaminated beer.'[294]   Victims 304

347 The potential for radically divergent views about victimhood and the pervasive contestation about this category, signal the importance

of attending to the social and political circumstances that condition the recognition of harm.   Victims 348

348   In the case of Project Coast and the special operations unit, Barnacle, the inability to name or even identify victims – particularly those who died after having been injected with an overdose of muscle relaxants – may also be an expression of racism or a lack of regard for the humanity of the victims. To date there have been no serious attempts to trace the families of these victims, no person or institution has taken any responsibility for doing this, and there has been no memorialisation.   Victims 64

349 **2001**

As the testimony in the criminal trial of Wouter Basson was drawing to a close, the *New York Times* published a story entitled 'US germ warfare research pushes treaty limits'. It questioned the permissibility of activities justified in the name of biodefence, namely: the Central Intelligence Agency's assembling and simultant testing of a Soviet-era, cluster, germ bomb; plans by the Defense Intelligence Agency to genetically enhance the potency of anthrax in order to test existing vaccines; and a Pentagon project to determine if a bioweapon facility could be fashioned from commercially available materials.

As in earlier debates about what constituted legitimate biodefence activities, competing assessments were given in 2001. These turned on what would count as an appropriate consideration. Would it matter, for instance, that the United States had not declared these projects in its reporting to the Biological Weapons Convention? Would it matter if many other countries did not make declarations at all under the treaty? Would it matter how the United States were to respond to another country undertaking such activities?   Offence 350

350   In posing the question of 'Is that offensive or defensive?' it is possible to get a sense of the scope for contestation about what labels to apply. Treating specific acts on their own can be countered by arguing that they should not be understood in isolation.

And yet, what counts as properly seeing things in 'the bigger picture' is itself often a matter of disagreement.[295] While for a specific issue a frame of reference might be agreed, it is potentially open to reinterpretation and reappraisals. Alterative descriptions of the activities can also fundamentally shift determinations of the bigger picture. In short, what is under question and the context in which it should be understood are defined in relation to each another.[296]   Offence 75

351 **2001**

While the Biological Weapons Convention is often hailed for building a norm against the weaponisation of disease, Richard Falk questioned this in a book chapter entitled 'The challenges of biological weaponry'. He situates the threat from bioweapons in relation to the wider issues of the growing importance attached to these by the US government in the 1990s. The most credible line of explanation for this focus is presented as that of diverting public attention from US nuclear capabilities. Whereas Washington's approach across successive administrations has emphasised the non-proliferation of nuclear capabilities and a selective focus on the unacceptability of chemical and biological weapons, an abolitionist approach, as championed by Falk, calls for the elimination of *all* weapons of mass destruction. It is against this understanding of how weapon prohibitions are being selectively (mis)appropriated that he asks whether:

> the ongoing process that supports CW [chemical warfare] and BW [biological warfare] regimes, as well as the nuclear non-proliferation treaty regimes, [should] be reevaluated and possibly rejected? From the perspective of the equality of states, a fundamental norm in international law, are these regimes embodiments of the hegemonic structure of world politics that controls and deforms diplomatic practice?[297]   IR END

352 2001

One of the many complications associated with determining truths about the complex fraud, human rights and drug charges against Basson was the ever-haunting spectre of deception. Witnesses for the prosecution were regularly challenged by the defence (and later by the judge in reaching his verdict regarding their motivations for testifying). All who testified against Basson, and who were themselves implicated in the crimes, did so on the basis that if they were found to have testified truthfully, they would be immune from prosecution.

As a clandestine programme, Project Coast necessitated some forms of deception. Basson testified to how he had misled numerous individuals and organisations – notably the programme's own front-company managers, foreign intelligence services and intermediaries – about the details of Project Coast, as well as about its overall existence.[298] A question in the context of the programme was, what counted as legitimate concealment? Basson contended that South Africa's own National Intelligence Agency might have information withheld from it. A question in the context of the trial was how such admissions of past deception should affect the standing of Basson.   Forgetting 372

As part of the trial, Basson's defence team set him apart from others in a variety of ways.

He was the only witness called in his support. For 53 days in the witness box, Basson was the only person who could be questioned in his defence.

At times as well, Basson was positioned as providing a unique and definitive insight into what took place in Project Coast. Claims that the details and justifications of certain actions were known only to Basson, as head of the programme, amounted to attempts to establish a relational authority over others. What Basson possessed, others lacked. That was said to give him the ability to really know what capabilities were developed.

Why produce umbrellas with poison at their tips? Why discuss scenarios for the use of these and other such murder weapons? To demonstrate how easily others might make assassination attempts on VIPs, came the retort: Why produce drug tablets with methaqualone? The answer: They didn't contain methaqualone, they were placebos for Special Forces trying to infiltrate the little-known arms-for-drugs activities of an armed wing of the ANC.

Why ask a military operator to distribute ecstasy? 'To test them to see if they were active in a covert international drug trade moving through South Africa.'

What? 373

The meaning of the Verkope list was a matter that arose in the criminal trial of Basson. Dr André Immelman indicated that, despite his suspicions, he could not say with certainty whether the substances listed were used as murder weapons. Basson reiterated that he had never seen the Verkope list prior to his 1997 bail hearing and, therefore, could not comment on it, save for the items given to him from it. These were needed for personal research or for Special Forces training instruction.[299]

What? 297 | Offence 371

The Rollback of South Africa's Chemical and Biological Warfare Program, Stephen Burgess and Helen Purkitt, US Air War College

The South African case also dramatically shows how thin the line is between defensive and offensive weapons. First the Iraqi, and now the South African, cases suggest that it is prudent to assume that if a country is suspected of developing covert nuclear capabilities, it is probably supporting research into the offensive uses of chemical and biological weapons as well. If efforts are being made in the more challenging and expensive nuclear arena, why would a regime not develop the more accessible and less costly chemical and biological weapons?

South African CBW programs also underscore the importance of control by civilians, of transparency, and of accountability. Some aspects of the *apartheid* regime's management of their CBW programs may be unique. However, this case vividly illustrates what will happen when there is loose accountability of covert [nuclear, biological and chemical] research and development by senior military and political leaders. This is especially likely when the government is besieged both at home and on its borders.[300]

Lessons 436

356 2001

Chandré Gould's reflections

Burgess and Purkitt[301] ascribed the establishment of the biological warfare component of Project Coast to the isolation of the apartheid state and the changing perceptions of threat in the southern African region in the late 1970s and early 1980s. Their report describes the programme as 'sophisticated' and 'secretive', open to little outside scrutiny. They identify the biological warfare programme as aimed at developing 'exotic means to neutralise domestic opponents'.[302] In asserting that the programme was sophisticated, they distinguish their own analysis from others who have claimed that the programme was of little scientific value, a view held by the TRC and me. Burgess and Purkitt provide little evidence that the programme was sophisticated. Indeed, much of the information on which they base this assessment has subsequently been found to be unreliable, particularly the work of BBC journalist, Tom Mangold, whose book *Plague Wars* provides a skewed and inaccurate picture of Project Coast.[303]

Burgess and Purkitt intended to determine the factors which led to the closure of the programme to understand better the proliferation dynamic. They ascribe the closure of Coast to four key factors: (1) the extensive financial corruption of the programme's directors; (2) the changing threat assessment in southern Africa in the late 1980s and early 1990s; (3) PW Botha's fall from power and De Klerk's subsequent attempt to bring the security forces under civilian control; and (4) the desire of the National Party government to ensure that the chemical and biological warfare programme did not fall into the hands of the ANC when it assumed power.

357 2002

Similarities between the South African chemical and biological warfare (CBW) programme and the Japanese World War II biological warfare

137

programme, as described by historian Sheldon Harris, are striking.[304] While the Japanese programme was significantly larger than the South African one, and made extensive use of Chinese prisoners of war for horrific human experiments, the Japanese programme, like the South African one, was initiated and driven by a single motivated individual, Dr Ishii Shiro. Like Basson, the Japanese military gave Ishii wide discretion and allowed him to travel extensively in the early stages of the programme's conceptualisation to collect information and determine the direction it would take. Like Basson, Ishii was admired by his colleagues for his 'brilliance',[305] his photographic memory and his intense patriotism. In the same way that Basson motivated the initiation of the South African programme, by claiming that other countries were developing a CBW capacity, the Japanese believed that the Soviets had already developed biological weapons capabilities and argued that mutual deterrence would increase Japanese security.

358 2002

In his criminal trial, Basson's defence lawyers argued that there was no proof that he knew about what was contained in the sealed, blue-steel trunks found after his arrest – a claim accepted by the judge.   What? 221

359 2000

Rancor between the prosecution and the judge was a recurring feature of the trial. Senior prosecutor Anton Ackermann and Judge Willie Hartzenberg openly traded words, which, if spoken at all, would normally be reserved for backstage conversations. In February 2000, Ackermann made an unsuccessful attempt to get Hartzenberg to recuse himself from the case on the grounds of bias and prejudgment. Sharp exchanges characterised the summing up of the prosecution in 2002, with allegations raised by Ackermann that the judge displayed a deference to Basson's version of the facts and an inability to believe Basson could be lying. Hartzenberg retorted with 'everything which the accused said that does not support your case was a lie… your entire argument boils down to a claim that the accused is incapable of telling the truth'.[306]   Forgetting 328

360 2001

Gould's notes on the Basson trial, 3 September

Wouter Basson is testifying in his criminal trial. He tells the prosecutor questioning him that during the later phases of Project Coast he acted as security officer and devised all the cover stories and misinformation necessary to maintain secrets. He also says that what had emerged from the research into interrogation techniques, was that you cannot manipulate people. The single most important lesson taught by Special Forces was: If the person interrogating you does not know what he is talking about, tell him any story that you like. Talk as much rubbish as you can within the first 24 hours after being taken prisoner so that your comrades have enough time to get away.

One cannot help but wonder how much of this advice Basson himself has followed.

Legacies 361

361 2001

Gould's investigative notes, 4 September

I meet with the former head of the SADF, General Jannie Geldenhuys at the Brooklyn shopping mall in Pretoria. I have a list of questions for him, but our conversation starts easily and conversationally. He tells me a joke.

> When one commanding general took over from another, the outgoing general gave the incoming general three envelopes and said, 'When things become tough and you are desperate you should open envelope one. The second time you are in a tight position open the second, and then the third.' He put the envelopes in the safe. When the problems started to build up and he was feeling down, he decided to open envelope one. On a piece of paper was written 'blame your predecessor'. So he did and that carried him through. Later when he was under pressure he opened the second envelope. On the paper was written: 'reorganise: we are in the process of reorganisation, please bear with us'. This tided him over. The third time he became desperate, he opened the third envelope and on the paper was written: 'prepare three envelopes'.

We talk, I ask questions, he responds. He tells me that:

> Internal security was a touchy subject. As the army, the idea came up – why can't we use something to make people more lackadaisical? Turn rabble rousing into a more placid mood. Other countries were searching for the same thing. Laughing gas was used in medicine – that type of thing.

I ask him about the 1 000 kilograms of MDMA (ecstasy) that was manufactured by Delta G Scientific, one of the front companies of Project Coast, under authorisation of the Surgeon General. He says: 'I was told that the MDMA was to put into tear gas. These things happened at the end of my tenure.'

He also tells me:

> Wouter Basson was a captain when I met him in the military hospital. When I left he was a major. I would have forgotten him if his name hadn't

139

come up... The Surgeon General would give me feedback about Coast, a summary of meetings. There was a policy of decentralised management. I was satisfied that I maintained control... CBW and nuclear were not very important projects to me.

He seemed very sincere. Legacies 362

362 2002

Notes from a telephonic discussion between Gould and one of the scientists from Roodeplaat Research Laboratory, 18 January

Never made powdered anthrax. The anthrax was freeze-dried and stored. When freeze-dried and stirred with a probe you get a rough powder. It was such a rough powder mixed with liquid that was put on the cigarettes. Theoretically the cigarettes could have worked.

Another fragment to add to the collection. Could it be used to dispute Basson's claims in the TRC? By whom? For whom? What value could these fragments of truths hold outside of any formal inquiry? Legacies 401

363 2002

Chandré Gould's reflections

An investigative reporter from the *Wall Street Journal* has been in South Africa working on a story about the scientists. He touches base with me regularly and passes on snippets of information which we discuss, analyse and try to make sense of. The story he intends to write will be themed: 'What to do with your old plague warriors'. He interviewed the Minister of Intelligence, Lindiwe Sisulu, who told him that a task force had been established to look into the activities of the scientists from the former chemical and biological warfare programme 'from a national sovereignty point of view'. The big question for the journalist was, 'Why engage Basson but leave the guys with technical assistance out there in the cold?'

This reporter says, 'it becomes difficult not to come to the conclusion that the government does not want to talk about these issues'. A new mantle of silence was being drawn.

He interviewed one of the scientists, who told him that one of his former colleagues from Roodeplaat Research Laboratories was doing something in his spare time 'to make ends meet, that he doesn't want to talk about'.

The scientist, he said, told him that he and his colleagues had been 'rebuffed by the system. Passed over for promotion and are not able to go back to universities. It's viewed as suspicious if scientists from the former project get together.' Legacies 364

364 2002

Gould's notes from an interview with a former South African intelligence agent, March

The discussion was filled with allegations of the most terrible kind. Chemical and biological weapons testing in African countries and hospitals; paedophilia and child trafficking run by the Minister of Defence to mention but a few. There is nothing here I can verify, or follow-up on. But each tantalising bit of information built on a base of rumour I have heard before.

He tells me that, in 1985, the ANC was also experimenting with biological agents. 'The ANC had a three-pronged approach: biovectors, drugs (the Lusaka drug trade run by a CIA agent); civil unrest.' And, he says, '20 SWAPO murdered by WB with thallium in 1982.'

These are the things I could not report – they were unverifiable. When placed here in this book, however, they no longer pose the kind of threat or risk they might have before, because this is not an attempt at a definitive factual account of Project Coast, and, as such, its form allows for greater freedom to say what otherwise might never be shared outside of these kinds of meetings.

Over time I reach the conclusion that the more horrific the things I am told, the less likely they are to be verifiable, but does that make them less likely to be true? For my own peace of mind, I decide it does.   Legacies 365

365 2002

Chandré Gould's reflections

I find a note in Seymour Hersh's book, *Chemical and Biological Warfare*, about the US chemical weapons programme.

> The [US] chemical corps answers its critics by arguing that the threat of biological warfare attack is too real to allow medical ethics to hamper research.[307]
>
> Legacies 366

366 It is easy, when investigating a case such as this one, to begin to imagine that apartheid South Africa was exceptional in its deception and the lengths that the state would go to defend itself against the indefensible. It offers some consolation – well of a sort anyway – to find that other nations have behaved badly with justifications that are equally weak.

Legacies 376

367 2002

General Constand Viljoen, who was the head of the South African Defence Force when the decision was made to establish the chemical and biological warfare programme, explained the reasons for establishing Project Coast to documentary film-maker, Liza Key, saying that:

> After the Sharpeville incident, when the ANC had decided to change their strategy ... to ... take the war to the people in the townships. And they... came with a new strategy and that is by causing uprisings in townships. One such uprising was the Sharpeville situation, in which the police started shooting, and killed a lot of people ... the defence force was very worried about this, because we didn't want to kill people ... So I then put to my staff the problem ... how could we deal with the crowd, with an angry crowd? ... my idea was to develop a kind of gas which was not known anywhere in the world as far as I know, that we would be able use on such crowds, that would incapacitate them to a degree, so that they could then thereafter in a calm position recover, and then we could solve any uprising, any urban uprising without shooting at the people.[308]   Victims 368

368 Such sentiments were echoed elsewhere.   Victims 455

369 But not everywhere.

370 2002

> Every step change in science has opened up new and more terrifying methods of killing and incapacitating; and in turn made more urgent that these means be subject to internationally enforceable control.
>
> UK Foreign and Commonwealth Office
> *Strengthening the Biological and Toxin Weapons Convention*[309] IR 85

371 2002

When Judge Hartzenburg delivered his judgment on 11 April, he painstakingly attended to each item on the Verkope list that had been linked by the prosecutors and witnesses to attempts to intimidate or murder individuals. He found in each case that the link between the items on the list – such as the organophosphate paraoxin – and the instances in which they were used – such as the poisoning of Frank Chikane – was tenuous and that there was no proof that Basson knew how the items would be used. He also dismissed testimony by SADF members who had implicated Basson in the provision of poisons. However, as to whether the crimes as described by the witnesses took place, the judge had no doubt that this was, indeed, the case, but the state had failed to prove that Basson was responsible.[310]   Offence 101

372 2002

In her trial report of Judge Willie Hartzenberg's judgment, journalist Marléne Burger contended:

Basson's evidence … is extensively reported in the judgment, which endorses much of the testimony as truth. The only reservation expressed by the judge is that he 'formed the impression' that Basson was 'not entirely frank' regarding his testimony on the fraud charges, claiming lack of memory in respect of anyone still alive who was involved in the transactions under review. The judge concluded that Basson had testified in 'such a manner as not to implicate anyone else' but said it would be 'all but impossible' to decide where he had lied and where not. Hartzenberg expressed no reservations about Basson's testimony in relation to the allegations of his involvement in human rights violations.[311]   Forgetting 359

373 2002

As part of acquitting Basson on all charges, Judge Willie Hartzenberg would argue that Project Coast had been a 'phenomenal' success, one whose achievements had 'thoroughly impressed' the United Kingdom and the United States.   What? 221

374 2002

Included within his ruling in the trial of Basson, Judge Hartzenberg concluded that the state prosecution had failed to prove to the court's standards of proof what had been used to poison Frank Chikane, whether this chemical derived from activities of Project Coast, or that those members of the security force who were identified as having smeared his underwear, had actually done so.[312]   Forgetting 199 | Victims 346

375 2002

Gould's notes on the judgment in the Basson trial, April

> The judge accepted that the CBW project was made more difficult by sanctions. Basson was instructed to obtain information and materials, even if that meant theft or bribery, as long as the funds couldn't be traced back to the SADF [South African Defence Force]. His superior officers didn't want to know how he obtained the information and materials. He had to use the cover of a rich businessman to do his work – this was accepted by his SADF commanders.

How simple, and yet masterful a way to conceal actions that may at some time in the future be revealed – by a deliberate and careful construction of unchallengeable deniability.   Legacies 360

From Gould's notebook, 18 November

> [Investigative reporter from the United States] – Woman at OVI [Onderstepoort Veterinary Institute] said she didn't want to speak to [a South African investigative journalist] and she said, 'oh yes, two Yemen's interested in Rift Valley and Sudanese interested in Bot [botulinum toxin]'. The Yemen's spoke in support of 11 Sep 2001. She said they were brought in by the IAEA [International Atomic Energy Agency] to SA to help with diagnostic techniques. 1993 [RRL scientist] was getting experimental Bot [botulinum] vaccines from Fort Detrick.

When I heard this, it seems important, but there is so little that one can do with this kind of information – to whom would one report it and to what end? Legacies 377

377 This kind of 'noise' is commonplace during investigations – and it is the noise that we usually leave out of clear narratives. Legacies 378

378 2002

Note in Gould's notebook, 1 December

Call to [South African diplomat]:

> The mines in Mozambique are aerial delivered butterfly mines which contain a liquid explosive. The casings in which they were reported to have been, were designed to go under an aircraft for delivery. The liquid explosive is leaking out. The SA government is currently devising a subtle strategy to ensure that the mines are destroyed. Mozambique shouldn't have them in the first place. Legacies 22

379 2002

At the end of this year, the United Nations Institute for Disarmament Research produced a 297-page report written by Chandré Gould and Peter Folb entitled *Project Coast: Apartheid's chemical and biological warfare programme.* This report drew on the material made available through the TRC, the trial of Basson, as well as interviews conducted by the authors. Forgetting 382

380 2002

Among the report's conclusions, the capabilities developed were said to include:

- The stated intention of Project Coast was to develop crowd control agents for domestic use and the provision of defensive equipment for

144

use by the SADF. Delta G Scientific was responsible for the production of ton quantities of CR. There is no evidence to suggest that Delta G Scientific produced or stockpiled chemical warfare agents on a large scale other than CS and CR. The production of a ton of methaqualone and a ton of MDMA [ecstasy] cannot be explained as having been for use as [chemical weapons]. The purpose of the production of these street drugs remains unknown.

- RRL [Roodeplaat Research Laboratories] was responsible for the research and development of chemical and biological agents which were untraceable post-mortem. Testimony from the scientists involved in these projects and RRL documents show that they believed that the substances would be used in covert operations to assassinate individuals. Animal experiments were conducted to test the efficacy of the poisons. A range of lethal poisons and bacterial pathogens was offered by RRL in their Verkope list.
- There is no evidence to suggest that RRL produced or stockpiled large quantities of chemical or biological warfare agents.[313]   What? 188

381 2002

We have a great deal to learn from Project Coast. It warns us of how a few people, with political and financial backing, lack of financial controls, lack of a moral and ethical framework, and lack of due civil process, can manufacture chemical and biological agents to achieve the assassination of individuals and threaten whole communities. Now, with the advances in genetic engineering leading to biological agents that could be engineered to affect only certain groups of people, who knows what the future holds and who knows who may get their hands on such organisms. If the apartheid regime of South Africa had been able to acquire such a capability, one can only shudder at how it might have been used.

It is our wish that this work will throw light on the murky world of chemical and biological agent proliferation and provide much food for thought about how such poison can be used and how its use can be prevented. We need to think about these issues now. Each day brings new developments in biotechnology and a new urgency. The biosciences are getting ahead of the mechanisms we have to control them and this could have far-reaching and disastrous consequences for humanity. If there is to be any benefit from the human rights abuses created by Project Coast, then let it be that we learned from it and prevented anything like it from ever happening again.[314]

Laurie Nathan and Patricia Lewis

'Preface' to *Project Coast: Apartheid's chemical and biological warfare programme* Lessons 355

145

382   The preface to *Project Coast* included the statement:

> The revelations over Project Coast and the transparency with which the South African government has dealt with them, has enabled South Africa to vigorously pursue the global effort to ban biological weapons and take a lead role in the negotiations for strengthening the 1972 Biological and Toxin Weapons Convention. South Africa's disarmament policy is coherent and consistent in its opposition to weapons of mass destruction in all their forms and in all countries. Having come clean on its experience during the apartheid years lends real credibility to South Africa's ethical and practical stance on international disarmament. South Africa went to the edge and beyond and then – under a new, enlightened regime – came back. Others can do the same.[315]   Forgetting 503

383   2002

'It is only when we have this understanding that we can learn and move on from the past. It is only then that we can prevent this happening again somewhere else.'[316]

'Foreword' by Archbishop Desmond Mpilo Tutu
Project Coast: Apartheid's chemical and biological warfare programme

Lessons 33

384   2002

The 2002 United Nations Institute for Disarmament Research report on Project Coast noted sources of concern regarding the proliferation of elements of Project Coast outside of South Africa.

In 1993, the technical expert to the programme, Dr Jan Lourens, was introduced to a Syrian by the name of 'Mr. Saroojee' through the last private secretary of South Africa's former president, Pieter Willem Botha. Would Dr Lourens be able to supply documentation and skills about the programme? As Lourens's employment had been terminated, this was not possible. Well then, what about just skills? Lourens and Dr André Immelman (head of research at Roodeplaat Research Laboratories) would meet with individuals purporting to be a general and a retired general from the Syrian Army at a house in Johannesburg to discuss capabilities for chemical and biological warfare. What, Immelman would ask, was the source of tension between Israel for which such weapons were needed?

No further contacts were made.[317]   IR 385

385   2002

Based on interviews with former research scientists, the United Nations

Institute for Disarmament Research report also stated that:

> There is uncertainty about what happened to [Roodeplaat Research Laboratories'] culture collection. Microbiologist Mike Odendaal said he gave it to André Immelman when he left the organisation, and he believed that Immelman was going to destroy it. Some of the scientists believe that the cultures could have been taken by their colleagues for their own research purposes. There is no evidence to confirm that the culture collection was destroyed at the official closure of the programme.[318] IR 386

386 2002

It has become clear that not all the biological products from Roodeplaat Research Laboratories (RRL) had been destroyed. The media reported that, in 2001, former RRL scientist, Dr Daan Goosen, had entered into a contract with two US intelligence agents who brokered a deal with the FBI that would have involved the transfer of '200 ampoules of hazardous biological materials' to the FBI.[319] Goosen claimed he entered the lucrative deal – initially for R20 million and later reduced to US\$ 5 million to 'counter the threat of biological terrorism'. Although the amount of money involved strongly suggests that the motive was financial, Goosen also hoped to secure green cards for himself, his family and former South African intelligence agent, Tai Minaar.

Ultimately, the deal fell through and the FBI alerted the South African Police Service to Goosen's intentions, thereby causing the National Intelligence Agency in South Africa a great deal of embarrassment as they had been unaware of Goosen's plans – despite them having maintained close relations with Goosen both before and after the TRC hearings.[320]

IR 484

387 One troublesome aspect of determining what took place under Project Coast has been the inability to take statements at face value. In events such as the TRC and the criminal trial of Basson, accounts of what took place were often questioned in relation to the underlying motivations of the speakers: how they might want to appear or make others appear? Offence 388

388 Grounds for doubt, though, extended beyond what was said as part of legalistic hearings. For instance, during the Basson trial, a formerly 'Top Secret' document, authored by him, was exhibited to the court. It makes explicit reference to the intention to develop 'offensive' chemical and biological weapons capabilities as part of Project Coast in suggesting that its objectives included:

Objective 4

(c) To conduct research with regard to basic aspects of chemical warfare (offensive)

(d) To conduct research with regard to basic aspects of biological warfare (offensive)…

(h) To conduct research with regard to covert as well as conventional systems…

Objective 6: To establish an industrial capacity with regard to the production of offensive and defensive CBW equipment…

Objective 7: To give operational and technical CBW support (offensive and defensive). This is usually divided into two sections:

a. Conventional. This kind of support usually entails supplying equipment (offensive and defensive) that has not yet been cleared for use by standard procedures. This includes storage of the equipment.

b. Covert. This support is given to the Commanding General Special Forces and his organisations, Chief of Staff Intelligence and his organisations and the SA Police and National Intelligence. This service includes the preparation of equipment, training with the equipment, transporting the equipment as well as support during application.

Objective 8. Conducting own CBW operations. This is similar to covert support, except for the use of own operators due to access and other circumstances.[321]

Might the revelations in this formerly secret document then be taken as a smoking gun, proving offensiveness?

As Gould and Folb commented in a report for the United Nations Institute for Disarmament Research, this document was originally produced for the proposed privatisation of Project Coast. In it, Basson made what appeared to be exaggerated claims about the nature of the programme to motivate how the front companies should be privatised.[322] If so, can this be taken at face value? Offence 248

389 2002

As noted in the 2002 book, *Secret and Lies*, by Marléne Burger and Chandré Gould, a review undertaken of the 'CD-ROMs stored as a "national asset" under the most stringent security, has concluded that, far from being the repository of Coast's deepest, darkest secrets, the discs contain little more than published literature on [chemical and biological warfare] in general.'[323] What? 77 | Forgetting 27

Handwritten notes by Chandré Gould from an interview with an SADF soldier, 5 February

He speaks about whether there was ever a real threat of chemical weapons use in Angola:

At the Lomba river valley – hills on either side of the river. The two opposing forces – SADF/UNITA/other allies on one side, and Soviet/FAPLA/Cubans on the other. The two opposing forces watched each other at fairly close range for about a week – sporadic shelling. Especially at night you'd hear the shells and 120 mm rocket-assisted mortars. They looked like firecrackers going overhead.

I believe that the Soviet-led forces had chemical weapons with them. We were briefed on the fact that an attack with chemical weapons was a possibility, and we had our gas masks and raincoats to use as protection. Of course, we were all aware that with modern chemical weapons this would be no protection at all, and it was therefore very unpleasant at night...

As I used to train members of UNITA, I had been informed by them – on many occasions – of the Cubans use of chemical weapons against them, and I had no reason to doubt their reports. They would have gained nothing by telling me of this, so there was no motivation for them to tell me a falsehood. Also, they were very reliable when it came to reporting events of the war in a factual way, as many of them had been fighting the war for nearly 20 years – first their war for freedom from the Portuguese, and then their war for freedom from what they called the Russo–Cuban colonisers.

This would have been the best time for the Soviet-led forces to use chemical weapons against the SADF – when we were all concentrated together in one area, before the war became more mobile and the forces more dispersed – but something deterred them from doing so... Legacies 47

Handwritten notes by Chandré Gould from an interview with an SADF soldier, 5 February

I ask him about the SWAPO prisoners of war whom the soldier, Johan Theron, claimed he had killed. His response:

There were not thousands of SWAPO prisoners of war... SWAPO soldiers were good and aggressive soldiers in the first place, and other than this, their political commissars indoctrinated them into believing that they would be tortured and killed if they were taken prisoner. They therefore often fought to the death. Those who were taken prisoner were taken to the prison camp in Mariental in SWA.

Would Theron have lied about killing hundreds of men? Was this soldier deliberately creating doubt, feeding me misinformation? Who to believe? And what about the men who were allegedly tied to a tree in the Dukuduku forest in KwaZulu-Natal?

Dukuduku was filled with National Servicemen and Permanent Force personnel from multiple different military units who were doing selection and pre-selection, the administrative, logistics and transport personnel who were needed to support this activity (also from multiple different units), the forestry people and so on. Other than that, part of the Zulu Battalion (I think 121 battalion) was also there – and large parts of Dukuduku were a restricted military area because of the Kentron missile test facility, so entrance was restricted. In my opinion, that story cannot be true. There are very few roads in and out of Dukuduku, and not much traffic, and it would not have been easy or possible to enter or leave without being detected. [Suggesting that it would have been impossible to tie men to a tree overnight without being seen or stopped, or somebody hearing them.]

His responses to my questions are so clear and so rational, I begin to doubt, wonder if part of Project Coast was a figment of imagination – and yet the documentary evidence, the accumulation of interview testimony says otherwise. But what motive could this soldier have for sowing doubt?

Forgetting 512 | Legacies 336

392 2003

The South African Supreme Court of Appeal dismissed an appeal made against the High Court ruling in the Basson case; this included Judge Hartzenberg's 1999 decision to throw out conspiracy to murder charges pertaining to events outside South Africa.[324]

Victims 393

393 2005

South Africa's highest court, the Constitutional Court, hears an appeal against the original High Court case against Dr Basson. It rules, among other things, that the six charges for conspiracy to murder outside of South Africa could be reopened. However, no such action has been undertaken since this ruling.[325]

Victims 210

394 2005

An animal-rights activist, Beatrice Wiltshire, first drew attention to the animal experiments being conducted at Roodeplaat Research Laboratory (RRL) in 1986. According to Michelè Pickover:

> When she [Wiltshire] tried to find out more, she came into conflict with the scientists who were at the forefront of one of South Africa's most clandestine operations. Attempts by anti-vivisectionists, who then began holding demonstrations outside RRL, to obtain answers from the government went unanswered. In 1984, when the *Weekly Mail* first ran a story on RRL, the only comment RRL's Animal Laboratory Services director made was that 'the extraordinary security was designed to protect the plant from industrial espionage' and 'irrrational animal rights groups'. The state's strategy against SAAV [South Africans for the Abolition of Vivisection] was to vilify them by portraying them as unscientific, emotional and irrational activists.[326] Victims 255

395 2006

Between 2006 and 2008, I (Gould) was the first, and only person from a non-governmental organisation, to be a member of the Biological Weapons Working Committee (BWWC), a subcommittee of South Africa's Council for the Nonproliferation of Weapons of Mass Destruction (NPC).

It was the first time I had participated in a formal structure of this nature and the arcane functioning of the body took some time to figure out. More complex was negotiating issues of trust and, particularly, whether I could be trusted not to be over critical, and not to be incautious with the confidential matters raised in meetings. This meant that I was cautious about what I said and how I said it, and did not challenge the way things were done. While I did not hold back on asking questions that I felt needed to be asked, it was made very clear when my questions were considered annoying or impolite.

I realised after some time that the extreme formality of the meetings acted as a restriction on the kinds of questions or views that could be raised. I also knew that if I overstepped the invisible line between what was acceptable and what was not, I could jeopardise the future inclusion of others from civil society in such forums.

When my term of office on the NPC ended in 2008 and was not renewed for reasons of needing to increase the racial diversity of the structure, I left feeling that my participation had failed to make much difference, if any at all, to the functioning of the structure – in part, at least, because of my caution. It certainly had not been possible in any formal meetings to raise the issue of changing South Africa's Form F declaration under the Biological Weapons Convention. Silence 499

Post-1994, racial categories have consciously been removed from some elements of state reporting. This includes the official crime statistics produced by the South African Police Service, a move deliberately justified 'to avoid the use of crime statistics to reinforce racial prejudices. Information on race and crime can be misused to stereotype people from one or other group.'[327] Racial categorisation has been retained for all manner of other administrative data collection, with the rationale that the state needs to track changes and to ensure that the country is reversing the discrimination of the past. However, this has meant enduring racial definitions and requiring individuals to define themselves in terms of race.

In addition, 'in the research and policy community racial descriptors are often used because they are believed to enable readers and peers to understand the phenomenon they are considering. We seem unable to make sense of our society, and discussions about our society, without reference to race.'[328]

Total war 463

397 2009

What lessons can be learnt from the past has long been a matter for reflection. Amid a climate of growing clamour for evidence-based government policy-making, the British Parliamentary Office of Science and Technology examined this topic in a document entitled *Lessons from History*. The contributions identified included:

Historical analogies: Drawing similarities between the present and the past can help avoid mistakes and make successful decisions.

New perspectives on current policy problems: Through understanding the many factors that shaped the past, it is possible to identify a wider range of choices available that might be perceived.

Challenging assumptions and correcting misconceptions: History can dispel myths today by showing how parallel concerns in the past were or were not borne out.

Evaluation of policy outcomes: Examples from the past can enable the questioning of contemporary expectations.

Policy implementation: Previous experiences can be drawn on to put policies into practice.[329]

Lessons 314

398 2009

But even as it extolled the many possibilities associated with history, the British Parliamentary Office of Science and Technology's *Lessons from History* signalled that just because lessons *can be learnt* from history, this does not mean that lessons always *are learnt*. Each example of the untapped contribution from history spoke to the failure to do so in practice.

Lessons 293

399 2009

Albeit briefly, *Lessons from History* also spoke to the limitations of history. Mechanically drawing on what was done in the past (for instance, how the 2001 outbreak of foot-and-mouth disease in the United Kingdom was responded to in the light of the 1967 outbreak) can lead to inappropriate choices. The adage that individuals too often 'fight the last war' applies far beyond generals in their bunkers. As further constraints, it was contended in *Lessons from History* that the kind of evidence sought in policy deliberations can be characterised by uncertainty, it can be open to contrasting interpretations, and it is only one kind of input into decision-making.

In attending to these limitations, this parliamentary report echoed conclusions voiced by scholars about evidence and analysis more generally. Be it of the past or present, analysis can neither resolve disputes about our basic values, nor tell us which problems can and should be addressed.[330]

Lessons 32

400 2011

Transitional justice has both positive and negative effects on democratization processes. Positive effects include, for example, when citizens' claims for transitional and/or criminal justice lead to governments having to react and respond by installing commissions of inquiry or initiating trials against perpetrators, etc. This level of responsiveness is one of the criteria to measure the quality of democracy. The assumption is that the more responsive governments are towards their citizens or victim groups' needs, the more efficient democratic institutions are. Nevertheless, government responsiveness is only one side of the coin. At the same time, parliamentarian and legislative powers also have to be capable of restricting executive powers.[331]

Anja Mihr
Associate Professor at the Netherlands Institute of Human Rights
University of Utrecht Justice 322

401 2011

Maggie Nelson addresses the practice of artists and activists, who represent acts of cruelty perpetrated by systems of power to mirror them back to society, in the hope that, by doing so, they might shame those in power and thus bring an end to the cruelty. She argues that this practice is fallacious.

Using Sister Helen Prejean (an outspoken critic of the death penalty in the United States) as an example, she writes that:

> Prejean's logic relies on the hope that shame, guilt, and even simple embarrassment are still operative principles in American cultural and political life – and that such principles can fairly trump the forces of desensitization and self-justification. Such a presumption is sorely challenged by the seeming unembarassability of the military, the government, corporate CEOs, and others repetitively caught in monsterous acts of irresponsibility and malfeasances. This unembarassability has proved difficult to contend with, as it has a literally stunning effect on the citizenry. *They ought to be ashamed of themselves!* We cry, over and over again, to no avail. But they are not ashamed, and they are not going to become so.[332]   Legacies 363

402 2011

The relationship between the state's use of violence and community-level struggles – creating a warlike situation – is best described in this quotation from the 2011 report by the Centre for the Study of Violence and Reconciliation entitled *The Smoke that Calls: Eight case studies of community protest and xenophobic violence.*

> [O]ur studies of community protests show that police actions escalated confrontation and tension which rapidly took the form of running street battles between protesters and police officers. There was widespread condemnation in communities of provocative violence against crowds of protesters on the part of police. Even more troubling were the incidents of random assault and allegations of torture against suspected protest leaders and their families in some of the communities... the counterpart to the police as protagonists is the role of the youth, mostly young men but including young women, in collective violence, both in spearheading xenophobic attacks as well as engaging in battles with the police and destroying public property during community protests.[333]

Here the 'war' between South Africans and African immigrants is also referenced, suggesting again a state of 'total war'.   Total war 403

403 2012

On 16 August 2012, 34 mineworkers died after the police opened fire on a crowd of striking workers at Marikana, a settlement in the platinum belt, north of Johannesburg. Striking mineworkers had been calling for improved wages at the Lonmin platinum mine. The deaths on this day were compounded by other ones, both before and after. In addition, some striking mineworkers that survived this day claimed that they had been tortured by the police.

The media coverage and subsequent Marikana Commission of Inquiry asked the same question, again and again: What could have prevented these deaths? Total war 453

404 2012

On 16 August 2012, South African police opened fire on a large crowd of men who had walked out on strike from a platinum mine at Marikina, about 80 miles north of Johannesburg. They shot down 112 of them, killing 34. In any country, this would have been a traumatic moment. For South Africa, it was a special kind of nightmare, since it revived images of massacres by the state in the old apartheid era, with one brutal difference – this time it was predominantly black policemen, with black senior officers working for black politicians, who were doing the shooting.[334]

The Guardian   Justice 329

405   The following letter appeared in *The Star* newspaper in 2012, claiming to represent the views of South Africans who believed that Basson had been the victim of a witch-hunt.

Later this year the hearing of the Health Professions Council of SA in which cardiologist Dr Wouter Basson is charged will resume.

One can only hope and pray that good reasoning will prevail and that the long witch-hunt against the good doctor – as it is perceived by his patients, including me, and many Afrikaners in general – will at last come to an end.

The court acquitted him in 2002 of 67 charges relating to his alleged actions as secret chemical and biological head in apartheid SA.

However, the council decided on its own hearing, stating that as a doctor he should not have done what it thinks he did.

What it boils down to is that every medical doctor who is sent to war with, say, a gun in his hand should remember the ethical code of the profession: 'Thou shalt not kill.'

That is, with all respect, ludicrous.

As a heart sufferer, I am very much dependent on Dr Basson to stay alive. I cannot conceive a more sympathetic and understanding doctor.

That one lonely person should for so many years stand in the dock to be crucified for the so-called wrongdoings of all Afrikaners in the past is an outright shame.

I can put it in no other words.

Ollie Olwagen

Bellville, Western Cape[335]

Victims 347

406   2013

As recounted in 2013 by one person interviewed by Brian Rappert, at the 13 January 1995 meeting between representatives from South Africa, the United States and United Kingdom,

> [British representatives] went to South Africa and my recollection – because I realise you are interested in this one – was we went very much in a mode of 'What will the South Africans tell us?'. I wasn't briefed or told, 'Oh no, there is such and such, such and such, such and such.' It was more to let them tell us what they wanted to tell us and I recall that what I saw as our role was to try and spell out what could usefully be put in [the Confidence Building Measure forms], and really sort of trying to make the message, 'You can build confidence by putting in details about what you've done', and so on. And it was – again, my recollection – very much left to the South Africans to decide what to do. It wasn't the sort of situation in which they were saying, 'Oh, this is what we think we'll say. What do you think of it?'
>
> IR 182

407   In 2013, the authors of this book along with others received a research grant from the Economic and Social Research Council (ESRC), the Defence Science and Technology Laboratory (Dstl), and the Arts and Humanities Research Council (AHRC) under the 'Science and Security' programme. Entitled 'The Formulation and Non-formulation of Security Concerns', the project set up to assess what is not taking place in relation to the analysis of the implications of science for security.

One of the foci was the apparent 'historical erasure' of the South African biological programme. We stated that we would:

> describe and examine the limited attention to the former South African programme within: (1) the diplomatic proceedings of the BWC and (2) the life scientists and professional science associations in South Africa. In relation to both, consideration will be given to the 'whys' and 'hows' by which this offensive programme became rendered a non-issue.

From here until Entries 426 (and beyond), we speak about how we went about doing this and what we found.[336]

Silence 408

To test our starting presumption that there has been an absence of attention to past programmes overall and particularly the South African one within the international diplomatic community, in mid-2013 we undertook a review of documents associated with recent meetings of the Biological Weapons Convention.[337] On the basis of this documentary review, we concluded:

1. CBMs [Confidence Building Measures] have been largely justified through restating their formal purposes of enhancing transparency and building confidence.[338]

2. Discussion about CBMs within the BWC since 2007 has been preoccupied with significant – but largely technical – issues of how to improve the quality and quantity of States Parties submissions.[339] This was an outcome of a 'two-track' approach agreed between States Parties, whereby efforts were made to first improve the user-friendliness and relevance of the CBM forms by the 2011 Review Conference, and then to revisit more wide-ranging questions about their purpose in the years that followed.[340]

3. The CBM form about past programmes has not been the subject of any significant attention in terms of its content or the need for revisions in recent times.[341]

4. The status of South Africa's declaration has received little, if any, attention within the discussion of States Parties. Nor have other declarations related to specific past offensive programmes.[342] Nor has the failure to mention either within the formal proceeding of the BWC itself been mentioned.

As such, we found it difficult to reconcile the CBMs' stated goals of securing transparency and confidence in the case of South Africa's declarations.

Silence 52

409 Outside of governments, in recent years, declarations of past programmes have attracted little attention in international civil society. One notable exception was the Hamburg Centre for Arms Control's 2006 report entitled *Transparency in Past Offensive Biological Weapon Programmes* written by Nicolas Isla. It provided a detailed analysis of six countries' declared Confidence Building Measures (CBMs) across varied activities, such as the quality of declaration about research, development, testing and stockpiling of bioweapons. In comparison to Canada, France, Iraq and Russia, South Africa stood out as providing no information across these varied activities on any offensive projects.[343]

As the author of the report argued, 'there is not necessarily a correlation between a consistent, longstanding and active support for the BWC and a high level of transparency regarding past activities. Providing only a limited level of transparency or no transparency at all undermines the CBMs and puts into question the commitment of a state to the full implementation of the BWC [Biological Weapons Convention]'.[344]

The report further suggested that for CBMs 'to function efficiently all BWC member states have to participate regularly and submission quality has to be improved. One way to help improve the quality of submissions is to assess, and if necessary revise, the individual CBM forms.'[345]

But should the limited level of transparency be said to undermine the value of the CBMs or, indeed, call into question states' commitments to implementation of the BWC? If – as we took it at the time – diplomatic processes consist of what is seen, declared and discussed in open forums, as well as interactions between states and their representatives, which are less visible or deliberately invisible, then assessing this question requires some nuanced consideration.   Silence 56

410 2013

In August 2013, as the first phase of conducting research, we undertook six interviews with individuals from South Africa as well as leading contributors to recent Confidence Building Measures (CBM) discussions. From these we hoped to gain an initial sense of what interviewees *would* (and *would not*) say about the history of the South African programme today as well as a sense of what they thought *should* (and *should not*) be said about it. In terms of the latter, if this research was going to assist ongoing deliberations within the Biological Weapons Convention (BWC) and elsewhere, it had to be done with an awareness of individuals' assessments of what was and was not helpful.

Isla's belief in the value of transparency as a means of holding states to account reflects a wider consensus, particularly within civil society, globally, that the more information that is publicly available, the better. WikiLeaks is perhaps the most well-known expression of the belief in the value of information to prevent states, and even non-state actors (such as large corporations), from behaving inappropriately.[346]

It is quite common to hear that transparency is fundamental to confidence, as expressed here by Hunger and Isla:

> To be able to regulate the behavior of states and assess regime effectiveness, actors must have information about the activities they want to regulate.

Transparency about and the willingness to explain the biological activities performed in a given country are of utmost importance in increasing confidence in their peaceful nature and preventing suspicion, hostility and aggression among states.[347]

According to this view, there is a direct relationship between a lack of transparency, or information sharing, and a lack of confidence.

Yet, the absence of a formal declaration about the offensive aspects of South Africa's apartheid-era, biological-warfare programme, seems not to have had this effect. Indeed, it has not even warranted comment in the context of the BWC. In contrast, repeated statements have been made about the constructive role of South Africa in strengthening the prohibition.

Taking this to be the case, in mid-2013 we drew the conclusion that merely 'outing' South Africa or challenging it to publicly alter or amend its declaration of past activities was unlikely to have the effect of either (1) convincing South Africa to submit a new declaration, or (2) increasing confidence among States Parties to the BWC. On the contrary, calling for increased transparency in this way could have the opposite effect. While, as a best-case scenario, pressure might result in South Africa submitting an amended declaration – it might also lead to states being more cautious of what they declare, or how openly they share their CBMs; this for fear of the risk of embarrassment or having to answer questions their diplomats may not be equipped to answer. In addition, it seemed there would be little value for the BWC in singling out South Africa for this kind of treatment, particularly in the light of the country's active engagement in BWC meetings since the end of apartheid. It would probably also take us no closer to understanding what does build confidence and how this might be enhanced to strengthen the BWC.   Silence 411

411 2013

'Outing' as a goal was also problematic because, even within the limited number of interviews in the first phase of our research, respondents offered substantially divergent assessments of fundamental issues, particularly about whether South Africa had an offensive biological weapons programme at all.

While most of those interviewed unproblematically characterised the programme as 'offensive', this was not universal. This suggests that what counts as 'offensive' cannot be assumed.   Silence 412

412 2013

For instance, in speaking with chemical and biological weapons expert

Volker Beck, he contended that the South African programme 'wasn't actually an offensive programme, it was an effort to try to find assassination weapons'.[348]

For him there was a difference between a biological weapons programme that targeted individuals and one that targeted larger groups or other states. The former, at least in his mind, was not relevant to the ban on biological weapons under the Biological Weapons Convention.

As he continued:

> [W]hen I followed the process of the South African programme, I often had doubts that in the context of the Biological Weapons Convention it was really something which, at that time was really a state-driven programme, or if it was something where people that lost control by state, did something on their own.
>
> Silence 447

413 All this raises many questions related to what is considered acceptable and by whom in relation to the use of force; more specifically, it raises the question of whether the diplomatic silence about the South African programme was related to the victims being (South) Africans. A further question arises about whether using biological assassination weapons against 'your own people' equates to offensive use or not. This could be informed by considerations of sovereignty and because 'assassination weapons' might be considered to fall outside of the scope of this treaty.

Silence 414

414 Moving to the question of whether the lack of a declaration about the offensive components of the South African programme was of concern, additional considerations arose as we undertook our research, such as whether state representatives to the Biological Weapons Convention (BWC) knew about South Africa's past bioweapon activities. Those interviewed all shared the perception that there were low levels of awareness about South Africa's past programme in the BWC; their estimations of the percentage of knowledgeable officials varied from one per cent to less than 10 per cent.

They did, however, differ over whether this mattered. The reasoning for alternative evaluations pointed to different assessments about what the BWC is for, as well as to how politics, truth and pragmatics should figure in its operation.

Silence 415

415 In response to being asked whether it mattered that one interviewee estimated that only five per cent of delegates attending the BWC knew of South Africa's programme, Beck said:

Volker Beck: 'No more today.'

Brian Rappert: 'Because it's the past and not germane or...'

Volker Beck: 'I think today the focus is on something else. It's similar to what, if you compare it with the Chemical Weapons Convention, the focus is no more on the old programmes and their destruction, even if it's not finished. But it's not where the focus... the focus today is Syria, or something. Nobody knows exactly if it's right or wrong to have the focus on Syria for the Chemical Weapons Convention. But today the focus of the Biological Weapons Convention is the progress in science. And even with the progress of science, I think the focus is only more or less on the potential of misuse of the science itself and less on possible state programmes. So you always have very selective views of items and especially what was past in programmes – and this is something that is past – it's over...'[349]   Silence 416

416 **2013**

Cédric Invernizzi, from the Swiss BWC delegation, argued that the lack of declaration did matter '[b]ecause I think that's what the BWC is all about: to prevent such programmes to [sic] happen again. If you don't really know the past, how can you prevent the very same things from happening again? So I think that's a big issue.'   Silence 417

417 **2013**

The divergence in reasoning among those involved in the Biological Weapons Convention (BWC) complicates any simple effort to 'come clean' about the past – what that would entail and whether it would be advisable or contribute in any meaningful way to improving confidence in South Africa's commitment to the BWC.   Silence 418

418 Because of these considerations, our plan for the research needed a rethink.

Our revised goal became to reveal the reasoning that informed alternative assessments. We set about analysing the interviews for the data, assumptions, meanings and inferences that informed individuals' evaluations of (1) the absence of an offensive declaration by South Africa; and (2) the absence of the consideration of this absence within the Biological Weapons Convention. By drawing on interview material, we hoped to display the often privately held considerations informing individuals' assessments of CBM-related issues. By then making these topics for collective discussion, through presentations and publications, we aimed to generate greater mutual understanding and scrutiny.

After relistening to the interview recordings, however, it became apparent that this strategy needed a rethink as well. In the interviews, the data, assumptions and inferences that informed assessments were often not aired. Instead, evaluations were simply stated. The prevalence of evaluations over detailed arguments, in part, stemmed from the structure of the interviews, which did not test thinking rigorously enough.

Defensive reasoning was also prevalent. Interviewees conveyed that, in their work, they avoided making statements that were threatening or could cause political embarrassment to others.

Upon reflection, we also noticed that we, as researchers, were engaging in this defensive behaviour ourselves. During the interviews, we avoided issues we thought would be too personally or professionally threatening to maintain our rapport (for instance, probing the role of some interviewees in the South African non-declaration). At times, this manifested in our hinting at concerns rather than explicitly stating them, expecting the interviewee to decipher our true intent in asking the question. Neither we nor the interviewees mentioned that this was taking place. At other times, to avoid any antagonism, we also failed to press interviewees when we thought they had made contradictory statements. Silence 419

419 2013

In the light of these experiences, we decided to revise our approach and take the prevalence of defensive reasoning as our focus. Silence 420

420 In their effort to bring about organisational change, Chris Argyris and others have concluded that many forms of interaction foster self-reinforcing and self-sealing defensive routines that inhibit robust inquiry.[350] As Argyris argues, '[d]efensive reasoning is omnipresent and powerful'[351] – it can be found across cultures and at all levels of organisations.

In this 'Action Science' model, there is a central distinction between two forms of learning: Model I (how people act in practice) and Model II (how people generally think they are acting). These can be contrasted as:[352]

Model I

- Offer unsubstantiated attributions and evaluations
- Unilaterally assert evaluations
- Make covert attributions
- Protect inquiry from critical examination

Model II

- Ensure reasoning is explicit and publicly test for agreement at each inferential stage
- Advocate position in combination with inquiry and public reflection
- Publicly reflect on reactions and errors
- Inquire into your impact into learning

This disjuncture between how people act and how they think they act has substantial implications for their ability to learn from past experiences. Attempts to stay in control of situations and to avoid threats to oneself or others means that there is often little testing of the basis for views and evaluations. Defensive reasoning leads to the use of covert attributions of motives, scapegoating, the treatment of one's own views as obvious and valid, and the use of unsupported evaluations. The silences and feelings of disempowerment, which form around certain issues, can easily spread.[353] The result is the reproduction of (perhaps invalid) assessments and inferences through self-reinforcing and self-sealing routines, which decrease the possibility of changing thinking and behaviour.

421   The overall prescription stemming from research in Action Science is not only to test reasoning overtly (even about embarrassing or threatening issues), but to also conduct research in a way that fosters further inquiry into the basis for claims. This requires fostering counter-intuitive thinking, developing the practical skills necessary for improving learning, and incorporating positive value goals into research. These conditions call for social researchers to adopt a form of investigation that is open to revision, based on experience and experimentation; to identify binds experienced by interviewees; to pose questions directly relevant to choices about action; to test the inferences and assumptions behind the choices advocated; to openly inquire into any voiced inconsistencies; to attend to how and whether we and the interviewees encouraged inquiry; and to employ as many forms of feedback as possible.

These aspirations are highly demanding.

As a first step, we revised the Confidence Building Measures interview plans to ensure respondents' reasoning was as explicit as possible. This meant committing ourselves to engaging with potentially threatening or embarrassing issues. This was only an initial step.

One of Argyris's techniques for exploring and altering learning patterns involves the production of so-called 'Action Maps'.[354] These seek to identify the interrelated variables that individuals identify as relevant to their learning; notably those self-maintaining and self-reinforcing patterns that limit learning.[355] In this way, they provide a basis for understanding the conditions for knowing. As hypotheses to be debated and refined over time, Action Maps also provide the basis for building agreement about what is taking place (and not), why, and what needs to be done to alter these circumstances. The latter objective can be obtained if Action Maps are used in cycles of dialogue, reflection and intervention, which can foster alternative situations. However, bringing about such desirable change might well require developing new skills and competencies. Silence 422

422 2013

In the light of our assessment of the importance of the themes raised by Argyris, by mid-2013 our research strategy became two-fold:

1. To produce a map of the practices and conditions that rendered the South African non-declaration of Confidence Building Measures (CBMs), a non-issue within the Biological Weapons Convention (BWC);

2. To use the formation and discussion of this map as the basis for encouraging reflection among government officials, members of civil society and others about what would need to take place to alter the South African non-declaration, the lack of discussion about non-declaration, as well as the lack of discussion about the lack of discussion in the BWC.

As conceived, the ways in which the South African past programme and declaration became non-issues is just part of a much wider set of countervailing pressures and competing imperatives within the BWC, which have negative consequences for international relations and weapon prohibitions, including how little time and opportunity there is for collective discussion.

We sought to identify the factors, specific to the case of South Africa, that our interviewees thought contributed to the lack of recognition or relevance of the past programme. We then identified more general issues, which led to some of the CBM-related concerns becoming non-issues. We then mapped the consequences that interviewees identified on group dynamics, which subsequently affect problem-solving and decision-making within the BWC.

We found that each set of issues shaped the others. For instance, the inability to recognise that there is a problem, which needs to be addressed, at least in the eyes of some, makes it more difficult to build a process in which CBMs are discussed and, where necessary, questioned. This, in turn, negatively impacts the collective ability to identify problems as there is no multinational forum in which to raise these. Silence 423

423 We wanted to acknowledge a set of 'general governing conditions' that influence and inform interactions between states and define possibilities for action, and constraints on action, by officials across the topics covered in the Biological Weapons Convention (BWC).

As interviewees conveyed to us, the work of civil servants and diplomats is characterised by demands and circumstances that often limit the scope for action. For instance, individuals in one government ministry need to negotiate their positions on matters (such as the CBMs) with those in another ministry with different concerns and priorities.

Reasons for an unchanged, official CBM declaration by the post-apartheid government, according to several sources, include:

- constraints on the accessibility of historical documentation in the BWC, which has resulted in inaction by officials;
- the non-declaration was raised only in specific contexts;
- officials did not test their views about South Africa's CBMs with others;
- officials assumed that others did not know about the programme; and
- officials would not raise concerns about the lack of discussion about the unchanged CBM within the BWC.[356]

The lack of discussion about the South African CBMs is just one example of how certain questions do not get raised about CBMs more generally. Reasons for this include the limited remit within the BWC for examining CBMs in recent years; the way in which states rarely openly voiced concerns about other states (whether inside or outside their regional grouping) for fear of the consequences of doing so (including appearing uninformed and being accused of making political attacks), as well as the absence of national capacity to analyse the CBMs.

The way in which these issues shape and constrain discussion within the BWC has knock-on implications for how states and others interact.

Many of these consequences relate to how individuals and organisations are perceived. For instance, the limited circulation of information creates disparities in who knows what, which in turn means that some people/states are deferred to as being more able to lead initiatives. This can mean that others feel disempowered. More generally, the previous issues reinforce existing groupings and coalitions.

Considering the consequences for group dynamics, we acknowledged the perceived binds related to raising contentious or challenging matters; for example, on the one hand, to do so would single one out in a manner that might well not be welcomed, while on the other, not to do so has the effect of making one – and the matters at hand – less relevant. While officials might be constrained by various diplomatic considerations, much the same could be said of those in civil society. Although the latter are, perhaps, freer to point out 'non-issues', doing so risks making them appear oppositional, a role that could reduce their ability to bring about the sought changes in the BWC.

Finally, we reflected on the consequences of these constraints and conditions for problem-solving and decision-making. These include low expectations for the quality of the CBMs and for what can be achieved through them, as well as ritualism in completing the forms.

Anyone seeking to raise a fundamental concern wrestles with a basic bind: if they do raise points of concerns, this could be regarded as politically motivated gesturing, while drawing attention to awkward matters could be viewed as counterproductive to achieving positive reforms. Yet, if points of concern about what is (or is not) being discussed are not raised, it is also not possible to achieve positive reform. These difficult situations can cause frustration and withdrawal. However, without airing varied perspectives, alternative options and conflicting viewpoints, collective reasoning is impaired.[357] As we argued, all these factors taken together reduce the overall confidence in the international prohibition of biological weapons. Silence 424

424 The map we eventually produced,[358] which set all this out, enabled us to have further conversations and interviews. While there was a great deal of agreement about the analysis offered and additional points were added, there was some reservation about whether this approach would be productive or counterproductive in diplomatic settings. We thought this was to be expected, given that we were trying to find ways of discussing issues that might be intractable, threatening or embarrassing. Indeed, criticism is to be welcomed as it provides an opportunity to test why some issues are regarded as intractable, threatening or embarrassing.

Additional consultations with officials, both inside and outside South Africa, raised a similar set of concerns about whether it is appropriate and useful to focus on South Africa to frame a discussion about the Confidence Building Mechanisms (CBMs) and confidence in their integrity; and, indeed, whether there is any value in discussing the CBMs at all. For some, focusing a discussion on the CBMs was regarded as a way of avoiding or bypassing more difficult discussions about a legally binding mechanism to verify whether states are adhering to the terms of the BWC. Silence 425

425 In the spirit of encouraging further inquiry about what needed to be done, we formulated a response to some of the points of concern to include in a report we produced about the publications:

- *Why are you undertaking a 'witch-hunt' of South Africa? Haven't other states not filled in their CBM [Confidence Building Mechanisms] properly?*

While, in many ways, the South African case offers an easy and unthreatening entry point to test the reasoning behind the CBMs and the role they play in the Biological Warfare Covention (BWC), it also presented some difficulties. South Africa has played a positive and constructive role in the BWC, at least since the early 1990s, so some voiced reservations about drawing attention to the South African CBMs and raising questions about its honesty as this could undermine this standing. It could also be construed as 'unfair' to point fingers at South Africa, when there are several other states whose CBMs about past activities have also been called into question – the most often cited example being Russia.

As we noted, our intention was not to single out South Africa. It is precisely because South Africa has played a constructive role in the BWC, that this can be discussed without it being detrimental. In addition, the fundamental change in government in South Africa after 1994 provides some distance between the present state and the actions of the former one. We also used South Africa as a starting point because of our own experiences – particularly Chandré Gould's nearly two decades of experience in South Africa, trying to prevent the malign application of the life sciences. We maintained this case provided a basis for identifying much more widespread communication dynamics that limit current international efforts in diplomacy; and for stimulating a more open, forward-looking and on-going discussion about transparency and confidence-building requirements in the context of the BWC.

- *What does bringing up the issues of the Action Map add to current discussions? Why are you not asking in a more positive spirit how the CBMs can be improved?*

From our interviews and past experiences, we contended that current international discussions about CBMs were stymied. This was the case despite the significant investments of time and money undertaken in recent years to improve these. As a result, alternative strategies were needed. [359] Our hypothesis was that addressing many of the reasons for this requires dealing with matters of *process*: how diplomats, non-governmental organisations, scientists, civil servants, academics and others, have collectively discussed issues of concern. The picture we painted indicated points for breaking out of the defensive thinking and routines, which constrain possibilities for positive action.

- *States will immediately turn off at the language.*

Earlier versions of work used a language of 'cover up and bypass' to characterise the non-discussion of the South African non-declaration. This language was taken directly from Argyris's work on the practices of leading companies. As it was suitable and arguably accurate in such contexts, we initially adopted it for this diplomatic setting. However, based on voiced concerns, we revised the wording to simply 'bypass'.

By explicitly addressing these criticisms in an open manner, we aimed to promote understanding about the reasoning for our analysis and its relevance to real-world situations. Silence 426

426 From the sort of thinking illustrated in the previous paragraphs, we concluded that promoting confidence in the Biological Weapons Convention (BWC) would require something other than just more discussion and time on the Confidence Building Measures (CBMs). In many respects, the nature of discussions had served to ultimately limit the terms of how the CBMs were handled in the BWC.

Working Papers submitted to the BWC for the States Parties meeting in December 2013 illustrated the need for a rethink. Many of these papers continued to deal with rather technical concerns about the practicalities of submitting and producing CBMs, which were discussed in preparation for the 2011 Review Conference (for instance, enabling electronic submission).[360] While perhaps useful in encouraging or stimulating participation, we felt that merely improving the user-friendliness of the CBM forms would, arguably, not be sufficient to address the malaise surrounding CBM participation. Instead, it is necessary to ask challenging questions about what limits the relevance of the CBMs.[361] Silence 57

427 For a nation or for a people to understand their situation as a state of war is highly consequential. To talk of war is to talk of 'us' and 'them', and typically an 'us' whose actions and motivations are unambiguously just, and a 'them' whose actions are equally unjust. Situations of war require unity and patriotic fervour. War also calls for the use of force-centred responses and a significant dedication of resources. Total war 428

428 The nation of South Africa was carved out of war, again and again.

Total war 429

429 The Voortrekker Monument outside Pretoria commemorates the movement of settlers between 1835 and 1854 from the Cape Colony into the hinterland. The Heritage Centre in the grounds of the monument seeks to 'preserve the heritage of the Afrikaans-speaking portion of South Africa's population and their contribution to the history of the country'.[362] Panelled storyboards at the centre provide a history of the struggles of Afrikaans speakers.

Prominent among those struggles is the Anglo-Boer War (1899–1902). Photographs, videos and text testify to the extreme hardship that befell those Boers who asserted their independence from British rule. This included the fate of 'More than *twenty-six thousand* Afrikaners, mostly women and children under the age of sixteen years, and *fourteen thousand* Blacks died in British concentration camps' (italics in the original).

The out-and-out opposition faced by the Boers against their repeated efforts to end the war is indicated in a panel that states:

> The suffering in the concentration camps and the resultant high morality rates, particularly amongst children, the increasing number of blacks who were taking up arms against the commandos and Boers in the veld (at the time of the peace negotiations there were between 12,000 and 14,000 women and children still wandering around in the veld), as well as the total destruction of thousands of farms with the resultant lack of food for the Burghers on commando, forced [the Boer leaders] to the negotiation table. Total war 430

430 Many periods of extreme hardship are recounted at the Heritage Centre. For instance, it is written that, 'After becoming a Republic in 1961, the onslaught against South Africa intensified from all sides.' Conflict within and without the national border meant that for 'nearly twenty years South Africa was engaged in a low-intensity war, which impacted on all levels of society. Hundreds of South African soldiers paid the highest price. The ANC's policy of urban and rural terror led to hundreds of casualties amongst innocent civilians.' Total war 432

431 An alternative approach would be to consider what gets left out of history. Forgetting 454

432 The Heritage Centre storyboards also state that constraints, resulting from international sanctions and the 1977 United Nations arms embargoes imposed on South Africa, had the effect of leading to 'the establishment of a munitions industry able to compete with the world's best'. Such a home-grown arms capacity was needed to counter both domestic troubles and the involvement of South Africa in neighbouring conflicts.

However, the South Africa government did not invest only in conventional arms in the 1970s and 1980s; substantial funds were also dedicated to nuclear, biological and chemical weapons. Total war 80

433 *Chandré Gould's reflections*

The common fallacies about truth, memory and reconciliation became clear to me when a colleague and I attempted to recall how the investigation into the chemical and biological warfare programme, for which we had been responsible at the TRC, started in 1997. We had not spoken about our investigation for many years. Prompted by the writing of this book, and by the recognition of the extent to which revelations about past activities rely on memory, I asked him if he would be willing to go back to the events of 1997 and 1998, leading up to the TRC hearings.

It did not take us long to see that neither of us could recall exactly how we came to investigate the programme, nor what brought the two of us together. We could not agree on where we had first found documentary evidence – whether it was in a covert office of the National Intelligence Agency or some other state agency. There was no documentation we could use to jog our memories, and even if there had been, the chances are that the documents would have been constructed for reasons other than to provide a jog to our memories – and for that reason may have concealed more about the 'truth' of the origin of the investigation than they would have revealed. As my colleague commented, 'Because now, you see, it's difficult to know what you're recreating and what you aren't recreating.' Legacies 452

434 2013

Interview, transcript excerpt, 19 August
Prof. Robin Crewe (in his capacity as President of the Academy of Science of South Africa, 2004 to 2012)

> Chandré Gould: 'So if you are thinking back now on the chemical and biological weapons programme, what would you say, aside from what you've just said now, what would you say its relevance is now, for us as South Africans, and the [Academy of Science of South Africa] particularly? If any.'
>
> Robin Crewe: 'Well, I think it raises some uncomfortable questions because in one respect we have a large conventional arms industry and we sell those arms and those kill people as effectively as the biologically engineered organisms do, so I think it raises larger questions about the extent to which you are actually a manufacturer of offensive weapons of some kind. But I think there's a particular horror about biological forms of warfare that is quite different from the conventional, other than the nuclear, forms. So I think from that point of view, it has raised the awareness of whether it's ethical to be involved in that kind of activity at all. And I think that there are many biologists who believe that it's not ethical. IR 435 | Lessons 440

435 2013

Interview, transcript excerpt, 19 August
Prof. Robin Crewe (in his capacity as President of the Academy of Science of South Africa, 2004 to 2012)

Brian Rappert: 'Does that distinctiveness for you come because of the possible effects in terms of the scale of casualties and so on, or because biology is different than...'

Robin Crewe: 'Well, I think that the horror of it is both in terms of the scale of the effects, in the sense that... well, I mean, when you explode a shell you explode a shell, when it's done, it's done, does whatever damage it does. But the biological organisms, the effect of the biological organisms, is potentially much larger and I think the concern is the degree to which that is actually under control, in the sense that if you release these things, you may actually no longer be able to control them very effectively. And so you know, I think those are some of the concerns that lurk behind people's worries.' IR 467

436 2013

Interview, transcript excerpt, 19 August

Prof. Robin Crewe (interviewed in his capacity as President of the Academy of Science of South Africa, 2004 to 2012)

Chandré Gould: 'I am just wondering, it was interesting that you say [the TRC] wasn't formally raised as an issue... who might have had the authority to raise such an issue in the scientific community? If it were to have been discussed, who would have had that kind of authority?'

Robin Crewe: 'Well some of the major scientific societies may have, or should have, considered whether it was an issue which they should discuss so, for instance, the Society of Microbiologists for instance, as an example or the South African Chemical Institute, and also given Wouter Basson's background, with some of the medical associations, and so you know from that point of view, I think there was a feeling that these were done by people who were unethical and, therefore, there was no need for it to be explored on a wider scale. But in retrospect I think that was probably incorrect. So I mean, there were the specialist societies that could have had a discussion about it. There were also the generalist societies like the Academy or like the Royal Society or the Akademie that could have considered and had a discussion, asked a number of their members, to make them presentations about it and then have a discussion, but I don't think they did.'

Chandré Gould: 'It didn't come up?'

Robin Crewe: 'It didn't come up, yeah...' To know 437 | Lessons 434

2013

Interview, transcript excerpt, 19 August

Prof. Robin Crewe (in his capacity as President of the Academy of Science of South Africa, 2004 to 2012)

> Robin Crewe: 'I think that for a lot of the societies they tend to get on with the science that they are interested in and they tend to ignore the larger social questions that may have arisen. But there's a... well, anyway, carry on.'
>
> Chandré Gould: 'No, carry on!'
>
> Robin Crewe: 'I was just thinking, you know, we tend to focus quite strongly on individuals with a professional background in that area but I was also curious why some of the social scientists were not interested in this as a social phenomenon, and how the interaction between the professional scientific societies and the people who are operating in that programme were related to each other.' To know 52

2013

Interview, transcript excerpt, 20 August

Project Coast scientist (requested anonymity)

> Project Coast interviewee: 'You know, in the scientific community, the whole community I worked in... people's attitude was, "I don't want to have anything to do with this. I am not doing this," even people that actually had to look into these things in terms of their work in the Department of Health, for instance. I experienced... just to tell you, a colleague – well, it's not a colleague, it was a Major-General at that stage – that was now after the TRC hearings, but the perceptions that stuck in people's minds because of this whole bizarre thing. And we still sit with some of those perceptions but I will come back to that. A Major-General took over from another one that retired, went through cabinets and he found some disks in these cabinets, these old floppy disks, and he called me and he said, "I don't know what this is. I want you to have a look at it, because I don't want to become contaminated. Alright, I'm contaminated already!" I checked them and they were all about tents but that was the sort of atmosphere that was there. There was always this... and still up to today, people believe that this is so *extremely* sensitive, *extremely* secret, and there is very little that we can do that's secret. It's all open but that perception stuck. Still people think that we do funny things, colleagues of mine' [emphasis in original].

439 2013

Interview, transcript excerpt, 20 August
Project Coast scientist (requested anonymity)

> Project Coast interviewee: '...as I said, this government sort of continued
> and keeping building on this mystery about the programme. Why, I
> don't know. I tried very hard to tell people, this isn't such a secret thing,
> but that perception has stuck. And it is still there.' What? 144

440 2013

Interview, transcript excerpt, 20 August
Project Coast scientist (requested anonymity)

> Chandré Gould: 'What can we learn from this whole thing?'
> Project Coast interviewee: [pause] 'I think it's very difficult because we
> want to translate things that happened in a very abnormal situation to
> a normal situation. The one thing that I've learned over the years since
> I took over and sort of went along, is that there are actually – and I
> think it's a difficult for many governments – maybe you should switch
> that off.'
> [Recorder stopped.]
> Project Coast interviewee: '...say how to manage programmes. I've learned
> two major things very early when I took over and when I had to keep
> this thing alive. And the one is what I said just now, is we became
> increasingly transparent. No funny things. And the other one is, how
> we use language.' Lessons 398

441 2013

Interview, transcript excerpt, 20 August
Project Coast scientist (requested anonymity)

> Chandré Gould: 'After the TRC, there was a meeting that I organised. I was
> working for the Centre for Conflict Resolution at the time and still going
> on with the research... [M]y belief was we needed to have a look ... we
> needed to see what lessons we could learn from this and what does it
> mean about the way in which we must go about things in the future? So
> we had a meeting and we invited to that meeting, all sorts of people from
> the Medical Research Council, all over. And one of the people who came
> to that was Eugene Lottering, who was at the time the head of the Non-
> Proliferation Secretariat. I don't know if you remember him? And he

came to that meeting incredibly angry and, in fact, he almost disrupted the meeting. He left before it was done and his words were, just as he was getting up to leave, he said, "There is nothing that I can learn from these people, nothing that we can learn from these people, that could in any way be useful. This is a waste of my time, basically." He was very angry and hostile when he said that, and I was wondering where that came from and whether you have any sense of what kind of ... what he was... I mean, there are various ways of interpreting what he said, but I am curious about whether there was a general sense that we were wasting our time trying to draw lessons from this past.'

Project Coast scientist: 'I can't really comment. I didn't know him that well, and it's one of those funny things, as I said, this government sort of continued and keeping building on this mystery about the programme. Why, I don't know. I tried very hard to tell people, this isn't such a secret thing, but that perception has stuck.' Lessons 443

442 2013

Interview, transcript excerpt, 20 August
South African archivist, Verne Harris

Chandré Gould: 'You know, I mean, I think that's exactly the point, is that very often that secret is a secret about the absence of a secret, you know?'

Verne Harris: 'It's like the TRC archive. There was this view, which I think – am I right? – was dominant in the years post-Madiba [Mandela] government, is that the TRC archive was full of incredibly sensitive...'

Chandré Gould: 'Explosive!'

Verne Harris: '... so that the 34 boxes were so ██ing dangerous they... you remember when the Minister of Intelligence was saying, "I won't give it to a court!" It's like a paranoia...'

Brian Rappert: 'Why, because I don't know what's in it!'

Verne Harris: 'Because when you open those 34 boxes and look inside and you say, "██! What?"'

Chandré Gould: 'What was all that about?! The question for me is, what is the necessity behind that secret-keeping? So what work is that secret doing? So is it concealing our ignorance? Is it creating an importance around something that needs to be created for some reason that's not entirely obvious? I mean, what function is that secrecy performing? I mean...'

Verne Harris: 'I think that's the right question.'

Chandré Gould: '...and the 34 boxes is exactly the right example of this because we now know that when you open those boxes, it's not that exciting, you know!'

Verne Harris: 'There's a mirror!'

Chandré Gould: 'It's just not that exciting and yet, how much time, money, did it take before those boxes were made available? I mean…'

Verne Harris: 'It cost a hell of a lot of money. It took several years.'

Chandré Gould: 'Exactly, and it took an organisation spending concerted effort on it, with a lawyer.'

Verne Harris: 'And still to this day, you don't say, you can't say anything.'

Chandré Gould: 'Exactly, exactly.'

Verne Harris: 'And we know that there's nothing there that should be kept out of the public domain, apart from insight into how the French secret services operated at that time.' What? 329

443 2013

Interview, transcript excerpt, 20 August
South African archivist, Verne Harris

Chandré Gould: 'You see, I am not interested in… I don't believe in truth so I am not really looking for a truth, looking for the truth. I think that what I am interested in, is how the way the story was told did or didn't resonate with various categories of people, that would allow it to result in something good and positive. So the logic that I started with was, we need to learn lessons from the past in order to prevent it from happening in the future. So if we tell the story about the past, we are going to learn something about how we need to act in the future so that we don't do that again. Well, that's a fiction. I mean, that is an absolute nonsense but one holds onto that for a while. I denied it! It foolishly informed a lot of what I did. So if you reflect back, and if you think about … if your purpose in doing this kind of absurd exercise is to kind of come up with new ways of doing things and seeing things so that you achieve a better outcome…'

Verne Harris: 'Yeah, so if you were to do a study of Idi Amin and you do really hard, empirical research and you are able to say how he was shaped in the military, his upbringing, you can tell exactly how many people died [pause] like, does it teach us a lesson? The more thorough your research, the more like compelling the lesson becomes?'

Chandré Gould: 'Isn't that the fiction we labour under?'

Verne Harris: 'No, you see, the lesson becomes the fiction that you tell. It's like African leadership is ▮▮▮▮, or whatever the story is that you want to tell… I think why do we do it, because human beings very seldom learn from the mistakes of the past, very seldom. My motivation is to find the inspiring story, the story of people who were in those spaces, who did extraordinary things and lived lives that were like... wow, how did you fucking do that in the context of Idi Amin, because that inspires me to deal with the challenges of today, where I am, right? I can't see any other reason for doing that. You see, Jacques Derrida makes the argument that this work is inspired by two imperatives, and these imperatives are articulated by ghosts. It's the ghosts of those who have done it, and it's the ghosts of those who are yet to be born, so my work has to be about honouring those who died, it's that you didn't die in vain but it's not about some kind of like... hidden, like a mausoleum, right? It's about doing something liberatory with that, with those stories, so that the ones who are coming will come into a world that is hospitable to them.'

Lessons 383

444 2013
Interview, transcript excerpt, 20 August
South African archivist, Verne Harris

> Verne Harris: 'Is it time yet for us to like, think about [memory and truth projects] that might take us into Mozambique and Botswana and Lesotho and do we want to go there? In terms...'
>
> Chandré Gould: 'Cross-border raids? No, it's not our domain.'
>
> Verne Harris: 'That's a great space of secrecy for us, I think, as a country you know. It's not unrelated to attacks against foreign nationals and xenophobia.'
>
> Chandré Gould: 'You think so?'
>
> Verne Harris: 'I think it's part of the price we pay.'
>
> Chandré Gould: 'For not having spoken about cross-border raids?'
>
> Verne Harris: 'For not having kind of engaged that... Almost like Freud, you know? It's like repression and compensation and ▇▇ like that.'
>
> Chandré Gould: 'Well, it's also about the only legitimate victim. So the only legitimate victim is the South African victim, on South African soil. And outside of that there are no victims, there are no legitimate victims and so in owning that victim status, you are justified in, what, committing xenophobic attacks?'
>
> Verne Harris: 'Who knows what the psychology of that is... I cannot even begin to explain that, but we need to read what was happening in the mid-1990s as not unconnected to what we are seeing now.' Forgetting 451

Interview, transcript excerpt, 20 August
South African archivist, Verne Harris

Verne Harris: 'How are you using truth, the concept, here? In your idiom and your language, because if you were to assemble all this evidence and now finally be able to say, well, the programme was authorised at this level and these are all the structures and this is what it had been doing, these were its plans for the next five years, would that be the truth? Is that the truth that we are looking for, or is it understanding what it meant?'

Brian Rappert: 'But are we primarily interested in truth? I don't know.'

Verne Harris: 'Maybe we don't give a ▄▄ about truth. We just want the ▄▄▄▄ evidence. People can work out their own truths, right?'

Chandré Gould: 'Well, not at that level, because here I think there's a few…'

Verne Harris: 'Because you know for me, that's increasingly becoming a question. It's like I don't know what it means. I don't know what truth means in relation to things like infiltration of family members, I don't know what that means, right? But I just have a profound conviction now that you need to give this stuff to people to work with. Like my own conscription, right? So I am only beginning to be able to engage it. For many years, it had to be hidden. I just needed it to be not there, but I'm not sure at what point I kind of realised I have to work out: what does it mean? What does it say about me? What is the truth about that? I don't know what the truth is actually, but it needs to be engaged, it needs to be made available to parts of myself, it needs to be made available to Ben and Kerry and others around me. But what the truth is about, fuck, it's to be determined through dialogical processes, right, and it will shift over time, new significances will emerge.'

Lessons END

446 Whatever the overall dubious standing of chemical and biological weapons in recent times, the activities of Project Coast were made sense of through the geopolitics of the day, but they also informed those politics.

Victims 447

447 2013

Interview notes
UK Foreign & Commonwealth official
Some discussion in Her Majesty's Government on whether the

assassination programme counted as an 'offensive' biological weapons programme. [The interviewee] argued it was. What was important was that the programme was tiny and insignificant in comparison to the Soviet programme. And since it was only intended for attacking the ANC and supporters, it was not seen in the same light as the Soviet/Russian offensive programme. Offensive as far as the Biological Weapons Convention is concerned, is largely perceived as [the] offensive use of weapons against other states.   Victims 543 | Offence 74 | Silence 413

448   2013

Interview notes

UK Foreign & Commonwealth official

No appetite within Her Majesty's Government to challenge South Africa about declarations about Project Coast for these reasons:

- turnover of staff a problem (there was a change of personnel and so the first-hand knowledge of it was largely lost in succeeding years);
- Soviet/Russia Confidence Building Measure situation much more of an issue (why hassle South Africa, if not do so for USSR?);
- South Africa seen as reforming enough: info from programme under control, Basson under control, formation of South African Non-Proliferation Council and enactment of export controls;
- South Africa constructive in Biological Weapons Convention Protocol negotiations, so there was no appetite to rattle the cage.

Between April 1994 and October 1994, there was (very) partial openness from the Soviets. The Russians had an easy way out: they could have used the end of the Soviet era as a basis for more transparency and openness, but didn't take it. South Africa did take that out. There was a clear contrast between the way the Soviets approached it and the way the South Africans did. The openness displayed through the Truth and Reconciliation Commission meant that Form F, about past offensive programmes, didn't have to be dealt with as a major issue. This was never a formal policy decision; more of a subconscious way of operating.

It may be cynical, but since South Africa is the only Non-Aligned Movement[363] country being constructive – while we should not turn a blind eye – we can be more accommodating.

South Africa were the good guys, you don't want to beat up on your friends. But at the same time, this is not something that is conscious and consciously discussed. It's not a matter of a formal policy decision adopted by British ministers.   IR 351

Article in the *Mail & Guardian*, 22 November

When Sharon Rudman had a massive heart attack just after 8 pm on a Sunday evening in January last year, immense panic descended on her family. Rudman lived in Calvinia in the Northern Cape and was visiting her family in Durbanville, north of Cape Town. Her own doctor was 360 km away.

Rudman's daughter rushed her to the nearby Mediclinic where she was admitted and sedated for the night.

When she awoke on the Monday morning, she was 'angry and aggressive', as heart attack patients often are.

The cardiologist on duty was waiting next to her bed, speaking Afrikaans.

'I yelled at my child: "I don't think I'm going to get on with this guy. I don't like Afrikaans doctors! They're bossy."'

Her daughter was annoyed. 'Have you any idea who this is?' she snapped. 'It's Wouter Basson. He's hands-down the best cardiologist on the planet! So, you're going to behave, and not tick him off.'

Rudman's child had heard of Basson's reputation from her mother-in-law, a nurse specialising in heart conditions.

'What? Isn't he "Dr Death"?' asked Rudman.

'Yes,' her daughter confirmed, 'But don't ever say that again.'

Rudman said that, at the time of this exchange, Basson 'just stood there, listening, calm and collected. I remember feeling soon afterwards that I was in incredibly safe hands.'

Rudman was transferred to Panorama Hospital, about 15 km away, for intensive heart surgery. She said Basson told her: 'We're going to do a five-way bypass, because that's what you need. We're not going to try this and that and then revert. We're going to do the whole thing and you're going to be fixed up and it's all going to be good.'

When she left for Panorama, Basson looked at her and said he'd see her within an hour.

'And there he was in the ward waiting for me when the ambulance arrived. I've had doctors who have kept me waiting for hours. He's not a bit like that. He treats you as an equal and doesn't think he's deputising for God. He makes your anger and fear go away, and puts you at ease.'

Rudman recovered within a few days. 'I was in the intensive-care unit for the shortest time of everybody who had had surgery at the same time as me, and it's thanks to Wouter Basson. In terms of my heart surgery, I think he's the greatest thing since sliced bread.' [364]

Rudman, a lawyer herself, says, 'I understand the law and I know about Basson's past. But we lived in a very different time 30 years ago. Robert McBride [ANC member] was responsible for deaths in the Magoo's bar bombing in Durban. He is now seen as a fit person to be the head of a police watchdog. Both Basson and McBride were soldiers in a war situation. In these situations, it's not fair to say, "You committed a crime and must now be punished because you were on the wrong side of the conflict." War is war and you take your orders from the people above you.'[365] Legacies 528

Over the past several months, the authors have been speaking to diplomats, representatives of professional associations of scientists in South Africa and people who were in some or other way associated with Project Coast.

We have been asking them why South Africa has been allowed to get away with an incomplete, if not inaccurate, declaration about its past chemical and biological warfare programme in the Biological Weapons Convention. We have also asked whether the revelations about the programme prompted action, discussion or changes to professional codes of conduct for scientists. For some diplomats, the TRC hearings demonstrated a willingness by a state to deal with the past, offered assurances of transformation and meant that a declaration was not regarded as necessary; for others; the lack of a declaration was not even an issue in 2013, and never was. For scientists and science organisations, the TRC hearings dealt with the past – it absolved them from the responsibility of dealing with the issues that arose about the conduct of scientists. It allowed for a distancing from the distasteful behaviour of some.

For many, then, the TRC enabled a deference – 'someone else was dealing' with it, which meant that we did not have to deal with it further.

In short, it was a mechanism of forgetting. Forgetting 30 | Justice 528

Chandré Gould's reflections, November

I wonder whether the lack of response I perceive – that so little seems to have changed in the education of scientists, or in the regulation of science by professional associations in response to the revelations about the chemical and biological weapons programme – is not an illusion born of my frustration at a lack of judgement, reckoning and justice? For example, barring one definite case, no professional association representing the professions of those engaged in Project Coast seem to have revised their codes of ethics, made recommendations about educational changes or taken action against their members who were involved in the programme.

Is this amnesia a conscious avoidance of the difficult issues or is it that we are so busy dealing with the complexities of the present that the present becomes all-consuming and a-contextual? Legacies 460

453 2013

Project Officer of Project Coast, Dr Wouter Basson, interviewed by John Maytham, Cape Talk radio, 18 December

In this interview, Basson was asked by the interviewer, John Maytham, how – knowing what was known about the attitudes in the defence force at the time towards 'the ANC and blacks and so on' – it was possible that the production of Mandrax and cocaine-laden tear gas under Project Coast could have been entirely peaceful in nature. To this Basson rejected the suggestion that 'the South African Defence Force as a whole had a negative attitude towards blacks'. After all, Basson himself had been 'involved in delivering books to blacks in the homelands'.

To this contention, there was the following exchange:

John Matham: '[It is hard to believe that what] you were trying to do is develop effective, more effective, and peaceful ways of pacifying large crowds, it's really hard to believe that.'

Dr Basson: 'Well I am sorry it is hard to believe. Show me the proof that it wasn't that. You can believe what you want. Perceptions are great but facts are different things. If they had the things that we developed at that stage, were busy developing, at Marikana, Marikana would never have happened. And that was our job, to prevent that sort of thing from happening. To stop people that were absolutely out of their minds at that stage, for reasons that might be good, but stop them damaging themselves and the environment. That's what we were doing and the things we developed were totally harmless, they would not have harmed a single person if they were ever used.' Total war END

454 2013

Doctor Basson's Cape Talk radio interview with John Maytham was given in response to a ruling by the Health Professions Council of South Africa (HPCSA) earlier in the day. The HPCSA had found him guilty of unprofessional conduct in relation to four charges associated with his time as head of Project Coast: coordinating the large-scale production of illegal psychoactive substances; weaponsing 'tear gas' for use against Angolan government soldiers; providing SADF operatives with disorienting substances for over-the-border kidnappings; and for making suicide, cyanide capsules available to members of the SADF.[366]

To these charges Basson had offered a series of excuses and justifications, each rejected by the HPCSA. Forgetting 459

455   2013
Project Officer of Project Coast, Dr Wouter Basson, interviewed by John Maytham, Cape Talk radio, 18 December

> Every single fact that has ever been involved in this court case has been through the court system, and there is not a single pointer that I am guilty of anything. Either intentionally or unintentionally or whatever, factually and there was never any perception or any intention to damage or harm anybody. The intention of the whole project was to protect South Africa and its people and to stop people from annihilating themselves, from burning and necklacing and burning down buildings and causing endless harm and damage to themselves and other innocents... Victims 456

456   The deeply racist, patronising tone adopted by Basson, in seeking to present his actions as benign – as offensive as they are – reveals the thinking that enabled not only Basson and military commanders to justify their actions, but scientists too. Victims 266

457   For many of his supporters, the many hearings to which Dr Wouter Basson has been subjected, constituted a witch-hunt. Legacies 458

458   2013
Dr Wouter Basson, Project Officer of Project Coast, interviewed by John Maytham, Cape Talk radio, 18 December

> John Maytham: 'I do try to understand, because you are getting a lot of support from our callers and from our smses, but you are getting even more condemnation, people unable to understand why you don't seem to understand why you did anything wrong in your work as soldier-stroke-doctor.'
>
> Dr Basson: 'It's very simple, they must just show me what I did wrong [voice higher pitch and speaking very rapidly]. It's easy, all they need to do is bring one single case of anybody that was either damaged and/or hurt in this process and I'll live with it. But nobody can do that. I mean its been 20 years that this has been going on and there is not a single scratch and/or blue mark and/or bruise on anybody that could be proven anywhere, so who did I damage and how?' Legacies 449

459   2013
Against the range of disturbing and bizarre allegations made about Project

Coast since the mid-1990s, the charges eventually brought against Basson by the Health Professions Council of South Africa (HPCSA) were unlikely to rank at the top for many. And yet, this remains the only case of a formal professional or criminal ruling against someone involved in the programme.

The origins of the professional-conduct ruling against Basson date back to a letter lodged by other doctors more than 13 years earlier. In eventually taking the case forward, the legal team representing the HPCSA had to decide what charges to bring against him. Whatever the findings and facts agreed through the TRC and the criminal trial, determinations of professional misconduct would have their own standards for proof and bases for guilt.

To the question of 'How to charge Basson?', the strategy adopted was to base the charges on the accepted history, as already established. Specifically, Basson was charged on matters of medical and ethical misconduct based on his own evidence, as given in his criminal trial.[367] As a result, within the HPCSA proceedings, central facts of the matter could be judged as 'not in dispute'.

However, binding Basson to his own account of the past in this way entailed simultaneously unbinding him from other histories of Project Coast.

Forgetting 178 | Legacies 472

460 2013

Chandré Gould's reflections

I was in the garden when the news came. The weeds had grown as tall as me in the short time we had been away. They formed a thick coating over the asparagus bed, hiding the delicate green shoots.

By 10 am the sun was scorching and I was already coated in sweat, fine particles of dust, seeds and grass. Mud smears my war paint. Helet called from the stoep. 'Have you heard? Wouter has been found guilty.' I whoop. Relief? Vindication? And then go back to the weeds.

I am not sure what I feel.

Sello (a friend and his family who had come for a visit from Johannesburg, and who is also involved in 'memory work') joined me in the garden a few hours later, just back from a family day out. He, too, had heard the news on the radio. 'Did you hear?' But we speak little about it. I am too confounded by my mixed emotions, not quite sure what to feel or think. I tell him so.

I know I will need to avoid the phone and media calls, which will start up soon, until I know what to say. I am wordless. Numb. A fitting end – the end of a doctor's career?

I know that for Basson this judgment by peers – even those he will dismiss as vindictive witch-hunters – will be, perhaps, more painful even than prison. The possibility of not having the status of doctor will hurt. Can I rejoice at another's pain – even his? I can't.

Is this justice, a fitting end? Could there have been another way? I wonder whether this moment holds meaning for many others. I think of all the things that cannot and have not been said. I think about how quickly the detail of atrocity dissipates and becomes smudges of memory without clear form.

I don't turn on the radio, don't answer calls, stick my head in the weeds.

Legacies 461

461 2013

Chandré Gould's reflections

For the three years of the hearing I was convinced that the Health Professions Council of South Africa (HPCSA) would be unable to make their charges stick. The case started badly with the HPCSA's main witness – a well-known and respected bioethicist – conceding during cross examination that a solider must follow orders during war time, even if he is a doctor.

Midway through the hearing, the lawyers for the HPCSA came to meet me over a weekend, at my home. I was touched by their commitment to the case, the depth of their research and their certainty that they would win. I did not share their optimism. I had closely watched the criminal trial of Basson. He appeared to be a master of deception, who easily blended truth and fiction into a powerful analgesic and amnesiac. He was also skilled at creating and recreating himself and his narrative to match the requirements of an audience. But this time the judges were not sympathetic and made the surprising and gratifying finding that he had acted unethically – the plan is that, in February 2014, we shall see whether he is to be struck off the roll of medical professionals, a strong possibility suggested by the ruling.

Legacies 462

462 2013

Chandré Gould's reflections, 19 December

A tenacious journalist from Radio 702 tracked me down last evening and asked me to speak to Xolani Gwala on the morning news show. Just after 7.00 am the phone rang to connect me. I listened to a clip played to introduce the discussion – a short excerpt from a much longer interview with Basson by journalist John Maytham the day before...

JM: 'You were working actively and produced tear gas that contained Mandrax and cocaine and it's really hard to believe, knowing what we know, about the defence force and its attitude towards members of the ANC and blacks and so on that this was an entirely peaceful programme, that you were trying.'

WB: 'You have no idea what the defence force as a whole was doing regarding the blacks, the amount of help that we gave in the homelands at that stage, and for the people – the education – we supplied the books. I was involved in programmes where we supplied lorries to take books to schools... the present government can't even do that. So, no, you cannot say that the South African Defence Force as a whole had a negative attitude towards blacks, that's...'

JM: 'I can say that significant proportions of the defence force... it's hard to believe that this programme was entirely, as you say in a letter, that the only [WB tries to interrupt] thing – let's try not to talk over each other please Wouter – thing you were trying to do is develop effective, more effective, and peaceful ways of pacifying large crowds, it's really hard to believe that.'

WB: 'Well I am sorry it's hard to believe. Show me the proof that it wasn't that. You can believe what you want. Perceptions are great but facts are different things. If they had the things that we developed at that stage, were busy developing at Marikana, Marikana [referring to the killing of miners by police in 2012] would never have happened. And that was our job to prevent that sort of thing from happening. To stop people that were absolutely out of their minds, for reasons that might be good, but stop them damaging themselves and the environment. That's what we were doing and the things we developed were totally harmless, they would not have harmed a single person if they were ever used.'

I respond with an accusation of historical revisionism – say that scientists who were involved in the programme believed that what was required of them was to develop, and make available to military operators, poisons, chemical and biological assassination weapons that would leave no trace post-mortem.

Mine is an easy story to tell; it is one the journalist interviewing me wants to hear. He wants to hear the refutation of Basson's appeal to an alternative truth. But the subtext – the racism implicit in his answers – that the [black] government can't help its people in the way the military helped 'blacks' in the past – the paternalist reference to protestors harming themselves – hangs like an unspoken, intangible blockage. Legacies 459

463 Crime, and particularly violent crime, has figured high on the list

of prominent social concerns in South Africa post-apartheid. Levels of incidents of crime like aggravated robbery, rape, assault with grievous bodily harm, common assault and murder have attracted national and international attention.

While rates for severe crimes peaked in the early 2000s, levels continue to be stable at notably high rates. With some 17 000 murders in 2013/14, or roughly 45 people a day, the murder rate in South Africa sits at roughly five times that of the global average.[368]

Stated differently, more people are murdered each year in South Africa than die in some war zones. For example, in the six years between 2007 and 2012, just over 16 000 (16 179) civilians died in Afghanistan, equivalent to an average of nine murders per day.   Total war 464

464 The attention to what crime is taking place has been followed by attempts to determine why it is taking place. What can explain these extreme levels of violence in South Africa? The shadow cast by apartheid has been identified as a reason for ambivalence to the law, feelings of low self-worth among the long-disenfranchised communities, and stark levels of inequality and unemployment. No longer a nation divided on strict racial classifications, South Africa remains divided nonetheless. Other general factors associated with crime include the lack of communication skills, substance abuse, and feelings of low self-esteem on the part of the perpetrators of violence. The sources for these can often be traced to family environments that are fracturing under economic and social stresses.

The widespread normalisation of violence – in other words, that it is perceived as a legitimate way to resolve disputes – means that it has been used in situations that might be judged as inconsequential and in ways that are deemed excessive.[369]

The 'normalisation' of criminal violence has been framed by the state as constituting 'a state of war'.   Total war 465

465 2013

'The war on crime is a people's war and as history has indicated, the people become victorious in the end.'[370]

Minister of Police, Nathi Mthethwa   Total war 466

466 2013

The violence committed by some individuals has its parallel in the punitive, harsh measures taken by the state. Being 'tough on crime' has become a rallying call of the ANC party, which has ruled South Africa since the end of apartheid. National policies have overwhelmingly defined responses to crime in terms of more law enforcement by the police.

186

As a consequence of this stance, there have been missed opportunities to reduce crime by addressing the social, economic and psychological factors that promote it.

As has been argued, the overreliance on the criminal justice system has sidelined social solutions such as giving help to families, supporting victims and providing basic social services. While the police population ratio in 2016 was 1: 681,[371] the ratio of social workers to members of the population is around 1: 3000.[372]

In fact, this approach has fostered the very conditions it seeks to address. It has been argued that this criminalisation of large swathes of the population (particularly young black men) through incarceration serves to habituate them into a life of violence and crime.[373]   Total war 546

467 To suggest that norms or taboos against chemical and biological weapons are prevalent in the international community should not lead to the conclusion that these norms are uniform or fixed. Rather, social norms are always subject to negotiation. The policing of what counts as an infraction is part of the process of reaffirming and renewing norms.   IR 468

468 2014

Much of the condemnation of chemical and biological weapons since 9/11 has been couched in terms of such weapons being 'weapons of mass destruction', which are indiscriminate because their effects cannot be controlled.

What counts as a chemical and biological weapon is part of the negotiation of the norm against them.

This is most evident in debates about the appropriateness of biochemicals. For example, under an exemption provided for the use of chemicals in 'law enforcement' in the Chemical Weapons Convention, some armed forces (for instance, the United States and Russia – much like South Africa under Project Coast) are actively pursuing anaesthetic and sedative drugs for incapacitation.[374] The use of a fentenyl gas (an opium-based narcotic) by the Russian security forces during the Moscow theatre siege in 2002 is merely one example of the types of options being pursued. Research is underway to find ways to alter consciousness, behaviour and emotions.[375]

The acceptability and permissibility of such biochemical agents is fought out, in part, through terminology. Proponents make use of labels such as 'calmatives' and 'incapacitants'.[376] In contrast, in 2013 the International Committee of the Red Cross labelled these agents 'toxic weapons', arguing that they presented 'serious risks to life and health, risks undermining international law prohibiting chemical weapons, and risks creating a "slippery slope" towards the reintroduction of chemical weapons into armed conflict'.[377]

IR 469

469 Who counts as a 'worthy victim' is part of the negotiation of the norm against chemical and biological weapons. That the Iraqi military employed chemical weapons to kill over 5 000 Iraqi Kurds in Halabja and elsewhere during 1988 was widely cited in the West, in the lead up to the 2003 Iraq War, as an indicator of the problematic nature of Saddam Hussein's regime.

And yet, the same condemnation was not evident in 1988 when Saddam Hussein was regarded as an ally in the containment of Iran.[378] While the chemical weapons experience of the Iraqi Kurds was highlighted in the build up to the 1991 Persian Gulf War, the plight of the Kurds faded into obscurity in the West in the years that followed, and was rekindled only after 9/11.[379]

IR 470

470 What counts as a breach of the existing international prohibitions is also part of the negotiation of the norm against chemical and biological weapons.

IR 471

471 Despite the TRC hearings into the chemical and biological warfare programme, its finding and the findings of the court in the Basson trial – that South Africa had an offensive and defensive chemical and biological warfare programme (and, in particular, that cholera was used in an attempt to poison a water supply to a SWAPO camp in Namibia) – a curiosity has remained since the 1990s; namely, not only has South Africa failed to declare an offensive biological research and development programme under the Biological Weapons Convention BWC), but other states have also made little or no mention of this non-recognition in the proceedings of the BWC.

IR 351 | Silence 55

472 2014

Chandré Gould's reflections, 8 January

Seventeen years is a long time for your life to be tied to another's, especially if that relationship is never consummated by so much as a conversation. This is the relationship I have with Wouter Basson: a barren relationship as far as personal interaction is concerned. And this is how I have contrived it, having had no desire to engage him beyond his multiple professional personas, but predominantly in his role as head of Project Coast, the apartheid chemical and biological weapons programme. I suspect he feels the same way. There is little point in our meeting to talk: neither of us will convince the other of our truth – we can never know each other. I did meet Basson during the TRC hearings. We bumped into each other as he entered the room in which we were to hold the public hearing. We were introduced. He had clearly heard my name from the people we had been interviewing during our investigation. He looked me in the eye: 'Oh, so you are Chandré Gould' – then slowly his eyes moved down my body and back up again. 'Not bad,' he said. I moved away quickly; there was nothing more to say. I felt infuriated, violated. Over the next three days we locked eyes across the hearing room, each silently daring the other to look away. It was a hostile and exhausting encounter.

Does the finding by the Health Professional's Council signal a change in this relationship? Will it bring some semblance of closure? Is there any healing in this closure – or only a standoff? Legacies 516

473   2014

> The language that should trouble us is the language of war and othering that has persistently characterised official statements about crime and violence since crime rates peaked in 2001. The fifth volume of the TRC's final report reminds us that the excuse that 'we were at war' was used to justify atrocities by state security forces, the African National Congress (ANC) and the Inkatha Freedom Party. The context of war allowed the protagonists to undertake violent actions 'with pride rather than distress or embarrassment'.[380]
>
> Editorial, *South African Crime Quarterly*   Total war 396

474   2014

On 4 February, Brian Balmer, Malcolm Dando and I [Rappert] presented an in-progress report to project members of the Defence Science and Technology Laboratory (Dstl). As part funders of the 2013/14 'The Formulation and Non-formulation of Security Concerns' project, as well as housing Britain's chemical and biological biodefence establishment at Porton Down, the project members sought feedback on emerging ideas and plans.

As part of our report on future work related to the Project Coast research, and in the spirit of Kurt Lewin's adage, 'If you want truly to understand something, try to change it', I indicated that Chandré Gould and I intended to try and convince South Africa to revise its Confidence Building Measures declaration to acknowledge its offensive dimensions. Seeing if this could be done – and if not, where the resistance would come from – was envisioned as not only leading to a positive outcome in terms of the Biological Weapons Convention, but also a basis for testing the Action Map developed. A meeting was planned to discuss this possibility with a South African official as part of the fieldwork planned for later that month. Silence 475

475   2014

Shortly after the 4 February presentation, I received concerns from members of the Defence Science and Technology Laboratory about the proposed plan of action. As noted in an e-mail:

> During the discussion, you mentioned that as part of the next steps of the project you are planning to speak with the Technical Expert on the South African BTWC delegation with the view of suggesting that South Africa declare their alleged historical biological warfare programme through a revision of their Biological and Toxin Weapons Convention's Confidence Building Measures submission.
>
> As discussed subsequently, in the phone conversation of 7th February 2014, Dstl is not comfortable with funding granted through project ES/K011308/1, which includes an element of UK Government (Ministry of Defence) contribution, to be used for such purpose. Any activity of this nature would have to be in line with UK Government policy, led by the Foreign and Commonwealth Office. We therefore agreed (verbally) with you that any action to encourage South African declaration is not undertaken as part of project ES/K011308/1, and that no explicit or implicit association (public or otherwise) is made between such action and MOD/Dstl's engagement with the 'Science and Security' programme.
>
> We reiterate, however, that we have no issue with project funding being used for the capture and analysis of the evidence base, relating to South Africa or elsewhere, as set out in your original project proposal, or for the articulation of conclusions resulting from such research.[381]   Silence 476

476 2014
Following on from this, appropriate disclaimers were made and related expenses charged to a personal research account to avoid any link between the efforts to get South Africa to declare its past offensive activities and the work being undertaken as part of the Science and Security programme.

Silence 477

477 The question of what sort of bounds should be placed on social research, which seeks to do more than describe the world 'as is', can be approached in alternative ways.

One common framing would be to pitch opposing principles against each another. For instance, 'academic freedom' or the importance of unfettered inquiry might be posed as competing with the prerogative of funders to shape research to their ends. Determinations of legitimate bounds would then amount to trials of strength between these considerations. Here, distinctions between 'research and advocacy' or 'knowledge and politics' could be evoked as a way of making sense of what counts as appropriate conduct. In tracing the competing principles and distinctions, one's attention is invariably drawn to the matter of 'Who?': who should have the authority to make the call about the limits to knowing or what counts as appropriate impact?

Another approach would be to use the consideration of limits to re-examine the assumptions that often underlie thinking about research. For instance, in line with a more collaborative orientation to inquiry, Argyris has questioned the reasoning that underpins conventional thinking. Here, all too often it 'is the researchers who are in unilateral control over the methods [and] who define the criteria of victory'.[382] For Argyris, acknowledging the grip of such defensive reasoning-inspired practices is at least a first step in encouraging robust forms of inquiry that reflect on reactions to, errors in, and the impacts of research. Loosening researchers' control makes it less possible for them to undertake their work in a fashion that protects them and others from questioning.

Silence 478

478 2014

While links between actions to encourage the South African declaration and our research project were avoided, one thing we did not do in our publications and presentations was to declare that officials from Her Majesty's Government had demanded this dissociation.

A lesson: even those that analyse the negative implications of defensive reasoning in delimiting thought and action can engage in defensive actions that protect them from critical examination.

Or at least for a time…

Silence 395

479 2014
Interview, transcript excerpt, 5 February
Project Coast scientist #2 (requested anonymity)

> Chandré Gould: 'And ███████ within your family, after the TRC and after the trial, was it difficult to discuss these things with your family?'
> Project Coast scientist #2: 'Ja, you see, my wife didn't know anything. She read everything in the newspapers, and that was quite a shock to her because she was… ag, and my friends as well, you know. I think… and to be quite honest, you know, I spoke to them about it and I told them about it, you know, my close friends, that was one evening and then it was over and done. So… and they didn't point fingers, you know. So, we just went on… went on with my life. And I think ███████ provided a very good outlet for me because I was in science again, you know, I was in veterinary science … cattle … vaccinating cattle and this is … personally it is me, to develop vaccines is one of the things that I really like, because

you develop something, you use it and it works, or it doesn't work. If it doesn't work, you try again. So that was what kept me busy…'

Chandré Gould: 'So, in some ways it was kind … I mean it was quite quick phased … that whole revelation phase, and then you could just get on with your life again.'

Project Coast scientist #2: 'Ja. I think, some people I suppose can ponder and think and sit and wonder why this, why that, but if you keep your mind occupied constructively, then I think you sort of… you move out of that and you just get on.'

480 2014
Interview, transcript excerpt, 5 February
Project Coast scientist #2 (requested anonymity)

Brian Rappert: 'OK, just one more question about the Project Coast. It would be interesting to know if there's anything you'd like to know now. Are there any lingering questions you might have which you would ask to anyone involved in it? Just things … I don't know … something that you've just got a curiosity about or…'

Project Coast scientist #2: 'You see, ja … you know, I still think sometimes … I think about it and think, "Why was it destined to be such an abortion?" Because we had good facilities, we had good equipment and why didn't they… Because I've been reading, I like military history, and I like the Angolan War and I've got most of those books and if you look at how those guys planned everything. Everything was planned to the detail. Typically in military style. If you look at a lot of the equipment that we designed, that we used in Angola was designed and built by ourselves. And if you look at all the detail that went into everything, you know, these guys didn't miss a thing, you know. Denel or Armscor, at that stage they designed flippin weapons… OK, it is still a weapon, it is something to kill a human. Why wasn't the same applied to Project Coast?'

What? 38

481 2014
Interview, transcript excerpt, 18 February
Project Coast scientist #3 (requested anonymity)

Chandré Gould: 'OK. So [Anon], if we just for a moment… I mean, one of the things that I'm interested in is how your involvement with the Truth Commission hearing, the later trial, impacted on your work in the future. So, I mean, you were one of the people who... you cooperated with the TRC, you came forward with the testimony and you testified against Basson. What sort of impact did that have on your career afterwards?'

Project Coast Scientist #3: 'I think it had a huge impact on my career. Basically, the truth sets you free. Now, it's a very interesting situation, and you will know this. I have never gone to the Truth Commission and say I'm sorry, I did this, that and the other. I know we spent a lot of time in the beginning, that I told you I don't want to go there and blah, blah, blah.'

Justice 264

482 2014

Interview, transcript excerpt, 18 February
Project Coast scientist #3 (requested anonymity)

Chandré Gould: 'I've been trying to ... speak to the Veterinary Council, because I'm interested in whether the revelations about Project Coast meant that they had any conversations on the Veterinary Council at all... Were there ever questions asked, discussions held?'

Project Coast scientist #3: 'Many... lots of it. I hate them. They are... they're afraid of me, because again, they don't... ja... the first thing that happened, they scrapped me.'

Chandré Gould: 'Oh really? They revoked your membership.'

Project Coast scientist #3: 'My membership.'

Chandré Gould: 'OK. And for [another scientist] ... sorry... do you know? Did they do the same?'

Project Coast scientist #3: 'Ja. And they didn't even tell us. They just decided in a meeting, "these guys, they are not in good standing with the council". So... and if you're not in good standing with the council... But anyway, I was then nominated ... to serve on the council for developing the laboratory animal technologist profession. And then the council wrote back and said, [Anon] is not in good standing with the council, he can't serve on the committee. So I said, that is not on. And I wrote them a letter and I cc'ed the letter at the bottom to everyone, including you, and the chairman, and Frank Chikane, and NIA [National Intelligence Agency] chief and everyone. I haven't sent it to any of them. I just put at the bottom there, cc. Because I would have if it was necessary, because all of them knew about this, and I said this is unacceptable and I demand an apology... a public apology, and they had to put it in a letter then and everything, that there's no

193

question… I'm in good standing. So that's where they lost then the first round.'

Chandré Gould: 'So they apologised?'

Project Coast scientist #3: 'They apologised, ja.' Forgetting 59

483 2014

Interview. transcript excerpt, 18 February
Project Coast scientist #3 (requested anonymity)

Project Coast scientist #3: 'Before the Truth Commission I went to the Presidency and I sat with Frank Chikane and he sat with Mandela and I said, "Look, we worked on this project. What do you want to know?" We told them, this is what we did and this is what we didn't do… We told old Frank Chikane he should have been dead, but he wasn't dead… And then he sat like that, and he was quiet, senior scientist Schalk was with me and my wife. She was my bodyguard, cloak and dagger days. You know that. So he sat there for a long time, maybe not that long but it felt like it. And then I said, "What do you think?" So he looked up and he says, "I think God loves me a lot."' Victims 203

484 2014

Interview, transcript excerpt, 18 February
Project Coast scientist #3 (requested anonymity)

Chandré Gould: '██████, you said very provocatively that all the scientists involved in Project Coast are involved in proliferation. I'm just wanting to understand what lies behind that.'

Project Coast scientist #3: 'To be a proper consultant we need to have laboratories to test and analyse. And then we test and analyse, and then from the analysis we see what needs to be the answers, and have to produce the answers, making vaccines and immuno-therapy. Then we have to produce and in the production, you proliferise [sic] the organism… that's the problem, here's the answer. Then the answer we proliferate. We use the technology exactly the same. The only thing we do is we tell everyone what we're doing [now].' IR 490

485 As to how silence, secrets and their revelation affected inmate relations, the scientists had this to say… To know 486

486 2014
Interview, transcript excerpt, 18 February
Project Coast scientist #3 (requested anonymity)

Chandré Gould: 'It's important what you said now, I mean, that their family…
you're implying that their silence has had an impact on their family life…
What has the conversation been in your family? How has it played out?'

Project Coast scientist #3: 'It had an effect on the family. Very strongly so,
because we were too close-knit and … there's no way of, how shall I
say, everything on this side, which is usually the way you handle this.
You don't know really what your dad is doing… they were small,
you know, but in the TRC they were grown up and then they were
faced with… when I got back from the TRC, at school the children
told my daughter, "Your dad is a murderer." So, she would come back
and say, Dad, what the hell is this? So… but you had to handle it. At
the end of the day we're still together. Whereas, if you don't do that,
then… they're not together. And, they are doing all extremely well in
difficult situations in South Africa for white males… economically.
So… and that wouldn't have been necessary… I doubt it whether it
would have been seen that they have come through the protected and
easy way for white males in the old times. So ja.'

Chandré Gould: 'And how, if I may ask, how did you explain it to your
daughter? I mean, when it came to that moment… I'm thinking about
it must have been a very difficult thing to have done.'

Project Coast scientist #3: 'Ja well, its first off a bit of a shock, and you
sit down and you … you're not expecting it, and she was really … but
again, it is just sit down and go through the truth and the facts of it,
and say this is what we did.'

Chandré Gould: 'Ja.'   To know END | Victims 253

487 In 2014 Gould and Rappert interviewed scientists who had worked
for a front company of Project Coast. In expressing his views on what
needs to be said now about Project Coast, one interviewee articulated
the central tension in any account of this chemical and biological
warfare programme – was it a scientifically competent and sophisticated
programme or was it a scientifically insignificant workshop for
assassination weapons?

Chandré Gould: 'So where does that … I mean, if we come back to that
original question, I mean, if it were up to you to decide what gets said now

about Project Coast, what would you want to be out there, if anything?'

Project Coast scientist #2: 'Not really anything. I think Project Coast has been proven to be scientifically very sound, a very high level of science. I think as far as biological weapons were concerned, the individual toxins and stuff were very good, which couldn't be controlled by anything, because those poisons and toxins were all off the shelf stuff that were just manipulated a little bit. So that side of it was very crude. And that was the side that was really but totally misused...'

Another scientist had this to say:

Project Coast scientist #3: 'The scientific side was based on ... but totally ... and the main reason was ... and this is what I was approached for ... to develop the vaccine to curb the birth rate amongst the black people, which I would still do today to curb the birth rate amongst the poor people, which most of them at the moment is black. But I still believe that if we can curb the birth rate, the quality of life for everyone will go up.'

Asked if there was anything he felt still needed to be answered about Project Coast, anything that needed to be said now, one of the scientists had only this to ask: 'So, that's the only thing I wanted to know from Project Coast is, why? Why didn't they offer me also money?'

[The money he was referring to was the millions of rands that were paid to the directors of the front companies when they were privatised.]

Legacies 525

488 2014

Interview, transcript excerpt, 19 February

Michael Schmidt, the Director of the Institute for the Advancement of Journalism

Chandré Gould: 'I am interested particularly in why you want to investigate Dual more.'

Michael Schmidt: 'In part I am hoping that what it will do is it will lay the groundwork for a future unravelling of what I call this pact of forgetting in the region, OK? And essentially what I am doing is, I am looking at the precedents being set in countries, in particular in the southern cone of Latin America, relating to Operation Condor. And what's happened there is firstly, precisely because Condor was a multinational operation, there were crimes committed, gross human rights violations, disappearances, massacres, tortures, etc., committed across various borders and the people who were the victims were not necessarily citizens of that country. They were often in exile, running away from the regime in the neighbouring country. Also, because of the different jurisdictions, not everybody covered their tracks up as well as the next, so in... I think – 1995, several terror archives were found in a rural police station outside of Asunción in Paraguay, that detailed a hell of a lot of these operations but transnationally, OK? And on that basis, a lot of prosecutions have started to arise. Now the situation is that, for instance, in Uruguay, there is a blanket amnesty, OK, but the former dictator, Juan María Bordaberry and his foreign minister, were both given life terms for crimes committed in Argentina and I think we have a similar situation here in southern Africa in that you have a series of crimes that were committed transnationally, you have a blanket amnesty, as in South West Africa as it was at the time. But these crimes involved people from South Africa, from Angola, that actual murders, if you will, took place outside territorial waters, and so I think that there is a loose thread there, that can be pulled at until this thing unravels. That's my long-term strategy with this.'

Chandré Gould: 'So you want to see prosecutions from this?'

Michael Schmidt: What I really want to see is some form of transformative justice really for the families involved, more than anything else, not so much a vindictive, prosecutorial process, although that might be part of it, because a lot of the people are actually dead now. But the knowledge is important. With Dual, we don't have a single victim named, which is crazy. We are talking about approximately 200 people. At least in places like Argentina, the disappeared are named and known. But I think what's operating in the region at the moment is a bit of a quid pro quo, where SWAPO has its own skeletons in the closet, they don't want to know about this. When I investigated, for instance, the Foreign Legion thing with Wouter Basson, I naturally approached the Zimbabwean authorities and the military authorities and said, "Look, these are your guys, who got murdered. Help me out here," and there was a resounding silence.'   Forgetting 391

489 2014

Interview, transcript excerpt, 20 February
South African lawyer that requested anonymity

Chandré Gould: 'And then you probably know more now, having looked through the lengthy transcripts of the trial and read books and consulted the files; you probably have more knowledge of Project Coast than most South Africans do. Is there anything that you think… on the base of that, what do you think should be left in South Africans' minds about this programme, if anything? What would you like South Africans to know?'

South African lawyer: 'Firstly, I think I got more knowledge out of the project through your book! And then obviously there was the evidence. No, I think that… I want to try to give you a good example. I don't know if it's applicable. It's like apartheid, something that went wrong, horribly wrong, you understand? It shouldn't have happened. If the objective was just for a purely defensive role, but so many things came out of it, under the umbrella, and this is where it went wrong.'

Chandré Gould: 'If I am hearing correctly, it's kind of an example of how apartheid went really wrong.'

South African lawyer: 'Yeah.'

Chandré Gould: 'One thing that it seems to have…'

South African lawyer: 'No, you know, let me just qualify that. I am not a supporter of apartheid but I think if you would have looked at the reason for Project Coast as being, "we just want to create a defensive mechanism," that in itself seems OK. But that didn't happen, you see, that's where it went wrong. And of course, the fact that it extended, I think that's another important point that I maybe can just make out of a personal position, it wasn't just for – and I don't want to go into the debate of if there was a war in the true definition of what a war is, but it became internal and it's for me difficult to say that there was a war in South Africa. I mean, in Angola we were fighting Angolans and we were fighting Russians and Cubans across the border, but to say to me that there was a war in South Africa, in Soweto and places like that, it's ridiculous.'

Brian Rappert: 'But in that sense is it a historical lesson, or is taking this case forward now still saying something about South Africa today? Are there any reflections that this raises for you in terms of contemporary issues?'

South African lawyer: 'Well the internal problem is being repeated. I think it was said by the defence, if you look at Marikana. Have we learned anything about it? What have we learnt if something like Marikana happens?'

Chandré Gould: 'Yeah. Well, I mean, and every day, the numbers of people being shot by the police now is unprecedented since the end of apartheid.'

South African lawyer: 'Yeah, exactly.' Lessons 538

Since the initial public indications of Project Coast, concerns about proliferation have been widespread. The programme and the investigations of it were queried as to how they might enable others to develop chemical and biological weapon capabilities.

But what counts as 'proliferation'? The citation of technical details at a public hearing? The spread of biological agents? The leaking of classified documents?

A corollary question can be asked: 'When might proliferation from Project Coast no longer be a concern?'

If we treat this programme as an assemblage of people, equipment, know-how, chemicals, documents, bioagents, formulas, samples and much else, the picture becomes complex. On the one hand, there are many elements that might contribute to proliferation. On the other, producing viable weapons requires bringing these together in the correct fashion.

Examination of weapons development suggests that far more is required to fashion weapons than just technical information – practical know-how, hands-on experience, and skills that are learnt through intensive training and trial and error.

For instance, despite signing the Biological Weapons Convention in 1972, the USSR had a massive bioweapons programme into at least the early 1990s.[383] Even with extensive research on weapon designs and previous experience with anthrax, Soviet bioweapons experts experienced many difficulties in weaponising it.[384] These related to the learning of practical know-how and skills, the establishment of protocols and the creation of an extensive infrastructure.

If this is the case, then as elements of the assemblage degrade or are destroyed, there is a prospect, over time, of curtailing or even eliminating the potential proliferation threats posed by former chemical and biological programmes.[385]

The likelihood of proliferation depends on the level of the envisaged threat. The demands of producing relatively crude chemical or biological weapons would be easier than weapons that inflict mass casualties. As illustrated in the 2001 anthrax letters in the United States or the 1995 Tokyo subway attack, relatively crude technical systems can lead to widespread disruption and fear.[386]

Since Project Coast, though, various individuals and governments have been asking questions such as: 'What can be done?' 'What can we do now?' 'What should others do in the future?' The value and threat posed by the elements of the programme will derive from and inform the hopes, events, fears and fantasies playing out on the world stage at the time. IR 491

That some countries might possess or be suspected of possessing, use or proliferate chemical and biological weapons in the 21st century can lead to a significant response in the international community. For example, concerns about these weapons drew condemnation and prompted action in the international community in the case of the 2003 invasion of Iraq and allegations that it possessed chemical and biological weapons, as well as in the case of the use of chemical weapons in Syria in 2013.[387] No government openly claims to operate such programmes. Within diplomatic and military circles, little credence is given to the suggestion that the categories of chemical or biological weapons should be treated as anything other than distinct and prohibited.[388] In short, as categories of weapons, they are taboo.   IR 434

492   2014

Interview, transcript excerpt, 4 June
Scientist #4 under Project Coast that requested anonymity

> Project Coast scientist #4: '[Y]ou know, the moment you give [the military] a tool, they either want to kill somebody or do something with it. So the moment they get these toxins… I did not give any toxins to anybody. But what did happen at Murrayfield, I was going through one of the intelligence documents and I picked up silatranes, which are basically a silicon molecule that has got a long carbon chain and so on, and they said, "This substance is deadly and there is no detection." So I went along to the guys and I said, "Can you make some that I can test and see if I can't work out some sort of biological enzymatic kind of process that will do this?" And I heard very little about it after that message. Lourens was busy making it. And next thing, they brought this rat into the lab and five minutes later the rat was dead and that was it, that was the last I heard of it. So I do not know what happened to that. And that's the one thing that really has troubled me, you know, because it would have been undetectable, you know, if my reading was correct. And that's not good.'   What? 268

493   2014

Interview, transcript excerpt, 4 June
Project Coast scientist #4 (requested anonymity)

> Project Coast scientist #4: '[My unit within the programme] was really focusing on defence. That was essentially detection, protective clothing, that kind of thing. The big problem was that you always

end up with the moment you have got that kit, the moment you have a kit, you have to test it and for that you need the toxin, and therein lies the problem.'

Offence 511

494 2014
Interview, transcript excerpt, 4 June
Project Coast scientist #4 (requested anonymity)

Chandré Gould: '███████, if I can just ask you, when you realised that what you were doing was... how did it turn out that you knew that you were part of this anti-fertility programme aimed at black women? I mean, how did that discussion happen?'

Project Coast scientist #4: 'Can you just turn off the recorder for a minute.'

To know 55

495 2014
Interview, transcript excerpt, 4 June
Project Coast scientist #4 (requested anonymity)

Brian Rappert: 'I suppose it would be interesting just to know a little bit about what it was like to work [at Delta G] and the relationship to these questions about what you knew or what you could ask.'

Project Coast scientist #4: 'Yeah, look, essentially... it's funny the way people keep secrets! When I was doing basic training in 1980, the Special Forces building was being built and I was just down the road at this military camp. It was basically the clerks' school where all the admin people went. And we were doing this long march down the hill, across the field, and we were stopped and so we said to the lieutenant, "What's that building up there on the hill?" He said, "That's secret, I can't tell you." We went to the corporal, "Corporal, what's that building there?" "Oh, that's the new Special Forces building!"

And the thing is that at ... the lab was kind of... [he starts drawing on a piece of paper] ... you had the analytical section this side and then there is basically a long lab like that and then there was a room, this was reception over there. And this was all open planning. So you know, when they made the Sarin, for example, somebody put on the gas mask. Why do you put on a gas mask unless there is something serious going down? So, you know, likewise with the silatrane that they made, my bench was just on the left and everyone saw the rat. I can't remember who said it but they said, "They were busy making the silatrane" so it was obvious it was being made. To know 238

496 2014
Interview, transcript excerpt, 4 June
Project Coast scientist #4 (requested anonymity)

Project Coast scientist #4: '[A]round 1994, 1993, it was around that time, I went to ▉▉▉ who is a black African cardiologist and I said, "▉▉▉▉, have you got an hour? I need to tell you something." And I told him pretty much what I am telling you [about my previous work as a scientist in Project Coast] and he went off to try and find somebody that would listen at all and he just came back and he said, "Nobody is interested."…So the trouble is that, you know, when you hear things like "Nobody is interested" and so on, and you are kind of desperate to tell somebody but there is just nobody that you can really turn to and speak to.' To know 163

497 2014
Interview, transcript excerpt, 4 June
Project Coast scientist #4 (requested anonymity)

Project Coast scientist #4: 'I haven't told anybody about [my involvement in Project Coast] because I think for… you know, as [my partner] said last night, she said, "Why don't you tell somebody? Because the longer you stay secret, that's…"'
Chandré Gould: 'The worse it gets.'
Project Coast scientist #4: 'And the perception is that you are covering up something and my feeling was that if I were to tell… the trouble is, there was not much interest as well, you know, until…'
Chandré Gould: 'Now.'
Project Coast scientist #4: 'Basson's [HPCSA] trial came up and the trouble is, you know, to go along and then speak to… just take [my current manager] for example, to go and sit with him and say, "▉▉▉, I have a story to tell and this is it." He would say, "Why haven't you told me before?" And I feel it's like dumping my shit on his shoulders. It is now his responsibility and it's not, it's my shit, that I am carrying around! And I just think that it's very difficult, it would be very difficult if suddenly my name comes up and stuff like that."
To know 527 | Victims 515

Interview, transcript excerpt, 4 June
Project Coast scientist #4 (requested anonymity)

> Chandré Gould: '[If] you had to think back now to what lessons might
> come out of this programme for…'
>
> Project Coast scientist #4: 'Scientists?'
>
> Chandré Gould: '…for scientists.'
>
> Project Coast scientist #4: 'Scientists don't do ethics. They have very
> little… ethics is one of those things where it's kind of feely-touchy,
> feel-good kind of stuff and you know, you go to a course, you tick the
> box and you move on…'   Lessons 441

Chandré Gould's reflections
After leaving the South Africa's Council for the Non-Proliferation of
Weapons of Mass Destruction, I remained involved in the Biological
Weapons Working Group. It is this committee that is tasked with ensuring
compliance with the Confidence Building Mechanisms to the Biological
Weapons Convention. However, Form F never came up for discussion,
because it had remained unaltered since 1995.

In 2014, I set about finding out how it might be possible to propose a
change to the Form F declaration. This required 'track two'[389] discussions
with people I am unable to name here. At first the idea was met with
some scepticism – doubt as to whether any suggestion for change would
be considered at all – but, more importantly, concern about how to phrase
a change. The best way seemed to be to start the process by proposing
some text. I was careful to make sure that I included only what had been
confirmed in the documents relating to Project Coast and in the criminal
trial of Wouter Basson. I was also cautious about claiming that the
programme had been officially sanctioned – a matter to which the post-
apartheid government had not conceded.

Informal exchanges between me and persons unnamed indicated that
this was going to be a difficult process. The response to the first draft of the
proposed amendment was:

> After reading your proposed text I am even more convinced that these
> changes will not add anything nor will they be of any help to the CBM issue.
> At best more questions may be raised.

If the programme was not officially sanctioned it means that it was not a government programme and therefore, not declarable hence no change required.

If you want to include the activities you described in the declaration as unofficial activities conducted by individuals then again the question is, why include it in the declaration.

You are correct this is more difficult than what even I have thought.

This led to a new draft, in which it was not claimed that the state had sanctioned a biological warfare programme, but rather couched the change as presenting new information about the past programme in the interests of transparency. I hoped that the new declaration would not only be regarded as non-threatening, but also that such a declaration by South Africa could be used as a way to encourage other states to follow suit. Silence 500

500 **2014**

Proposed text for an amended South African CBM Form F:

Declaration of past activities in offensive and/or defensive research and development programmes

1. Date of entry into force of the convention for the state party:
   Signed: 10 April 1972
   Ratified: 3 November 1975

2. Past offensive biological research and development programmes
   South Africa had no offensive biological research and development programmes in the past.

   Note: In the interest of transparency the following information is provided:

   Under the auspices of the military chemical and biological warfare programme (Project Coast), both offensive and defensive work was conducted. Project Coast was managed by a committee appointed by the Minister of Defence and chaired by the Chief of the Defence Force. Although the committee was responsible for the project, it was never fully informed of the details and the Head of Project Coast (1981–1992) exercised significant latitude in directing activities.

   Since 1992, a number of investigations and public hearings have taken place relating to Project Coast, the apartheid-era chemical and biological warfare programme. These included an investigation and public hearing by the Truth and Reconciliation Commission (June and July 1998) and the criminal trial of the project officer, Dr Wouter Basson (4 October 1999–11 April 2002).

During the Chemical and Biological Warfare hearings of the Truth and Reconciliation Commission and the criminal trial of Dr Wouter Basson evidence was presented that scientists employed at a military front company [a seemingly private research institute that was in fact run and owned by the military], Roodeplaat Research Laboratories (RRL), undertook research that could be interpreted as offensive in nature.

A document from Roodeplaat Research Laboratories, dated 1986, lists H-code projects. Employees of RRL testified during the TRC hearing that these were 'hard' projects or projects they understood to be undertaken for military purposes. Relevant research projects listed in the document are:

Table 1: Extract from RRL document setting not research projects to be undertaken

Code	Project title
86/H/19/80	The development of a fertility test model in baboons
86/H/30/60	The preparation of the alpha toxin of Clostridium perfringens Type A
86/H/38/70	The evaluation of the anti-fertility potential of hCG-derivatives
86/H/398/70	The evaluation of the anti-fertility potential of LDH-C4 combinations
86/H/40/70	The evaluation of the anti-fertility potential of LDH-C4 inhibitor combinations
85/H/11/70	Carcenogensis and chronic toixicity of Fusarium moniliforme

A document entitled Verkope ('Sales') authored by the head of research at RRL was presented as evidence during the TRC hearing and criminal trial. According to the author of the report, the document lists items prepared at RRL and made available to military and police operators. Each item is dated. The items containing pathogens or toxins are:

Table 2: Extract from 'sales' list authored by the head of research at RRL

Date	Item	Quantity
22.06.1989	Sugar and Salmonella	200 gm
04.08.1989	Vibrio cholerae	16 bottles
11.08.1989	Cigarette Bacillus anthracis	5
	Coffee chocolate Bacillus anthracis	5
	Coffee chocolate Clostridium botulinum	5
16.08.89	Vibrio cholerae	6 bottles
08.09.89	Vibrio cholerae	10 bottles
08.09.89	Mamba toxin	1
06.10.89	Brucella melitensis c	1 x 50
	Salmonella typhimurium in deodorant	1
11.10.89	Cultures from letters (2)	2
21.10.89	Brucella melitensis c	
	Salmonella typhimurium in deodorant	1

The judgment in the *State vs Wouter Basson* concluded that in 1989 operators of the Civil Cooperation Bureau, seeking to destabilise the elections in Namibia, contaminated the water supply to a camp outside of Windhoek with *Vibrio cholerae*. Since the water supply was chlorinated, the contamination attempt was unsuccessful.

Aside for these items listed on the Sales list, no evidence exists regarding the development or use of biological weapons inside or outside South Africa.

The South African Defence Force developed no military doctrine relating to the use of biological weapons and authorised no offensive biological weapons research and development.   Silence 501

501 2014
The proposed amendment to the South African Confidence Building Mechanism Form F was ultimately tabled for discussion at the Non-Proliferation Council – and somewhat unsurprisingly – rejected on the basis that there would be no advantage for South Africa to make such an amendment.   Silence END | Lessons 445

502 Notes from an interview by Chandré Gould and Brian Rappert in which the interviewee requested anonymity.

Interview notes
Disarmament expert

> Chandré Gould: 'The UNIDIR monograph [*Project Coast: Apartheid's Chemical and Biological Warfare Programme*] met with a lot of resistance before its publication: what were South African diplomats worried about?'
>
> Disarmament expert: 'I am not sure. I think that they were concerned about ▮▮▮, and about his reputation – they wanted to protect him. ▮▮▮ is a powerful character and he didn't want this to undermine the work he was doing in the BWC, or his reputation. ▮▮▮ is quite different and he felt quite differently about this, you should try to speak to him. ▮▮▮ also tried very hard to discredit you, saying that you were just a journalist, had no expert knowledge and were in no position to write an authoritative account of the programme. It was really only because I knew you, knew what work you had done and had faith in it, that I could go ahead with this.
>
> Individuals play an important role in the BWC – and personalities drive or hold back the process. ▮▮▮ was one of the people who drove the process. But I could never get ▮▮▮ to talk about his own role in holding up/representing the apartheid government.'
>
> Chandré Gould: 'Was the UNIDIR monograph more threatening than the TRC? Why?'
>
> Disarmament expert: 'I am not sure that it was, it just was in a different context.'
>
> Forgetting 19

Interview notes
Dr Boitshoko Ntshabele, President of the South African Veterinary Council, and Dr Lynette Havinga, Registrar of the South African Veterinary Council

13 August

The authors wait in a large, square room to speak with representatives of the South African Veterinary Council about its past (in)actions in sanctioning members who participated in Project Coast.

Snacks are put out. The authors continue to wait. The room is adorned with images of its former leaders. A framed newsletter from the 1990s hanging on a wall, which includes a photograph of a leading member of

Project Coast, Dr André Immelman. The accompanying text announces that he and others have been elected to the Veterinary Council's central governing board.

The interviewees enter. Salutations and greetings. Dr Boitshoko Ntshabele, President of the Council. Dr Lynette Havinga, Registrar of the Council. The interviewees pose various questions about the purpose of the research and its confidentiality.

The interviewers' questioning begins.

Forgetting 505

505 2014

Interview transcript excerpt

Dr Boitshoko Ntshabele, President of the South African Veterinary Council, and Dr Lynette Havinga, Registrar of the South African Veterinary Council

13 August

Chandré Gould: 'Just for the sake of the recorder, the date is the 13th of August, we are at the South African Veterinary Council and it's Chandré Gould and Brian Rappert. OK, so should we begin with our questions? The first question really is very simple... the Truth Commission hearings were public, they took place in 1998, '97/'98, and we are just interested in how the Council responded to the revelations that were made. Was it an issue that the Council took up or not?'

Boitshoko Ntshabele: 'We've discussed it, that the general principle is that we went back to Council minutes, having received your e-mail, to try and get a sense of whether the issue was ever tabled. It does not appear that there was a specific issue from the TRC but there were possibly unsubstantiated allegations around some individuals. But the issue itself has not surfaced.'

Clarification is then provided of the Veterinary Association's procedures for allegations of misconduct. Given its role as judge of professional conduct, the Association does not initiate investigations into members; even if they are widely reported in the press, unless the coverage includes *prima facie* evidence of its own. In the case of Project Coast, as explained by the interviewee, minutes from that time indicated that all the Association had heard were unsubstantiated allegations. While members of the Association might have implicated themselves in misconduct through their affidavits and oral evidence, substantiated written evidence of misconduct had to be

208

submitted to the Association for it to start proceedings. Since it was not, no action was taken.

> Lynette Havinga: 'So I assume at the Truth and Reconciliation, somebody had to send "it" to us to say, "These are the revelations."'   Forgetting 506

506   Yet, despite the background on procedures, in a previous interview one of the scientists, who had worked in a Project Coast front company (and who was a registered veterinarian at the time), told us that he had been sanctioned by the Council for his role in the programme.   Forgetting 482
507   2014
When Dr Boitshoko Ntshabele as President of the South African Veterinary Council was asked whether the discussion of professional conduct issues stemming from Project Coast evoked the following feelings:

> Brian Rappert: '[O]h gosh, this was way in the past and why are they asking about this?! Or do you think there is something we can learn?

There was the following exchange:

> Boitshoko Ntshabele: 'You said your exploits are academic so maybe our academics tend to teach so many desk lessons today. We will take your question and ask our Review Committee. We've got a Review Committee, so we will ask them to reflect over a long period of time as to... and maybe your finished material will be much more... because it will provide insights. You said you interviewed the involved individuals. Did you interview them?'
> Chandré Gould: 'Yes. But I mean, I've interviewed them all in the past and it's all in the document... these are publications that were published, one in 2004, 2002, so these are publications that came out a long time ago.'
> Boitshoko Ntshabele: 'I'm trying to say that there is no exact answer to the question, maybe that's what I should say, and that perhaps before us, as a Council, we've got a Review Committee, and its function is to review, and the question you are asking is a real reflection on that question, and they would have a look and say, "How do we strengthen our systems?" and the lessons learnt really are, I am still insisting that they are always in books and articles that individuals read, all these things, and there is always a society collectively that will learn from those experiences. I don't know, that's my honest gut-feel answer at this point in time.'   Lessons 489

Through the back and forth exchange of the interview with the South African Veterinary Council, information was generated that could serve as a basis for devising an account of the past.

At times the interviewees were keen to emphasise that what could be said today needed to be said, but it had to be grounded in the existing historical records:

> Boitshoko Ntshabele: 'Sure, but remember that the trouble is that we are dealing with history and we were trying to respond to those questions based on history. An accurate account, I have said to you, is only the minutes [of the Council's board].'

Here the minutes provided a bedrock – and seemingly the only authoritative one – for knowing. Currently, according to Ntshabele, any move beyond that bedrock would be 'speculative'. Grounding the past in this way also provided a guard against questions of doubt within the context of the 2014 interview. All that could be relied on were the minutes – minutes that were never provided to us as interviewers. This guard was provided by the fact that neither interviewee was party to the events in decades gone by and so could not offer personal memories.

However, at other times in the interview, the historical record, as given in minutes, was treated in a more nuanced fashion.

> Chandré Gould: 'OK. Now I understand the procedures, thank you very much. The question is really, as a Council, whether seeing this unfold, whether it didn't… perhaps it might not have… you know led to the observations, "There is something happening and that's the Truth Commission and that's their business, it's got nothing to do with us," or "We see members of the Council in front of this Commission, what does that mean for us? What does it mean for vets professionally in South Africa and how do we respond?" So the Council didn't have that conversation?'
> Lynette Havinga: 'Council didn't have that conversation…'
> Boitshoko Ntshabele: 'I would like you to remember that I said to you that we went back to the minutes because we had to give you an accurate account of Council's thoughts, and Council's thoughts are distilled in a record of the minutes so that's as far really, factually, what we can say, that it appears that it was not considered by Council at that point in time. The matter that was considered had to first be dealt with in terms of that process, so to trigger Council to proceed.'

Lynette Havinga: 'But you know, you can't read the Councillors' minds!'
Chandré Gould: 'No, of course not!'

In this exchange, Dr Ntshabele and Dr Havinga initially speak to the minutes in an unambiguous and unqualified manner. They are definitive. As such, the unstated implication is that the interviewees themselves could not be questioned as to how they interpreted or represented the minutes. They simply said what they said.

The later contention that 'what we can say, that it *appears* that it was not considered by Council at that point in time', introduces some grounds for hesitancy and doubt about the ability to know the past by reviewing historical records. The follow-on suggestion by Dr Havinga, that it is not possible to read the board members' minds from the historical record, opens a space for consideration beyond those codified in the records. This provides further reasons for hesitancy and doubt about what history can be assembled from the official records.

Within the interactions of the interview then, the minutes were treated as both authoritative and somewhat less than that. Through this, the interviewees presented themselves as possessing both a firm and a loose grasp of how past allegations were addressed. Forgetting 509

509 For interviewees to locate the past in records that are available only to them, confers several interactional advantages in the context of an interview. They are excluded from needing to offer their personal assessment of past events – that would be mere speculation. In addition, when interviewers do not have access to the records, their ability to dispute the history given is severely undermined.

Such a reliance, though, can turn into an awkward dependency. If that record of history can be established as flawed, then the offered account of the past and the credibility of those offering it, are severely dented. Forgetting 510

510 2014
In the case of the South African Veterinary Council, after the interview, the authors found a string of online correspondence, sent to the Council in the late 1990s, raising questions about one of its members, based on the work of the TRC.[390]

With this case in hand, several questions followed: Was this correspondence deliberately left out of the minutes at the time? Was it deemed unsubstantiated?

This alternative record was pointed out to the two representatives interviewed from the Veterinary Council, but there has been no response as yet. Forgetting 20

511 Pairs in opposition – self/other, offence/defence, leaders/followers, etc. – take their meaning in relation to one another. As a result, holding on to one invariably entails holding on to its opposite. A sense of self requires a sense of other, defence requires offence, and followers require leaders.   Total war 262 | Offence 249 | Victims 513

512 Any reference to the chemical and biological weapons programme necessarily involves a reference to Wouter Basson. Since the TRC hearings, it has been Basson, and not the other scientists or military leaders, who is identified most readily with the programme. As head of the programme for most of its secret existence, this is unsurprising. However, the focus on one individual, the personification of the Project Coast, has served to distract attention from the many others who held leadership positions in the military, or even in the companies that made up the programme. Why try Basson for the crimes associated with Project Coast and not those who testified against him? Why were those responsible for the decision to authorise the programme and its activities not called to book? The answers to these questions lie in the practicalities of process, rather than in principle or in the call of justice.

And yet, the focus on Basson alone allows – even encourages – a perception that the criminal trial and even the Health Professionals Council of South Africa hearing were 'witch-hunts' that unfairly targeted the most visible, most exposed person.

Could the situation have been any other, given that the high levels of secrecy meant that information about the entirety of the programme was not only withheld from those taking instruction, but also from those in the military who held more senior positions than Basson?   Forgetting 330

513 As noted by Nils Christie, it typically follows that 'the more ideal a victim is, the more ideal becomes the offender. The more ideal the offender, the more ideal is the victim.'[391] Thus, when widely recognised offenders become identified as victims, the ultimate contingent bases of victimhood are evident.

In the case of Project Coast, because of his identification with the programme and his lack of expressed repentance, many position Basson at the extreme end of offenders. And yet, others regard the continuing attention on Basson as evidence that he merits the status of victim.

                                                                    Victims 405

514 Online petition presented to the Health Professional Council of South Africa by Mark Heywood from the NGO Section 27 (a public-interest law centre), and signed by medical professionals.

A STATEMENT OF CONCERN FROM HEALTH PROFESSIONALS IN SOUTH AFRICA: DR WOUTER BASSON

I, the undersigned health professional, add my name to other health professionals calling on the Health Professions Council of South Africa to remove Dr Wouter Basson, head of the apartheid Chemical and Biological Warfare Programme, from the medical register in South Africa, as an appropriate sentence for his egregious violations of medical ethics.[392]

During the hearing, the number of signatories would come into question, with Basson's lawyers showing that some had signed it more than once.

515 To speak about those typically thought of as 'offenders' as 'victims' – even repented offenders – is challenging because it undermines many commonplace assumptions. Victim is often defined in opposition to offender.   Victims 511

516 2014

Chandré Gould's reflections, 26 November

The Health Professionals Council of South Africa's sentencing hearing starts today. We are at The Villa's – a guest house across the road from the imposing American Embassy. The hearing struggles to get going. There is no PA system and it's difficult to hear against the clicking of cameras. The three adjudicators from the HPCSA are seated with their backs to the audience. Despite the many years that Basson has been under examination, the media retain their interest in this case and the man.

Basson and his legal team are seated in a row opposite the lawyers for the HPCSA.

Basson catches my eye – smiles and winks. He is not looking good. His eyes are bloodshot and he seems tired – but still up for a game.

Presumably his fate will be decided by medical peers in this forum, but neither the journalists nor the doctors nor activists present believe that this day will conclude the process. Legal process is slow, tedious and filled with legal manoeuvring that leads to delays.

During the first break of the day, Basson comes over to greet me, shakes my hand and comments on how well I look. I greet him back. It's a familiar play. A few weeks before, responding to my radio interview, he had dismissed me, questioning my credentials and ability to comment about the military, while I had dismissed his claims that he had simply followed orders and had done nothing wrong.   Legacies 517

517 During the Health Professionals Council of South Africa's sentencing hearing, Basson's advocate, Jaap Cilliers, argues that it is absurd to judge a man now for something that happened 30 years before in entirely different

circumstances and ignore the good he had done in the 30 years since. Indeed, it is vindictive. Legacies 450

518 2014

Notes from the HPCSA hearing, 26 November

Heywood is questioned by Cilliers. He asks why the petitioners seek Basson's removal from the roll of medical professionals?

Heywood responds, saying that 'people have to trust health professionals, that they would act in the best interests of patients'.

Cilliers objects to Heywood's's testimony. He is not a health professional, nor an expert on ethics. His testimony should not be admissible. It is unfair for him to testify against Basson.

In attempting to establish his right to comment, Heywood makes the case that 'users of health care professions also have an interest in ethics of medical professionals. I am a user, and have rights.'

'Should I respond to that nonsense?' Cilliers counters.

519 2014

Notes from the HPCSA hearing, 27 November

The Health Professionals Council of South Africa's hearings have been attended by members of the Khulumani Support Group, since it started. Khulumani's members are victims and survivors of apartheid human rights violations. It was started by survivors who testified at the Truth and Reconcilition Commission and is now a social movement with over 100 000 members.[393] Those attending the hearings are family members of disappeared people, some of whom were believed by the families to have been affected by medicines or products from Project Coast.

This exchange takes place between Basson's advocate, Jaap Cilliers, and Dr Marjorie Jacobson, representing the Khulumani Support Group:

> Jaap Cilliers: 'Not even all lawyers understand this. The committee found that, listen, your sin that led to the finding of guilty, is that you accepted and relied on a senior doctor, General Nieuwoudt [former Surgeon General] that what you were doing was legally and ethically correct. You complied with his clear guidelines. That no lethal or harmful substances may be developed, but what we find is that you transgressed in the sense that you should not have relied solely on Nieuwoudt's order. If that is the sin, he has to be punished for, are you sitting there as a human being and arguing that the punishment should be removal from the roll?'
>
> Marjorie Jacobson: 'I do because he has to take responsibility for his actions.'

Jaap Cilliers: 'Don't you believe him when he says he follows orders? And you disbelieve the correctness of the findings of the committee?'

Marjorie Jacobson: 'He has taken no personal responsibility for the activities he was involved in and as a doctor, you have a responsibility for doing no harm.'

Jaap Cilliers: 'The fact is that committee found that there were no harmful consequences, that all substances were not harmful. Are you still saying that 30 years later, he should... are you suggesting that all doctors who involved themselves in the military should be struck from the roll?'

In the audience are journalists, members of the Khulumani Support Group from Mamelodi and health professionals. As far as I can determine, Basson has no supporters here. The argument being made by Cilliers causes visible discomfort and distaste. Why?

520 2014

On 27 November, Majorie Jacobson argues in the Health Professionals Council of South Africa's hearing that, 'Only when sanctions [are] imposed on people that there is any reflection on what their activities caused to citizens of South Africa. Vlok [former Minister of Police] and De Kock [jailed police hit-squad commander] are examples of that. Sanction gives opportunity to reflecting on their activities.'

521 2015

On resumption of the Health Professionals Council of South Africa's hearing in January, a small group of women and men from the Khulumani Support Group patiently followed the HPCSA hearings – being present on most days. These are families of the disappeared, of young men who were duped by the security forces into believing they were joining the ANC and then murdered. Artist, Kathryn Smith, who attended the hearings, asked them why they were coming to the hearings, how they felt about Basson and whether they believed he was guilty. Here Manoko Mokgonyana, the coordinator of the group, speaks on their behalf:

Manoko Mokgonyana: 'All right, most of the families – after they appeared at the TRC. Neh. So there were some of the things, you know, which were unbelievable, and then they were so, you know, amazed because the only thing they hoped that their children would be coming back from exile. As they, you know, they knew that most of the children maybe they could have slipped the country, but after the TRC findings, that most of their loved ones were killed, brutally killed, and more especially they were drugged. Kidnapped. They were drugged. And then eventually they were, you know, bombed, and then their remains, they don't know where they are buried. So they thought that coming to this – you know – trial, maybe some of the truth could be revealed about the whereabouts of their loved ones.'

Kathryn Smith: 'Okay. And do they think that... how do they feel about Basson and his, his guilt maybe? Or his involvement in the deaths of their loved ones. Do they think he is directly responsible? How do they understand him and the role that he played?'

Manoko Mokgonyana: 'Umm, ja. More especially when they said, ja, the Nietverdiend 10. They were injected with a certain substance, you know, they don't understand which kind of a substance. And then when they have to hear, hear the trial that Basson was producing chemical weapons, or substances, and more especially some of them, they were used in the tear gas in the townships. So they feel that the substances which was used, they don't know, but which substance was used, maybe he could tell you, you know, that this kind of a substance was used, you know, to drug. Ja, after injecting them they were drugged. And even, there is this case of the youth in Mamelodi. You know there were ... there was a powder, I heard from the families that they were firstly injected and then there was a powder, which was spread amongst them, and then this when they were bombed, you know there, you know, there was fire inside, but, you know, when they have to go and, you know, touch the bodies, you know, their flesh, you know, their bones were whitish and what-what, you know, and that shows that there was a substance which was used.'

And then later...

Manoko Mokgonyana: 'They say that coming here, it was like okay. It was like healing, yeah. When they walk, you know, coming here, going back home when they have to listen to the radio, they were so confident, saying that "haai, in the end things are going to be completed". But now when they postpone, you know, their spirits are so low.'

Kathryn Smith: 'I feel the same...'

Manoko Mokgonyana: 'Even me today.'

Mrs Ledwaba: 'Because you don't have money. You come here with the money and then ... struggling to ... it's disappearing.'

522 2015
Interview by Kathryn Smith with members of the Khulumani Support

Group at the Health Professionals Council of South Africa's sentencing hearing of Wouter Basson.

> Kathryn Smith: 'Do... How have you felt about these particular proceedings and the one that... the first session [in] November, the sentencing hearing? Has it been frustrating? Has it been productive? ... You said your spirit is very low?'
>
> Member #1: 'Yeah, you know some days... my spirit is down, down, down, down, down.'
>
> Kathryn Smith: 'I personally find it very frustrating, and it must be exhausting. I mean you guys have been observing, and present, at these hearings for many years?'
>
> Member #1: 'Yes.'
>
> Kathryn Smith: 'What keeps you coming back?'
>
> Member #2: 'We want to know the truth and justice must be made, for all.'
>
> Kathryn Smith: 'Do you think this process is going to deliver what you want.'
>
> Member #2: 'Yeah, we hope so, because we've got hope about the justice system around here.'
>
> Kathryn Smith: 'So you still believe...' Justice 523

523 **2015**

In 2009, South Africa was faced with a choice between appeasing the political elites of Africa or abiding by its own law and Constitution. This choice had to be made following a decision taken at an African Union assembly to withhold cooperation from the International Criminal Court (ICC) in respect of executing the arrest warrant for Sudanese President Omar al-Bashir. As a responsible member of the community of nations, South Africa chose to respect its international treaty obligations. A government spokesperson announced that, while South Africa had reservations about pursuing the case against al-Bashir, he would be arrested if he entered South African territory. The same spokesperson said that his government would not act 'outside the framework of the law'.

In 2015, South Africa was faced with a similar choice. This time around, rather than offend the big men of Africa, our government chose to trash our Constitution and the rule of law – the very fabric of our post-apartheid democratic order.[394] Justice 400

524 **2015**

Foraging through my archive in preparation for this book, I perused a file labelled 'Frank Chikane'. This was assembled after I [Gould] had received a request from Reverend Chikane in 2004 to assist him to obtain more information about his poisoning. In it were several declassified documents about STRATCOM, the strategic communications component of the police's security branch, and two pages of a manuscript entitled 'Confessions of an apartheid killer', clearly stamped 'declassified'. No date and no publication details were provided. However, it appeared to be written by Paul Erasmus, a member of STRATCOM, who had applied to the TRC for amnesty, and whom I had interviewed several times in the past. Under the heading 'Johannesburg 1990' appeared the following:

> I returned to John Voster Square on Monday 20 August 1990, on my first day with the new formal Stratcom Unit. One of my tasks was to sort out the Stratcom kit in the strong rooms on the ninth floor. It was a large tool box containing an assortment of 'hard Stratcom' aids – *Digitalis* for inducing heart attacks, syringes, rubber gloves, paint remover, sneezing powder, CS powder (tear gas), an assortment of powerful laxatives, several medicines, including one that negated the effect of the contraceptive pill, containers of arsenic and strychnine and several vials of 'Bokpoort', a poison developed by the forensic science laboratory.[395]

Concealment and concealing harm was not the preserve of any single unit, section or branch of the security forces. Victims 242

525 2015

In June, the South African government defied an arrest warrant for Sudanese President Omar al-Bashir issued by the International Criminal Court. For senior programme adviser of the International Centre for Transitional Justice and human rights lawyer, Howard Varney, the act of inviting al-Bashir to South Africa and aiding him to leave the country, a free man, was a violation of the moral obligation South Africa had made by engaging in a formal, transitional justice programme, and signalled a serious threat to the rule of law. As he commented:

> South Africa is no longer a beacon of hope and inspiration to the world. Of all nations, we were expected to side with victims of mass murder, rape, mutilation and torture; not with their persecutors. South Africa can no longer be counted upon to stand up for oppressed peoples and victims of mass atrocity. However, we can be counted upon to side with those accused of perpetrating genocide and crimes against humanity. Since South Africa does not consider itself bound by treaties that it ratifies, and is willing to

break international law to serve narrow geo-political interests, it poses a serious threat to the creation of a viable system of international justice. In short, we are well on the road to becoming a rogue state.[396]   Legacies 337

526 2015

Opening statements by Anja Mijr at a conference entitled Memory, Justice and Reconciliation, Sarajevo, 10–12 June:

The good news is that transitional justice measures (broadly defined and including a potpourri of measures from truth-telling to memorialisation, amnesty and justice) over a period of about 25 years deliver stronger democracies.

Based on empirical research into transitional justice processes around the world, there are four key findings:

1. Transitional justice measures such as memorials or commissions of inquiry and trials only show effect in stabilizing democratic institutions over a period of 20+ years, thus a generation.

2. Transitional justice measures can only contribute to building new (democratic) institutions on the one side and thus legitimizing them. They can also delegitimize the past, corrupt, violent or unjust dictatorial regime through means and measure of accountability. In this context, they have a deterrent effect on recurrence of past violence.

3. Most Transitional justice measures are forward looking. They are a 'communicative enterprise' and have thus an exemplifying effect on how rule of law, justice or even institutions on local and national level can work beyond hybridity, corruption and political ideology.

4. Transitional justice measures can contribute to reconciliation if they are applied in a non-biased way, but in an inclusive way that does not differentiate among ethnic or social background. Most post-conflict societies, however, are not able to do this, because fear, hate, vengeance and mistrust prevail and are often even perpetuated by current governments, for reasons of power.

Generally speaking, the expectation that TJ can rebuild institutions, establish trust among citizens and rule of law-abiding institutions as well as among the different conflict parties and citizens as such, are high. They can, nevertheless, have a positive effect if applied in a non-biased and ethical way to all those who committed violence (on all sides) and those who suffered violence and injustice (on all sides). Even though it takes time to overcome distrust and feelings of vengeance, small steps of single trials, behaviour of truth commissions, memorials or reconciliation projects, gain in support over the years and will have a positive effect on democratic institutions building over a longer period of time. Justice 522

527 The history of Project Coast needs to be approached in a robust way to examine what can be said about it, as much as what cannot. In other words, it is necessary to ask what issues have not been addressed and have not been aired. How and who produced the absences? To know 436

528 *Chandré Gould's reflections*

One of the questions in relation to Project Coast and the security-force operations associated with it, is why this part of our history remains so marginal in any account of apartheid. While most South Africans of a certain generation are likely to be familiar with the name Wouter Basson, artefacts, documents or accounts of the programme are not to be found at significant sites of memory, such as Freedom Park or the Apartheid Museum. What is the reason for this absence of a narrative? I would posit that this has to do with the absence of a coherent, easy-to-relate narrative. With no victims and no voices, or testimony post-TRC to assert the needs or interests of victims, the narrative, staccato and broken as it is, becomes a narrative of 'perpetrators'. It becomes a story of motives, intentions and possibilities, all of which have been contested. The stories told by willing witnesses were both ridiculous and horrific, a science fiction of apartheid. Basson, as the person who holds all the answers but refuses to release them, becomes not only the secret-keeper (and in this maintains tremendous power over those who believe they might have fallen victim to the programme) but also the focus of all the attention.

The absence of a victim narrative or account also serves to strip the narrative of credibility or resonance. Personalising the violence of apartheid through victim narratives and testimony rendered it visible. In this case, there was no victim (other than Frank Chikane) to associate clearly with the programme, and no one other than the investigator to keep making the case for its importance or relevance. In this situation, the person investigating becomes the story-teller and the person responsible for the victims' untold victim stories, the placeholder until a more legitimate voice can be heard. Legacies 529 | Justice 529

529 Working with perpetrator narratives raises several difficult personal and professional issues. On the one hand, the story of violation, the details of the manifestations of a system like apartheid cannot be told only through victim narratives. These can typically present only the experience of violation – not the motivation or experience of perpetration – and thus

can present only a portion of the story. The story of violation cannot answer questions about *why* the violation occurred; and in cases where victims died, they could not even share their experiences of violation. Thus, perpetrator narratives are essential to piecing together what happened and how – and even to locating the remains of those who died.

This understanding is what lay at the heart of the amnesty exchange at the TRC – amnesty was regarded as necessary currency for a transaction that would reveal some truth – with the expectation that victims and their families would need information that had previously been held in secret by the police, the military and intelligence services as institutions, and by individual perpetrators – torturers, murderers. Partly because only a select number of perpetrator narratives can be told – both because only some come forward to tell their stories, and because of practical constraints (time and resources) – a curious moral lacuna occurs during a formal process of the telling of perpetrator narratives. For a moment, perpetrators who come forward and who are seen to be telling their stories fully and honestly can be 'heroes' – the 'good guys'. Their story buys them credibility. It means that they can get jobs without difficult questions being asked, even with the new government, as several who were involved in the chemical and biological warfare programme did.

It means also that they are not required to transform, to confront their role in the violence of apartheid or their motivations or responsibilities. For the investigator – who works closely with them and gets to know them and even their families – the contrast between the willingness of such 'perpetrators' to tell the story and those who defy the process, creates somewhat of a blinker or blindness to the absence of a real reckoning with their past. This was my [Gould] experience. As I came to know each of the scientists, who spoke about their roles in Project Coast – learnt about their pasts, their motives, their justifications, their children's progress through school, their personal trials and dilemmas, drank their tea and sat in their lounges – it was easy to assume that personal transformation was occurring. And so, when after 16 years, we as authors returned to interview two of the scientists and found them uncritical of their own roles in the programme, unconsciously expressing deeply racist views – and very comfortable in their new positions, with the same access to resources and power they had had in the past – I was deeply disturbed. Saddened. Ashamed at my role in enabling them to feel absolved through the TRC process and, like the professional associations, able to defer responsibility for their actions. Legacies 530 | Justice 537

530 Three themes emerge from the interviews conducted with professional

associations, diplomats and officials in relation to their engagement with Project Coast: complicity, justification and deferral.

Complicity in silence – during apartheid, scientists in the programme were members of scientific communities and academic structures, and were well-regarded by peers. These bodies have not addressed the ethical implications of this for their current or future members. One suspects that merely tabling this issue in a meeting conjures the fear of complicity by association.

Professional associations have justified their silence by saying that drawing attention to this aberration risks contaminating science in the minds of the public and may lead to anti-science attitudes. And in any case, someone else is dealing with the issue – the TRC, the courts, etc.

All those involved in the revelation and concealment of the programme, whether as members of the military responsible for the programme, as diplomats in the Biological Weapons Convention, as police or intelligence investigators, as TRC staffers or members of the media, were complicit/ involved in one way or another in apartheid. Whether we were bystanders or participants in the maintenance or downfall of apartheid – we were present and our own roles and experiences are carried with us as emotional, ideological and/or experiential baggage, which strongly influences our views on what should and can, or should not and cannot be said about the past.

There was a significant overlap between the people involved diplomatically, politically and in the intelligence services and security forces during the transitional period – 1994 until well after the end of the TRC. Not only did each of these actors have an institutional interest in the nature of the revelations and concealments, they also had and have a personal stake. As the TRC unfolded, strange new alliances formed and dissipated.

Those from the security forces that were seen to be open to the process, and honest about their participation in human rights abuses, were welcomed, gained almost hero status in some cases, such as that of Eugene De Kock (former head of a police hit squad), whereas others, who were seen to be uncooperative, were vilified (such as Basson).

The irony was that the stories that were regarded as most 'believable' were those that confirmed the tropes of good and evil. It was, therefore, in the interests of the scientists who cooperated with the TRC to present themselves *badly*.

Legacies 487

531 There are many things that do not add up about this chemical and biological weapons programme, and which remain unsatisfactorily

answered by the documentary evidence, or by the accounts given by those who worked in the project. Legacies 532

532 There are the more obvious questions that have stubbornly remained unanswered: What happened to the collection of micro-organisms (the culture collection) from Roodeplaat Research Laboratories when it was shut down, and should we be worried about it? (Probably not.)

There are also questions about the rationale for the programme. Why would scientists research and develop chemical or biological substances that could be used for purposes of assassination or disruption, when very much less-sophisticated products could have achieved the same end? Was this merely an elaborate way of siphoning off state funds to individuals who had already resigned themselves to the inevitability that apartheid would be dismantled? Legacies 533

533 Also, why were scientists from Roodeplaat Research Laboratories making poisons available to the police and members of the military in 1989, if the wars in the neighbouring states were over, the internal conflict was ending and negotiations were about to start? And if chemical weapons use was ruled out around the same time, why continue with the expensive procurement and testing of chemical defence equipment? Why, too, would a British engineering firm, Foster Wheeler, be contracted at this late stage to draw up blue prints for a new, larger, chemical and biological laboratory? Legacies 534

534 Further still, if Project Coast was prompted by a concern that South African troops could fall victim to chemical weapons use in Angola, as has been alleged, why was the procurement and provision of protective clothing left until late into the 1990s – and troops were never prepared for this eventuality? Was this defensive component of the programme nothing more than window dressing? Legacies 390

535 Another set of remaining questions about Project Coast relates to its boundaries: could we, for example, conclude that the Namibians – whom Johan Theron claimed to have injected with muscle relaxants and thrown into the sea – were victims of Project Coast, based on his allegation that Dr Wouter Basson had provided him with the drugs? Probably not, and yet since Project Coast has become synonymous with Basson, the distinction between what he might have done as a military doctor and what he did as head of the chemical and biological programme has become blurred over time and in the recounting of the narratives that remain. Legacies 391

536 2016

The threat of prosecutions for those who did not apply for amnesty in the TRC has yet to be realised. Justice 176

As time passes, the chemical and biological warfare programme feels less and less important and real, and there seems to be less reason for it to inform or be the basis for any action. It is this that has enabled Basson – the personification of the programme – to recreate himself, repeatedly, in the imagination of some (white) South Africans, who see him as victim of a witch-hunt.
Justice 200

538 In the 21 years between 1992 and 2013, the apartheid chemical and biological weapons programme (code-named Project Coast), and particularly its head, Dr Wouter Basson, were the subject of more investigation, revelation and legal inquiry than almost any other manifestation of apartheid, and yet there remain as many questions as there are answers. Revelation does not seem to have brought us either healing or closure; neither has it brought us any closer to preventing something similar from happening again.
Legacies 539 | Lessons 399

539 2016

Chandré Gould's reflections

In preparation for an exhibition about the chemical and biological weapons programme at the Nelson Mandela Foundation, I started scratching again, hoping to come a little closer to the names of SWAPO members who may have been thrown into the sea. I contacted a former member of the South African Security Branch. He put me in touch with one of his colleagues (a former student spy for the police), who is now a Namibian and a member of SWAPO. I told him what I was looking for and he responded by saying:

> There is a sensitivity involved in all enquiries of this nature – as a Namibian I must be sensitive to the feelings of my fellow countrymen. As a country, and enshrined in our Constitution, we have decided to let the past be the past (as opposed to the approach South Africa took, with the Truth and Reconciliation Commission, of dragging everything into the public eye, and the various court cases that resulted from that). Basically, we drew a line at Independence, everything that preceded it was regarded as the past, not to be dragged up again.
> Legacies 24

540 2016

In February, consultative workshops were held at the Nelson Mandela Foundation with scientists, memory workers, artists and medical practitioners about how we might represent Project Coast in an exhibition planned for later that year. Here participants stressed their concern about creating 'equivalence' between animal and human victims (and between victims from the liberation movements, and victims who were members of the security forces). They felt that treating animal and human victims in the same way would dehumanise the human victims, who had already been dehumanised by apartheid. They believed that equating humans with animals would devalue the human lives affected by Project Coast. Victims 254 541 2016

Press Release: Institute for Security Studies and Nelson Mandela Foundation

Exposing the ghosts of SA's toxic past
A new exhibition sheds light on the pain of our past and prospects for a happier South Africa.

Today, 6 October, the Nelson Mandela Foundation and the Institute for Security Studies opened the exhibition *Poisoned Pasts.*

This year marks four decades since the 1976 Soweto student uprisings in South Africa, which spurred the decision of the apartheid military to establish a secret chemical and biological warfare programme, code-named Project Coast. This year also marks 20 years since the Truth Commission started its investigations, which led to the public hearings about Project Coast.

'Today, South Africa is again experiencing a wave of student protests and a state under severe pressure. It is an appropriate moment to consider how the past has been dealt with, and what implications this holds for the future,' says Sello Hatang, CEO of the Nelson Mandela Foundation.

The burden of a toxic past will haunt future generations in ways that we cannot always anticipate, and South Africans will continue to grapple with questions on how to deal with the past, what is required to bring healing, and where to find assurance that historic harms will never be repeated.

Poisoned Pasts is a collaborative undertaking by forensic artist Kathryn Smith (Liverpool John Moores University/Stellenbosch University), ISS researcher Chandré Gould and sociologist Prof. Brian Rappert (University of Exeter).

In the exhibition, facts and testimony are set against contested and conflicting accounts, putting visitors in the position of an investigator. Concise, meticulously researched commentary accompanies powerful visual reportage. Original artefacts, reconstructions and historical documents – many of which are available for visitors to consult at their leisure – illuminate the many narratives that Project Coast has produced.

'This exhibition leads us to examine how we reckon with difficult pasts, while it also acknowledges and honours unidentified victims. It also raises questions about how scientists and medical practitioners can be protected from becoming involved in similar programmes,' says Chandré Gould.

Poisoned Pasts, ultimately, is not about the past: it is about the futures we want to be building. And for the Nelson Mandela Foundation, it is about realising the South Africa of Madiba's dreams.

542 Having been involved in the various investigations, revelations and recordings of Project Coast, I [Gould] am left no more satisfied than when I started. This raises several difficult questions about the relationship between 'truth', revelation, justice and transitional justice. Legacies 457

543 Who then was a victim of Project Coast? Such a question is impossible to answer in the abstract. Practically, it cannot be definitively answered because so much about what took place under apartheid in South Africa remains hidden in the shadows. Politically, any answer would need qualification with respect to what and whose harm counts. Pragmatically, determinations of victimhood depend on the reasons for asking the question in the first place. Victims 544

544 Rather than seeking a set answer, another way to approach this topic is to ask how the posing of this question itself can help further inquiry and understanding.

For instance, we might consider how an appreciation of the negotiation of victimhood helps to inform an understanding of how notions of 'the enemy' were, and are being, fashioned in South Africa. Victims 545

545 Or we could ask how notions of what counts as 'legitimate suffering' can inform the continuing search for justice today. Victims END

546 As in other wars, the casualties in the 'war against crime', being fought in post-apartheid South Africa, have included those resulting from excessive force; in other words, excessive force used by the state against its own people.

As in other wars, the documentary evidence of this is fragmented, partial, and often gets compiled by those accused. Some official figures on official actions exist. For the period 1994–1997, the Minister of Safety and Security recorded the following charges against members of the South African police:

Murder 256
Culpable homicide 125
Attempted murder 630
Assault with intent to do grievous bodily harm 1 119
Common assault 3 564
Pointing of a firearm 660

Between April 1997 and March 2000, 2 174 individuals were recorded as dying because of police action, with 70 per cent of those resulting from the use of force. Over April 1998 to March 1999, the Independent Police Investigative Directorate recorded 128 cases of torture.[397] Total war 547

547 Violence by the state has been met with collective violence at community level. Between 2009 and 2016, there was a slow but steady increase in the number of violent protests in South Africa[398] by communities that have responded to nepotism, corruption and failures of the state to meet their expectations. Total war 402

548 2016

Writing in the exhibition guide to the *Poisoned Pasts* exhibition at the Nelson Mandela Foundation, the CEO of the Steve Bike Foundation had this to say about who we should consider 'insider' victims:

> *Poisoned Pasts* also tells the stories of other casualties of Project Coast: the collaborators, askaris and soldiers who made the deployment of Project Coast's creations possible. In some instances, for a myriad of reasons, these individuals themselves were poisoned or killed through means developed by the chemical and biological warfare programme.
>
> This aspect of Project Coast raises the question of whether those who ultimately had to 'take a dose of their own medicine' should be considered victims in the same manner that activists, freedom fighters and the public are? Is there equivalency between those who sought to end apartheid, and were poisoned for their efforts, and those who actively worked to uphold the regime? Morally, should perpetrators also be considered victims?
>
> For many, this may seem like an academic question, one which unnecessarily underscores the divisions of the past and undermines the narrative of the rainbow nation. Yet, the question of equivalency is a critical one as it speaks to justice, personal responsibility and the creation of a culture of human rights.
>
> Apartheid was declared a crime against humanity by the United Nations; Project Coast, facilitated to uphold the criminal state, was therefore also inimical to human rights. Its existence and perpetuation was only possible through the active engagement of, not only the security forces, scientists and researchers, but also the doctors – who despite swearing to uphold the Hippocratic oath – took part in unethical research.
>
> Regardless of Project Coast's service on behalf of apartheid, as has been noted in assessments of the project, some of the scientists and

researchers involved do not consider their engagement wrong; rather, they were involved as foot soldiers in the war that was apartheid. Others were there for the 'science'.

This is not to say that raising the alarm would have been easy; or that the rewards for scientists – such as the ability to conduct their own innovative research alongside Project Coast – would not have been tempting. But the notion that they were neutral participants in the programme is problematic in that it strips them of personal agency, and their ability to bring about change. Similarly, the notion that soldiers and other collaborators were victims is problematic.

Why problematic? In short, because the choices of individuals matter. They determine the course of history. Neither apartheid nor Project Coast were natural disasters; they were man-made tragedies that could have been averted or ended earlier. Had the individuals involved in Project Coast made different choices, perhaps this exhibition would be entitled *Proud Pasts,* and would recount the ways in which South Africa's scientific and medical communities worked to advance human rights, instead of chemical and biological warfare.

By classifying perpetrators as morally equivalent to victims, and scientists as neutral participants, individuals are distanced from their responsibility to make choices and to be accountable for the personal and societal impact.

Rather, by holding perpetrators accountable, society has an opportunity to communicate the responsibility of all towards creating a culture of human rights. To quote Steve Biko, *'History works through people, and we have availed history to work through us.'* In this light, Project Coast raises a critical question for contemporary society: today, what type of history is at work through individual and collective choices? Victims 323

NOTES

Transcripts of the Truth and Reconciliation Commission's Special Hearing into the Chemical and Biological Warfare Programme are available from the South African History Archive and from the website of the Department of Justice: http://www.justice.gov.za/Trc/special/index.htm#cbw

Military documents referred to in the text and the endnotes are available from the South African History Archive. These are formerly top secret documents that have now been declassified.

1 Rappert, B and Gould, C (2014) Biological Weapons Convention: Confidence, the prohibition and learning from the past. ISS Occasional Paper No. 258, 14 July 2014. Pretoria: Institute for Security Studies.
2 Meyer, M (2012) Placing and tracing absence, *Journal of Material Culture*, 17(1): 103–10.
3 Lindqvist, S (2003) *A History of Bombing*. London: Granta, p i.
4 Tutu, Archbishop DM (2002) Forward, in *Project Coast: Apartheid's chemical and biological warfare programme*, UNIDIR/2002/12. Geneva: UN Institute for Disarmament Research, p v.
5 Or, at least, this quote is often attributed to him. See, for instance, Kindersley, D (2012) *The Psychology Book*. London: DK Publications, p 123.
6 Truth and Reconciliation Commission (1998) *Truth and Reconciliation Commission of South Africa Report: Special investigation into Project Coast*, Volume 2, Chapter 6, p 521.
7 John Maytham interview with Dr Wouter Basson, 18 December 2013, Cape Talk radio.
8 Republic of South Africa (1995) *Confidence Building Measure Form 'F'*. Pretoria, p 64.

9   Dlamini, J (2014) *Askari*. Johannesburg: Jacana Media, p 250.
10 Truth and Reconciliation Commission (1998) *Truth and Reconciliation Commission of South Africa Report*, Volume 1, p 7.
11 Namely, the Steyn Commission; see Burger, M and Gould, C (2002) *Secrets and Lies*. Cape Town: Zebra Press, p 1.
12 See Neumann, K and Anderson, D (2014) Introduction, *International Journal of Conflict and Violence*, 8(1): 4–15.
13 Nelson Mandela Foundation and the Global Leadership Academy (2014) *The Mandela Dialogues, Dialoguing Memory Work: Report on the Dialogue Series*. Johannesburg: Nelson Mandela Foundation and GIZ Global Leadership Academy, p 6.
14 Bellman, B (1981) The paradox of secrecy, *Human Studies*, 4: 1.
15 Taussig, M (2003) Viscerality, faith and scepticism, in B Meyer and P Pels (eds) *Magic and Modernity*. Stanford, CA: Stanford University Press, pp 272–306.
16 Aftergood, S and Blanton, T (1999) The securocrats' revenge, in S Marget and J Goldman (eds) *Government Secrecy*. London: Libraries Unlimited, pp 457–59; and Teeuwan, M (2006) Introduction, in B Scheid and M Teeuwen (eds) *The Culture of Secrecy in Japanese Religion*. London: Routledge, pp 1–34.
17 See Johnson, PC (2002) *Secrets, Gossip and Gods*. Oxford: Oxford University Press, p 25, for a discussion indebted to the work of Georg Simmel.
18 Much of the analytical work along these lines is from anthropologists concerned with culture, ritual and initiation. See Bellmen, B (1984) *The Language of Secrecy*. New Brunswick: Rutgers; De Jong, F (2007) *Masquerades of Modernity*. Edinburgh: Edinburgh University Press; Taussig, M (1999) *Defacement: Public secrecy and the labour of the negative*. Stanford, CA: Stanford University Press.
19 Balmer, B (2012) *Secrecy and Science: A historical sociology of biological and chemical warfare*. Farnham: Ashgate.
20 Rappert, B and Balmer, B (2007) Rethinking 'secrecy' and 'disclosure', in B Rappert (ed.) *Technology and Security*. London: Palgrave, pp 45–65.
21 On the last of these, see Mellor, F and Webster, S (2017) *The Silences of Science*. London: Routledge.
22 Rappert, B (2012) *How to Look Good in a War: Justifying and challenging state violence*. London: Pluto Press, Chapter 3.
23 As developed in Wooffitt, R and Holt, N (2011) *Looking In and Speaking Out*. Exeter: Imprint Academic, pp 65–7.
24 From ESRC. *Why Make an Impact?* Available at http://www.esrc.ac.uk/funding-and-guidance/impact-toolkit/what-how-and-why/why-impact.aspx> [Accessed April 2014].
25 Edwards, D (1997) *Discourse and Cognition*. London: Sage Publications.
26 Edwards, D (1997) *Discourse and Cognition*. London: Sage Publications, p 14.
27 Edwards, D (1997) *Discourse and Cognition*. London: Sage Publications, p 16.
28 For a wider historical analysis of this, see Zanders, JP (2003) International norms against chemical and biological warfare, *Journal of Conflict & Security Law*, 8(2): 391–410.
29 Mayor, A (2009) *Greek Fire, Poison Arrows and Scorpion Bombs: Biological and chemical warfare in the Ancient World*. London: Overlook Duckworth.
30 Zanders, JP (2003) International norms against chemical and biological warfare, *Journal of Conflict & Security Law*, 8(2): 391–410.
31 Wheelis, M (2002) Biological warfare at the 1346 siege of Caffa, *Emerging Infectectious Diseases*, Sept. Available at http://wwwnc.cdc.gov/eid/article/8/9/01-0536 [Accessed March 2017].

32 Taken from the 1868 *Declaration of St Petersburg*.

33 Quoted from Weiss, P (1999) Legal theories and remedies, in LR Kurtz and JE Turpin (eds) *Encyclopaedia of Violence, Peace & Conflict*. San Diego, CA: Academic Press, p 327.

34 See SIPRI (1971) *The Problem of Chemical Biological Warfare*, Volume 4. Stockholm: Almqvist and Wiksell.

35 Jenkins, D (2002) *The Final Frontier: America, science and terror*. London: Verso Books.

36 See Rappert, B (2006) *Controlling the Weapons of War: Politics, persuasion and the prohibition of inhumanity*. London: Routledge, Chapter 4.

37 Van Creveld, M (1997) Technology and World War II, in C Townshend (ed.) *The Oxford Illustrated History of Modern War*. Oxford: Oxford University Press, pp 175–93.

38 Jenkins, D (2002) *The Final Frontier: America, science and terror*. London: Verso Books.

39 During World War I, for instance, only Germany undertook serious steps to utilise the emerging scientific understanding of infectious disease for destructive ends by seeking to infect draft animals with glanders and anthrax.

40 International Committee of the Red Cross (ICRC) (2013) *Chemical and Biological Weapons: Overview*, 8 April. Available at http://www.icrc.org/eng/war-and-law/weapons/chemical-biological-weapons/overview-chemical-biological-weapons.htm [Accessed March 2017].

41 International Committee of the Red Cross (ICRC) (2013) Chemical and Biological Weapons: Overview, 8 April. Available at http://www.icrc.org/eng/war-and-law/weapons/chemical-biological-weapons/overview-chemical-biological-weapons.htm [Accessed March 2017].

42 Price, R (1997) *The Chemical Weapons Taboo*. Ithaca, NY: Cornell University Press; and Price, R and Tannenwald, N (1996) Norms and deterrence, in P Katzenstein (ed.) *The Culture of National Security*. New York: Columbia University Press.

43 Tannenwald, N (2008) *The Nuclear Taboo*. Cambridge: Cambridge University Press, p 463.

44 Roosevelt, FD (1943). *Public Papers of the Presidents of the United States*, Volume 12, p 4. Available at http://presidency.proxied.lsit.ucsb.edu/ws/ [last accessed 26 May 2017].

45 Geissler, E and Van Courtland Moon, JE (eds) (1999) *Biological and Toxin Weapons: Research, development, and use from the Middle Ages to 1945*. Oxford: Oxford University Press; and Wheelis, M, Rózsa, L and Dando, M (eds) (2006) *Deadly Cultures*. Cambridge, MA: Harvard University Press.

46 See Legro, J (1995) *Cooperation Under Fire*. Ithaca, NY: Cornell University Press, Chapter 4.

47 Wiseman, Lieutenant Colonel DJC (1948) *The Second World War, 1939–1949. Army. Special weapons and types of warfare*, Vol. I, Gas warfare. London: The War Office, p 46.

48 UN Commission on Conventional Armaments (2012) UN document S/C.3/32/Rev.1, August. Quoted from Carus, WS. Defining 'Weapons of Mass Destruction'. CSWMD Occasional Paper 8. Washington, DC: NDU Press, p 9.

49 Price, R (1997) *The Chemical Weapons Taboo*. Ithaca, NY: Cornell University Press.

50 Gould, C and Folb, P (2002) *Project Coast: Apartheid's Chemical and Biological Warfare Programme*. UNIDIR/2002/12. Geneva: UN Institute for Disarmament Research, pp 31–45.

51 Mortimer, B (1996) SA Defence Force involvement in the internal security situation in the Republic of South Africa. Submission in respect of the former SADF to the TRC, Cape Town, 21 October.

52 Seegers, A (2003) The role of the military in state formation in South Africa, in P Batchelor, K Kingma and G Lamb (eds) *Demilitarization and Peace-Building in Southern Africa*, Volume III. Aldershot: Ashgate, p 96

53 Cawthra, G (1986) *Brutal Force: The apartheid war machine*. London: IDAF, pp 24–5.

54 Hanlon, J (1986) *Beggar Your Neighbour* London: James Currey Press, p 7.

55 Quoted from Robinson, J (1994) Disabling chemical weapons. Working Paper for Pugwash Study Group on the Implementation of the CBW Conventions.

56 Dando, M (1996) *A New Form of Warfare*. London: Brassey's Military Books, Chapter 5.

57 Escalante, F (2007) *638 Ways to Kill Castro*. Minneapolis, MN: Ocean Press.

58 Hearing of the Subcommittee on Africa of the Committee on Foreign Affairs - US House of Representatives, On the Implementation of the US Arms Embargo (against Portugal and South Africa, and related issues), 22 March and 6 April 1973.

59 Gould interview with Vernon Joynt, Pretoria, 6 October 1999.

60 94th Congress, 2nd Session Senate Report No. 94-755. Foreign and Military Intelligence, Book 1. *Final Report to the Select Committee to Study Governmental Operation with Respect to Intelligence Activit*ies Volume XVII: Testing and Use of Chemical and Biological Agents by the Intelligence Committee, 26 April 1976. Available at https://www.archive.org/details/finalreportofsel01unit. [last accessed 11 October 2016].

61 94th Congress, 2nd Session Senate Report No. 94-755. Foreign and Military Intelligence, Book 1. Final Report to the Select Committee to Study Governmental Operation with Respect to Intelligence Activities, Volume XVII, p 388.

62 Geldenhuys, J (1990) Bestuursdiriktief: Project Coast. SADF document GG/UG/302/6/COAST/5/1, 15 June. Appendix A: Purpose and Management of Project Coast, p1. Available at from the South African History Archives, AL2922: The chemical and biological warfare collection.

63 Geldenhuys, J (1990) Bestuursdiriktief: Project Coast. SADF document GG/UG/302/6/COAST/5/1, 15 June. Appendix A: Purpose and Management of Project Coast, p1. Available at from the South African History Archives, AL2922: The chemical and biological warfare collection.

64 Hearings before the Select Committee to Study Governmental Operations with respect to Intelligence Activities of the United States Senate, 94th Congress, First Session (1976) Volume I: Unauthorized Storage of Toxic Agents, 16–18 September 1975. Washington, DC: US Government Printing Office, p 2.

65 Hearings before the Select Committee to Study Governmental Operations with respect to Intelligence Activities of the United States Senate, 94th Congress, First Session (1976) Volume I: Unauthorized Storage of Toxic Agents, 16–18 September 1975. Washington, DC: US Government Printing Office, p 6.

66 Fig, D (1988) Apartheid's nuclear arsenal: Deviation from development, in J Cock and P McKenzie (eds) *From Defence to Development: Redirecting military resources in South Africa*. Cape Town: David Philip, p 164.

67 Cawthra, G (1986) *Brutal Force: The apartheid war machine*. London: International Defence & Aid Fund for Southern Africa, p 29.

68 Hanlon, J (1986) *Beggar Your Neighbour*. London: CIIR, p 25.

69   Selfe, J (1987) The Total Onslaught and the Total Strategy: Adaptations to the security intelligence decision-making structures under PW Botha's administration. Thesis submitted in fulfilment of the requirement for the degree of Master of Arts, University of Cape Town, p 120.

70   Taken from Malan, Gen. M (1997) *Submission to the Truth and Reconciliation Commission*, 7 May, p 13.

71   Taken from Malan, Gen. M (1997) *Submission to the Truth and Reconciliation Commission*, 7 May, p 25.

72   Selfe, J (1987) The Total Onslaught and the Total Strategy: Adaptations to the security intelligence decision-making structures under PW Botha's administration. Thesis submitted in fulfilment of the requirement for the degree of Master's of Arts, University of Cape Town, p 119.

73   Cawthra, G (1986) *Brutal Force: The apartheid war machine*. London: International Defence & Aid Fund for Southern Africa, p 29.

74   Quoted in Selfe, J (1987) The Total Onslaught and the Total Strategy: Adaptations to the security intelligence decision-making structures under PW Botha's administration. Thesis submitted in fulfilment of the requirement for the degree of Master of Arts, University of Cape Town, p 120.

75   Minter, W (1994) *Apartheid's Contras: An inquiry into the roots of war in Angola and Mozambique*. London: Zed Books, p 6.

76   While the US signed the Geneva Protocol in 1925, it ratified it only on 10 April 1975.

77   See Goldblat, J (1970) Are tear gas and herbicides permitted weapons? *New Scientist*, April: 13–16.

78   Parks, H (1982) Classification of chemical and biological warfare, *University of Toledo Law Review*, 13: 1145–72.

79   Neethling, Gen. L (1998) Testimony to the Truth and Reconciliation Commission, Chemical and Biological Warfare Hearings, 11 June.

80   South African History Online (n.d.) Soweto students march against government's language policy. Available at http://www.sahistory.org.za/dated-event/soweto-students-march-against-government039s-language-policy [Accessed June 2015].

81   De Villiers, JP (1976) Current anti-riot chemicals. Unpublished paper, September. Available from the South African History Archives, AL2922: The chemical and biological warfare collection.

82   De Villiers, JP (1976) Current anti-riot chemicals. Unpublished paper, September. Available from the South African History Archives, AL2922: The chemical and biological warfare collection.

83   De Villiers, JP (n.d.) Handleiding *vir die SAW Bevelstelsel Vol I: Nationale Veiligheid en Totale Oorlog*. Available from the South African History Archives, AL2922: The chemical and biological warfare collection.

84   De Villiers, JP, McLoughlin, GE, Joynt, VP, Van der Westhuizen, CP (1971) *Chemical and Biological Warfare in a South African Context*. Available from the South African History Archives, AL2922: The chemical and biological warfare collection.

85   Ellert, H (1989) *The Rhodesian Front War*. Gweru: Mambo Press; Flower, K (1987) *Serving Secretly*. Johannesburg: Galago; and Stiff, P (1985) *See You in November*. Johannesburg: Galago.

86   Stiff, P (1985) *See You in November*. Johannesburg: Galago.

87   Peta Thornycroft interview with Jan Lourens, Johannesburg, 1997.

88   The underwear found by Van der Spuy at EMLC may, therefore, have been of Rhodesian origin.

89   Peta Thorneycroft interview with MJ McGuinness, Officer Commanding
      Counter Terrorist Operations, Central Intelligence Organisation, Pretoria,
      October 2000.
90   Mike Woods, e-mail communication with Peta Thornycroft, 2000.
91   Reports from the Officer in Charge of Operations to Officer Commanding
      Special Branch Headquarters and the Director-General Central Intelligence
      Organisation. Rhodesian Special Branch documents dated June–November 1977.
92   Mortimer, B. SA Defence Force involvement in the internal security situation in
      the Republic of South Africa. Submission in respect of the former SADF to the
      TRC. Cape Town, 21 October 1996, p 4.
93   Central Intelligence Agency (1976) Soviet and Cuban Aid to the MPLA in
      Angola during January 1976. Document ER M 76-1009, 2 March, release date
      November 1998. Available at http://www.foia.ucia.gov/browse [Accessed 26 May
      2016].
94   Central Intelligence Agency (1985) Soviet Military Support to Angola: Intentions
      and prospects. Special National Intelligence Assessment. Available at http://
      www.foia.ucia.gov.
95   Stiff, P (1999) The Silent War: South African recce operations, 1969–1994.
      Johannesburg: Galago, p 204.
96   Central Intelligence Agency (1976) Soviet and Cuban Aid to the MPLA in
      Angola during January 1976. Document ER M 76-1009, 2 March, release date
      November 1998. Available at https://www.cia.gov/library/readingroom/docs/
      DOC_0000681965.pdf [accessed 26 May 2017].
97   Minter, W (1994) Apartheid's Contras: An inquiry into the roots of war in Angola
      and Mozambique. London: Zed Books, p 6.
98   Basson, W and Knobel, DP (1993) Voorligting aan die Minister van Verdediging
      oor die verloop en huidige status van Projekte Coast en Jota te George op 7
      January 1993. SADF document GG/UG/302/6/J1282/5, 7 January, p 1.
99   Knobel, DP (1992) Ondersoek kragtens Artikel 5 van die Wet op die Ondersoek
      van Ernstige Ekonomiese Misdrywe, 117 van 1991: Krygkor, met spesifieke
      verwysing na Brigadier W Basson, January.
100   Truth and Reconciliation Commission (1998) Truth and Reconciliation Report of
      South Africa, Volume 2, Chapter 6.
101   'Verkleinde Verdedigingsbevelraad: Notule van vergadering gehou om 07H30
      op 25 Oktober 1990 te Samik. Aanhangsel A: Voordrag aan Verkleinde VBR:
      Voorgestelde filosofie vir chemiese oorlogvoering vir die SA Weermag – Beginsels
      en teurgvoer oor huidige stand in die SA Weermag', SADF document HS PLAN/
      DP/302/6/COAST.
102   Chandré Gould interview with General Constand Viljoen, former Chief of the
      South African Defence Force, Cape Town, 18 May 2000.
103   Gould, C and Folb, P (2002) Project Coast: Apartheid's chemical and biological
      warfare programme. UNIDIR/2002/12. Geneva: United Nations Institute for
      Disarmament Research, pp 36–7.
104   Personal electronic communication between Chandré Gould and Dr WS
      Augerson, 15 February 2001.
105   Basson, W and Knobel, DP. Voorligting aan die Minister van Verdediging oor die
      verloop en huidige status van Projeckte Coast en Jota te George op 7 Januarie
      1993. SADF document GG/UG/302/6/J1282/5, 7 January 1993.
106   Basson, W and Knobel, DP. Voorligting aan die Minister van Verdediging oor die
      verloop en huidige status van Projeckte Coast en Jota te George op 7 Januarie
      1993. SADF document GG/UG/302/6/J1282/5, 7 January 1993.

107 Basson, W and Knobel, DP. Voorligting aan die Minister van Verdediging oor die verloop en huidige status van Projeckte Coast en Jota te George op 7 Januarie 1993. SADF document GG/UG/302/6/J1282/5, 7 January 1993.

108 Basson, W and Knobel, DP. Voorligting aan die Minister van Verdediging oor die verloop en huidige status van Projeckte Coast en Jota te George op 7 Januarie 1993. SADF document GG/UG/302/6/J1282/5, 7 January 1993.

109 Basson, W and Knobel, DP (1993) Voorligting aan die Minister van Verdediging. SADF document GG/UG/302/6/J282/5, 10 August, p 2.

110 Mortimer, B (1996) SA Defence Force Involvement in the Internal Security Situation in the Republic of South Africa. Submission in respect of the former SADF to the Truth and Reconciliation Commission, Cape Town, 21 October, p 5.

111 Malan, General M (1997) *Submission to the Truth and Reconciliation Commission*, 7 May, p 9.

112 De Villiers, JP (1982) Perspectives in chemical warfare. Lecture given to a joint meeting of the Northern Transvaal Branch of the South African Chemical Institute and the Institute for Strategic Studies, University of Pretoria, August.

113 Knobel, DP in *The State vs Wouter Basson*, 15 November 1999.

114 Alibek, K and Handelman, S (1999) *Biohazard: The chilling true story of the largest covert biological weapons program in the world told from inside by the man who ran it*. New York: Random House, p 98.

115 Infladel was established before the Internet but had access to computerised international search vehicles, including a link to US databases. Infladel was one of only two facilities in South Africa that had this capability at the time. The person responsible for this was Antoinette Lourens.

116 Jan Lourens, telephonic discussion with Chandré Gould, 21 May 2000.

117 Judgement in *The State vs Wouter Basson*, para. 48 (referencing the testimony of Knobel regarding the structure of Project Coast and its front companies).

118 Van Rensburg, S (1998) Testimony of at the TRC Hearing into Chemical and Biological Warfare. Cape Town, 9 June.

119 Gould interview with Hennie Jordaan, 18 January 2001.

120 Despite having the same surnames, Willie and Wouter Basson are not related.

121 Chandré Gould interview with Professor Willie Basson, former Managing Director of Delta G Scientific, Cape Town, 2 April 1998.

122 Chandré Gould interview with Geoff Candy, former Project Coast scientist, 24 May 2000.

123 Chandré Gould interview with Geoff Candy, former Project Coast scientist, 24 May 2000.

124 Gould interview with Willie Basson, 2 April 1998.

125 Gould interview with Willie Basson, 2 April 1998.

126 Gould interview with Willie Basson, 2 April 1998.

127 Goosen in *The State vs Wouter Basson*, 22 May 2000.

128 Goosen in *The State vs Wouter Basson*, 22 May 2000.

129 Goosen in *The State vs Wouter Basson*, 22 May 2000.

130 Goosen in *The State vs Wouter Basson*, 22 May 2000.

131 Burgess, S and Purkitt, H (2001) *The Rollback of South Africa's Chemical and Biological Warfare Program*. Montgomery, AL: Air War College, Maxwell-Gunter Air Force Base, p 23.

132 McSmith, A (2013) Margaret Thatcher branded ANC 'terrorist' while urging Nelson Mandela's release. *The Independent*, 9 December.

133 For further details, see Pickover, M (2005) *Animal Rights in South Africa*. Cape Town: Double Storey, p 134.

134 Hofmeyr, CFB (1988) Conference with Dr JM Erasmus, Director Veterinary Services, Department of Agriculture and Water Affairs on 4 June 1988, 6 July.

135 Huxsoll, D (1992) Narrowing the zone of uncertainty, in R Zilinskas (ed.) *The Microbiologist and Biological Defense Research*. New York: New York Academy of Science.

136 Novick, R and Shulman, S (1990) New forms of biological warfare? In S Wright (ed.) *Preventing a Biological Arms Race*. Cambridge, MA: MIT Press.

137 See also King, J and Strauss, H (1990) The hazards of defensive biological warfare programs, in S. Wright (ed.) *Preventing a Biological Arms Race*. Cambridge, MA: MIT Press, pp 120–32.

138 Leitenberg, M (2001) Biological weapons in the twentieth century: A review and analysis, *Critical Review Microbiology*, 27(4): 267–320.

139 Leitenberg, M (2001) Biological weapons in the twentieth century: A review and analysis, *Critical Review Microbiology*, 27(4): 267–320.

140 Piller, C and Yamamoto, KR (1988) *Gene Wars: Military Control over the New Genetic Technologies*. New York: Beech Tree Books.

141 Basson, W and Knobel, DP (1989) *Approval for Destruction of Project Documentation: Project Coast*. Top Secret GG/UG/302/6/COAST/5/1, 21 November. Hennopsmeer: SAMS Headquarters.

142 De Klerk, FW (1998) *The Last Trek: A new beginning*. London: Macmillan, p 199.

143 Landgren, S (1989) The CBW industry, in *Embargo Disimplemented: South Africa's military industry*. Oxford: Oxford University Press, p. 151.

144 Burger, M and Gould, C (2002) *Secrets and Lies*. Cape Town: Zebra Press, pp 73–4.

145 Basson, W (1990) *Projek Coast: Voorligting aan Staatspresident*. GG/UG/302/6/ C123/BK, 26 March, paras 23 and 27.

146 De Klerk, FW (1998) *The Last Trek: A new beginning*. London: Macmillan, p 156.

147 Knobel, DP (1992) Fondsbehoefte en fondshantering: Projek Jota, 6 July, p 2. Exhibit K2 in *The State vs Wouter Basson*, South African High Court, Transvaal Division.

148 De Bruyn, Cmdt JG (1993) *Certification with Regard to the Destruction of Chemical Products on 27 January*. TOP SECRET AI/UG/302/6/C123-2, 30 March, p 1.

149 Notule van die vergadering van die beheerkomitee van Projek Jota gehou op 29 Jan 1993 in die HF Verwoerd gebou, Kaapstad (GG/UG/ 302/6/J1282/5).

150 De Bruyn, Cmdt JG (1993) *Certification with Regard to the Destruction of Chemical Products on 27 January*. TOP SECRET AI/UG/302/6/C123-2, 30 March.

151 Handwritten notes by Basson on De Bruyn, Cmdt JG (1993) *Certification with regard to the Destruction of Chemical Products on 27 January*. TOP SECRET AI/UG/302/6/C123-2, 30 March.

152 Convention on the Prohibition of the Development, Production, Stockpiling and Use of Chemical Weapons and their Destruction, Art. 1.

153 Notule van die vergadering van die Beheerkomitee van Projek Jota gehou op 31 Maart 1993 in die HF Verwoerdgebou, Kaapstad. SADF document GG/ UG/302/6/J1282/5, 31 March 1993.

154 Knobel, DP and Steyn, B (1993) *Voorligting aan die Minister van Verdediging*, 7 January. Signed acceptance and authorisation from the Minister of Defence.

155 Notule van die vergadering van die Beheerkomitee van Projek Jota wat gehou is

op 9 Januarie 1995 by die Kantoor van HNW. SADF document GG/UG/302/6/J1282, 9 January 1995.

156 See Lyman, P (2002) *Partner to History*. Washington, DC: United States Institute of Peace Press, pp 189–94.

157 Knobel, DP (1994) Briefing to President Mandela on the Defensive Chemical and Biological Warfare Programme of the SADF and the RSA's position regarding the CWC and BWC. GG/UG/302/6/J1282/5, 18 August.

158 Lyman, P (2002) *Partner to History*. Washington, DC: United States Institute of Peace Press, pp 189–94.

159 Truth and Reconciliation Commission (1998) *Truth and Reconciliation Commission of South Africa Report*, Volume 1, p 48.

160 Tutu, D (1998) Forward to *Truth and Reconciliation Commission of South Africa Report*, Volume 1, p 1.

161 Republic of South Africa (1995) Promotion of National Unity and Reconciliation Act, Act 34 of 1995.

162 Sanders, M (2007) *Ambiguities of Witnessing*. Johannesburg: Wits University Press, p 3.

163 Republic of South Africa (1995) Promotion of National Unity and Reconciliation Act, Act 34 of 1995.

164 South African Council of Churches (1994) Minutes of SACC Consultation on Reconciliation, Peace and the Truth Commission, held in Khotso House. Historical Papers, South African History Archive.

165 Republic of South Africa (1995) Promotion of National Unity and Reconciliation Act, Act 34 of 1995.

166 Human Rights Watch (1998) HRW welcomes release of South African truth report: Criticises attempts to censure report. New York: Human Rights Watch.

167 Republic of South Africa (1995) Promotion of National Unity and Reconciliation Act, Act 34 of 1995.

168 Gould, C (2016) Open secrets: 'Truth-telling' and transitional justice in revealing biowarfare programs, in F Lenzos (ed) *Biological Threats in the 21st Century*. London: Imperial College Press, pp 159–68.

169 Department of Justice and Constitutional Development (2015) [accessed 30 December 2015] Amnesty hearings and decisions: Summary of amnesty decisions. Available at http://www.justice.gov.za/trc/amntrans/index.htm [Accessed June 2016].

170 Gould, C (2016) Open secrets: 'Truth-telling' and transitional justice in revealing biowarfare programs, in F Lenzos (ed) *Biological Threats in the 21st Century*. London: Imperial College Press, pp 159–68.

171 Abrahamsen, T and Van der Merwe, H (2005) Reconcliation through Amnesty? Applicants' views of the South African Truth and Reconciliation Commission. Johannesburg, Centre for the Study of Violence and Reconciliation. See Gould, C (2016) Open secrets: 'Truth-telling' and transitional justice in revealing biowarfare programs, in F Lenzos (ed.) *Biological Threats in the 21st Century*. London: Imperial College Press.

172 Gould, C (2016) Open secrets: 'Truth-telling' and transitional justice in revealing biowarfare programs, in F Lenzos (ed.) *Biological Threats in the 21st Century*. London: Imperial College Press, pp 159–68.

173 Gould, C (2016) Open secrets: 'Truth-telling' and transitional justice in revealing biowarfare programs, in F Lenzos (ed.) *Biological Threats in the 21st Century*. London: Imperial College Press, pp 159–68.

174 Republic of South Africa (1995) Promotion of National Unity and Reconciliation

Act, Act 34 of 1995. Quoted in Sanders, M (2007) *Ambiguities of Witnessing*. Johannesburg: Wits University Press, p 3.

175 Dignan, E (2014) *Reconciliation Lessons: Verne Harris on South Africa*. Belfast: Northern Ireland Foundation. Available at https://northernireland. foundation/2014/03/19/reconciliation-lessons-verne-harris-on-south-africa/ [Last accessed 11 October 2016].

176 Burger, M and Gould, C (2002) *Secrets and Lies*. Cape Town: Zebra Press. See also Lenzos, F (ed.) (2016) *Biological Threats in the 21st Century*. London: Imperial College Press.

177 Lyman, P (2002) *Partner to History*. Washington, DC: United States Institute of Peace Press, pp 249–54.

178 Republic of South Africa (1995) *South Africa Confidence Building Form 'F'*, p 64.

179 Brummer, S (1996) Secret chemical war remains secret. *Mail & Guardian*, 23 August.

180 Burger, M and Gould, C (2002) *Secrets and Lies*. Cape Town: Zebra Press.

181 Gould, C (2005) South Africa's Chemical and Biological Warfare Programme, 1981–1995. Thesis submitted in fulfilment of the requirements for the degree of Doctorate of History, Rhodes University, August.

182 Van Rensburg, S (1998) Testimony of at the TRC Hearing into Chemical and Biological Warfare. Cape Town, 9 June.

183 As in Odendal, M (1998) Testimony of at the TRC Hearing into Chemical and Biological Warfare. Cape Town, 9 June; and Van Rensburg, S (1998) Testimony of at the TRC Hearing into Chemical and Biological Warfare. Cape Town, 9 June.

184 Christie, N (1986) The ideal victim, in E Fattah (ed.) *From Crime Policy to Victim Policy*. Basingstoke: Macmillan.

185 Gould, C and Folb, P (2002) *Project Coast: Apartheid's Chemical and Biological Warfare Programme*. UNIDIR/2002/12. Geneva: United Nations Institute for Disarmament Research, p 84.

186 The documents can be found on the website of the International Security Network, Zurich, Switzerland. Available at http://www.isn.ethz.ch/infoservice/ secwatch/za_cbw/ [Accessed July 2015].

187 Nelson Mandela on receiving the report of the Truth and Reconciliation Commission, South Africa, 29 October 1998. Quoted in Hatangh, S and Venter, S (2011) *Nelson Mandela by Himself: The authorized book of quotations*. London: Macmillan, p 33.

188 Nelson Mandela, address at the opening of the President's Budget Debate, Parliament, Cape Town, 2 March 1999. Quoted in Hatangh, S and Venter, S (2011) *Nelson Mandela by Himself: The authorized book of quotations*. London: Macmillan, p 33.

189 Minty, A (1998) Testimony of at the TRC Hearing into Chemical and Biological Warfare. Cape Town, 8 June.

190 As one official warned, the new South Africa needed 'to be seen not like in the past when the regime acted as an outlaw violating all basic norms of international behaviour but as a new member of the international community that acts as a good and responsible world citizen which will honor and comply with the letter and spirit of our international obligations.' See Minty, A (1998) Testimony of at the TRC Hearing into Chemical and Biological Warfare. Cape Town 8 June.

191 Minty, A (1998) Testimony of at the TRC Hearing into Chemical and Biological Warfare. Cape Town, 8 June.

192 Haysom, N (1998) Testimony of at the TRC Hearing into Chemical and Biological Warfare. Cape Town, 8 June.

193 Haysom, N (1998) Testimony of at the TRC Hearing into Chemical and Biological Warfare. Cape Town, 8 June.

194 Haysom, N (1998) Testimony of at the TRC Hearing into Chemical and Biological Warfare. Cape Town, 8 June.

195 Haysom, N (1998) Testimony of at the TRC Hearing into Chemical and Biological Warfare. Cape Town, 8 June.

196 Knobel, DP (1998) Testimony of at the TRC Hearing into Chemical and Biological Warfare. Cape Town, 12 June. Only one official foreign trip was made by a South African Defence Force official other than Basson; a trip to Israel and West Germany in 1986.

197 Knobel, DP (1998) Testimony of at the TRC Hearing into Chemical and Biological Warfare. Cape Town, 12 June.

198 Basson, W (1998) Testimony of at the TRC Hearing into Chemical and Biological Warfare. Cape Town, 31 July.

199 Basson, W (1998) Testimony of at the TRC Hearing into Chemical and Biological Warfare. Cape Town, 31 July.

200 And further it was asked: did Lourens consider that this person would be an 'agent who was going to use that one someone in Europe?'. It did occur to him he said, but because of this arm's length to the activities of the project 'it didn't dawn on me until I actually woke up after the poison exercise, and then it was real. I was in England for a few days thereafter, and I cannot remember how many days, and I remember very well buying every single newspaper that I could lay my hands on to try and find out, you know, had somebody died mysteriously, and so on. So, yes it – I was very aware of that aspect then.' Lourens, J (1998) Testimony to the Truth and Reconciliation Commission Chemical and Biological Warfare Hearings, Cape Town, 8 June.

201 Lourens, J (1998) Testimony of at the TRC Hearing into Chemical and Biological Warfare. Cape Town, 8 June.

202 Lourens, J (1998) Testimony of at the TRC Hearing into Chemical and Biological Warfare. Cape Town, 8 June.

203 Lourens, J (1998) Testimony of at the TRC Hearing into Chemical and Biological Warfare. Cape Town, 8 June.

204 For a general overview of the production of ignorance, see Gross, M and McGoey, L (eds) (2015) *Routledge International Handbook of Ignorance Studies*. London: Routledge.

205 For other examples, see Masco, J (2001) Lie detectors: Of secrets and hypersecurity in Los Alamos, *Public Culture*, 14: 441–67; Rappert, B and Balmer, B (2007) Rethinking 'secrecy' and 'disclosure', in B Rappert (ed) *Technology and Security*. London: Palgrave, pp 45–65; and Reppy, J (ed.) (1999) *Secrecy and Knowledge Production*, Ithaca, NY: Cornell University Peace Studies.

206 Van Rensburg, S (1998) Testimony of at the TRC Hearing into Chemical and Biological Warfare. Cape Town, 9 June.

207 See Goffman, E (1970) *Strategic Interaction*. Oxford: Basil Blackwell, for further discussion of so-called 'expression games'.

208 Van Rensburg, S (1998) Testimony of at the TRC Hearing into Chemical and Biological Warfare. Cape Town, 9 June.

209 For a consideration of white South Africans and victimhood, see Krog, A (2013) *Conditional Tense*. London: Seagull Books, Chapter 6.

210 Testimony of Trevor Floyd in *The State vs Wouter Basson*, South African High Court, Transvaal Division, 9–12 May 2000, as reported in the daily trial report prepared by Marléne Burger.

211 Lourens, J (1998) Testimony of at the TRC Hearing into Chemical and Biological Warfare. Cape Town, 8 June.

212 Huxsoll, D (1992) Narrowing the zone of uncertainty, in R Zilinskas (ed.) *The Microbiologist and Biological Defense Research*. New York: New York Academy of Science, pp 177–91.

213 Folb, P (2001) Inside track, *Tract Two*, 10(3).

214 Pickover, M (2005) *Animal Rights in South Africa*. Cape Town: Double Storey, p 134.

215 Van Rensburg, S (1998) Testimony of at the TRC Hearing into Chemical and Biological Warfare. Cape Town, 9 June.

216 Wandrag, S (1991) *Progress Report with regard to Specific R-Projects*, July. Pretoria: Roodeplaat Research Laboratories.

217 Extract taken from a non-dated and non-signed document entitled *Available Data about Brodifacum*.

218 While much research in recent years has sought to establish how animal abuses is a prelude and predicator for abuse to humans (for instance, as in Linzey, A (2009) *The Link between Animal Abuse and Human Violence*. Eastbourne: Sussex Academic Press), it seems non-contentious to suggest that this relation can exist in the reverse.

219 Pickover, M (2005) *Animal Rights in South Africa*. Cape Town: Double Storey, pp 137–8.

220 Lourens, J (1998) Testimony of at the TRC Hearing into Chemical and Biological Warfare. Cape Town, 8 June.

221 Koekemoer, J (1998) Testimony of at the TRC Hearing into Chemical and Biological Warfare. Cape Town, 9 June.

222 Koelemoer, J (1998) Testimony of at the TRC Hearing into Chemical and Biological Warfare. Cape Town, 9 June.

223 Quotes in this entry taken from the testimony: Koelemoer, J (1998) Testimony of at the TRC Hearing into Chemical and Biological Warfare. Cape Town, 9 June.

224 Testimony of van Rensburg, S (1998) Testimony of at the TRC Hearing into Chemical and Biological Warfare. Cape Town, 9 June.

225 Van Rensburg, S (1998) Testimony of at the TRC Hearing into Chemical and Biological Warfare. Cape Town, 9 June.

226 Van Rensburg, S (1998) Testimony of at the TRC Hearing into Chemical and Biological Warfare. Cape Town, 9 June.

227 Goosen, D (1998) Testimony of at the TRC Hearing into Chemical and Biological Warfare. Cape Town, 11 June.

228 Goosen, D (1998) Testimony of at the TRC Hearing into Chemical and Biological Warfare. Cape Town 11 June.

229 Nyatsumba, K (1998) The full horror of apartheid exposed, *Sowetan*, 19 June, p 16; Brand, R (1998) Lid lifted on military's box of horrors, *The Star*, 10 June; and Smith, C (1998) A peek behind the doors of apartheid's laboratory of death, *Saturday Argus*, 13/14 June.

230 Brand, R (1998) Front company "sold' poison to SADF, *The Star*, 10 June, p. 7.

231 Brand, R (1998) SA's chemical warfare horrors, *The Star*, 10 June, p. 7.

232 For example, Beresford, D (1998) Apartheid's lab rats under the microscope. *Mail & Guardian*, 12–18 June, p. 10; and Brand, R (1998) Inside the poison death factory, *The Star*, 10 June.

233 Knobel, DP (1998) Testimony of at the TRC Hearing into Chemical and Biological Warfare. Cape Town 17 June.

234 Knobel, DP (1998) Testimony of at the TRC Hearing into Chemical and Biological Warfare. Cape Town 12 June.

235 Knobel, DP (1998) Testimony of at the TRC Hearing into Chemical and Biological Warfare. Cape Town, 12 June 1998.

236 Knobel, DP (1998) Testimony of at the TRC Hearing into Chemical and Biological Warfare, Cape Town, 8 June.

237 Knobel, DP (1998) Testimony of at the TRC Hearing into Chemical and Biological Warfare, Cape Town, 8 June.

238 Knobel, DP (1998) Testimony of at the TRC Hearing into Chemical and Biological Warfare, Cape Town, 8 June.

239 Knobel, DP (1998) Testimony to the Truth and Reconciliation Commission Chemical and Biological Warfare Hearings, Cape Town, 8 June 1998.

240 Rappert, B and Balmer, B (2015) Ignorance is strength? Intelligence, security and national secrets, in M Gross and L McGoey (eds) *Routledge International Handbook of Ignorance Studies*. London: Routledge, pp 328–37.

241 Knobel, DP (1998) *Testimony to the Truth and Reconciliation Commission Chemical and Biological Warfare Hearings*, Cape Town, 8 June 1998.

242 Knobel, DP (1998) *Testimony to the Truth and Reconciliation Commission Chemical and Biological Warfare Hearings*, Cape Town, 8 June 1998.

243 Knobel, DP (1998) *Testimony to the Truth and Reconciliation Commission Chemical and Biological Warfare Hearings*, Cape Town, 8 June 1998.

244 Testimony of Gen. DP Knobel in *The State vs Wouter Basson*, South African High Court, Transvaal Division, as reported by Marléne Burger in the daily trial report prepared for the CCR's CBW research project, 22 November 1999.

245 Basson, W (1998) *Testimony to the Truth and Reconciliation Commission Chemical and Biological Warfare Hearings*, Cape Town, 31 July 1998.

246 Knobel, DP (1998) Testimony of at the TRC Hearing into Chemical and Biological Warfare, Cape Town, 12 June.

247 Mijburgh, P (1998) Testimony of at the TRC Hearing into Chemical and Biological Warfare, Cape Town, 7 July.

248 Knobel, DP (1998) Testimony of at the TRC Hearing into Chemical and Biological Warfare. Cape Town, 7 July.

249 The Citizen (1998) Chemical warfare papers not destroyed – witness, *The Citizen*, 9 July; Smith, A (1998) One man understands content of computer disks storing poison info, *Saturday Argus*; Cape Argus (1998) Wouter's disk 'key to germ warfare', *Cape Argus*, 8 July.

250 Swanepoel, W (1998) Testimony of at the TRC Hearing into Chemical and Biological Warfare, Cape Town, 10 June.

251 Basson, W (1998) Testimony of at the TRC Hearing into Chemical and Biological Warfare, Cape Town, 31 July.

252 Author unknown, date unknown, Betalings van Coast Projekte: Fondsevloei (Payments of Coast Projects: Flow of funds], document now numbered CBW 54 is available from the South African History Archives chemical and biological warfare collection.

253 Exchanges cited from Basson, W (1998) Testimony of at the TRC Hearing into Chemical and Biological Warfare. Cape Town 31 July.

254 Basson, W (1998) Testimony of at the TRC Hearing into Chemical and Biological Warfare. Cape Town, 31 July.

255 African National Congress (1998) ANC on Apartheid Plans to Poison Nelson Mandela. Department of Information and Publicity, 10 June.

256 Basson, W (1998) Testimony of at the TRC Hearing into Chemical and Biological Warfare. Cape Town, 31 July.

257 Basson, W (1998)Testimony of at the TRC Hearing into Chemical and Biological

Warfare. Cape Town, 31 July.

258   For instance, Steyn, C (1997) Basson's human guinea pigs horror. *The Star* 7 February.

259   Basson, W (1998) Testimony of at the TRC Hearing into Chemical and Biological Warfare. Cape Town, 31 July.

260   Basson, W (1998) Testimony of at the TRC Hearing into Chemical and Biological Warfare. Cape Town, 31 July.

261   Basson, W (1998) Testimony of at the TRC Hearing into Chemical and Biological Warfare. Cape Town, 31 July.

262   Basson, W (1998) Testimony of at the TRC Hearing into Chemical and Biological Warfare. Cape Town, 31 July.

263   Basson, W (1998) Testimony of at the TRC Hearing into Chemical and Biological Warfare. Cape Town, 31 July.

264   Basson, W (1998) Testimony of at the TRC Hearing into Chemical and Biological Warfare. Cape Town, 31 July.

265   Odendal, M (1998) Testimony of at the TRC Hearing into Chemical and Biological Warfare. Cape Town, 9 June.

266   Basson, W (1998) Testimony of at the TRC Hearing into Chemical and Biological Warfare. Cape Town, 31 July 1998.

267   Basson, W (1998) Testimony of at the TRC Hearing into Chemical and Biological Warfare. Cape Town, 31 July 1998.

268   Truth and Reconciliation Commission (1998) *Truth and Reconciliation Commission of South Africa Report - Special Investigation into Project Coast*, Volume 2, p 511. Available at http://www.justice.gov.za/Trc/report/index.htm [accessed 26 May 2017].

269   Truth and Reconciliation Commission (1998) *Truth and Reconciliation Commission of South Africa Report*, Volume 1, p 49.

270   Truth and Reconciliation Commission (1998) *Truth and Reconciliation Commission of South Africa Report*, Volume 2, p 510.

271   Truth and Reconciliation Commission (1998) *Truth and Reconciliation Commission of South Africa Report*, Volume 2, p 521.

272   Truth and Reconciliation Commission (1998) *Truth and Reconciliation Commission of South Africa Report*, Volume 2, p 519–20.

273   Truth and Reconciliation Commission (1998) *Truth and Reconciliation Commission of South Africa Report*, Volume 2, p 514.

274   Laurence, P (1998) Report of SA Truth Commission spares no one in its censure. 30 October. Available at http://www.irishtimes.com/news/report-of-sa-truth-commission-spares-no-one-in-its-censure-1.208685 [Accessed 29 August 2015].

275   Norton-Taylor, R (1998) 'Germ war' deaths to be re-examined. *The Guardian*, 30 December.

276   Norton-Taylor, R (1998) 'Germ war' deaths to be re-examined. *The Guardian*, 30 December.

277   Norton-Taylor, R (1998) 'Germ war' deaths to be re-examined. *The Guardian*, 30 December.

278   Testimony of National Intelligence Agency deputy director-general Mike Kennedy at *The State vs Wouter Basson*, 1 December 1999. Trial diary prepared by Marléne Burger and Chandré Gould for the Centre for Conflict Resolution. Available at http://www.issafrica.org/uploads/Wouter_Basson_Trail_Summary.pdf [Accessed 20 August 2015].

279   Mangold, T and Goldberg, G 1999. *Plague Wars: A true story of biological warfare*. London: Macmillan.

280 Mangold, T and Goldberg, G 1999. *Plague Wars: A true story of biological warfare*. London: Macmillan.

281 Kouzminov, A (2005) *Biological Espionage: Special operations of the Soviet and Russian foreign intelligence services in the West*. London: Greenhill Books.

282 Alibek, K and Handelman, S (1999) *Biohazard: The chilling true story of the largest covert biological weapons program in the world told from inside by the man who ran it*. New York: Random House.

283 Alibek, K and Handelman, S (1999) *Biohazard: The chilling true story of the largest covert biological weapons program in the world told from inside by the man who ran it*. New York: Random House, p. 22.

284 See van Zyl, P (1999) Dilemmas of transitional justice: The case of South Africa's Truth and Reconciliation Commission, *Journal of International Affairs*, 52(2); and Truth and Reconciliation Commission (1998) *Truth and Reconciliation Commission of South Africa Report*, Volume 1.

285 Van Zyl, P (1999) Dilemmas of transitional justice: The case of South Africa's Truth and Reconciliation Commission, *Journal of International Affairs*, 52(2); and Truth and Reconciliation Commission (1998) *Truth and Reconciliation Commission of South Africa Report*, Volume 1, p 9.

286 van Zyl, P (1999) Dilemmas of transitional justice: The case of South Africa's Truth and Reconciliation Commission. *Journal of International Affairs*, 52(2); and Truth and Reconciliation Commission (1998) *Truth and Reconciliation Commission of South Africa Report*, Volume 1, p 7.

287 Swiss parliamentary delegation report (1999) *Le rile des services reassignments suites dan le cadre des relations entrée la Sies et l'Afrique du Sud*, 12 November.

288 Haefliger, M (2001) Swiss investigate alleged secret service links to South Africa. *SWI* 22 August. Available at http://www.swissinfo.ch/eng/swiss-investigate-alleged-secret-service-links-to-south-africa/2202122 [Last accessed 1 May 2016].

289 Haefliger, M (2001) Swiss investigate alleged secret service links to South Africa. *SWI* 22 August. Available at http://www.swissinfo.ch/eng/swiss-investigate-alleged-secret-service-links-to-south-africa/2202122 [Last accessed 1 May 2016].

290 Mangold, T and Goldberg, J (1999) *Plague Wars*. New York: St Martin's Griffin, pp 242–3.

291 Peeren, E (2014) Lumumba's ghosts: Immaterial matters and matters immaterial in Sven Augustijnen's *Spectres, Transformations Journal of Media & Culture*, 25: 1–12.

292 Serfontein, S (1980) Organisasie-Ondersoek na Projek Barnacle, 12 December.

293 For further details on Operational Dual, see Burger, M and Gould, C (2002) *Secrets and Lies*. Cape Town: Zebra Press, Chapter 5.

294 Burger, M. and Gould, C. Trial diary. Daily reports from the trial of Dr Wouter Basson. Available at https://www.issafrica.org/uploads/Wouter_Basson_Trail_Summary.pdf [Accessed 26 May 2017].

295 Wright, S. and Ketcham, S (1990) The problem of interpreting the US biological defense program, in S Wright (ed.) *Preventing a Biological Arms Race*. Cambridge, MA: MIT Press, pp 169–96.

296 See Rappert, B (2006) *Controlling the Weapons of War*. London: Routledge, Chapter 6 for a more in-depth consideration of these issues.

297 Falk, R (2001) The challenges of biological weaponry, in S. Wright (ed.) *Biological Warfare and Disarmament*. London: Rowman & Littlefield, p 29.

298 Burger, M (2002) *Trial Report: 31 July 2001*. Pretoria: Institute for Security Studies.

299 Burger, M (2002) *Daily Reports about the Trial of Dr Wouter Basson: 4 October*

1999–11 April 2002. Pretoria: Institute for Security Studies.

300 Burgess, S and Purkitt, H (2001) *The Rollback of South Africa's Chemical and Biological Warfare Program*. Maxwell Air Force Base, Alabama: Air War College, p 82.

301 Burgess, S and Purkitt, H (2001) *The Rollback of South Africa's Chemical and Biological Warfare Program*. Maxwell Air Force Base, Alabama: Air War College.

302 Burgess, S and Purkitt, H (2001) *The Rollback of South Africa's Chemical and Biological Warfare Program*. Maxwell Air Force Base, Alabama: Air War College, p xi.

303 Mangold, T and Goldberg, G (1999) *Plague Wars: A true story of biological warfare*. London: Macmillan.

304 Harris, S (2002) *Factories of Death: Japanese biological warfare, 1932–1945, and the American cover-up*. New York: Routledge.

305 Harris, S (2002) *Factories of Death: Japanese biological warfare, 1932–1945, and the American cover-up*. New York: Routledge, p 77.

306 Harris, S (2002) *Factories of Death: Japanese biological warfare, 1932–1945, and the American cover-up*. New York: Routledge.

307 Hersch, S. 1968. *Chemical and Biological Warfare: America's hidden arsenal*. New York: Bobbs-Merril, p 108.

308 Liza Key interview with General Constand Viljoen (2002) transcript from film footage, available from the University of Cape Town, Special Collections, Jagger Library. Exact date of the interview is unknown.

309 Foreign and Commonwealth Office (2002) *Strengthening the Biological and Toxin Weapons Convention*. London: HMSO.

310 Burger, M and Gould, C (2002) *Secret and Lies*. Cape Town: Zebra Press, pp 202–03.

311 Burger, M (2002) *Trial Report: 11 April 2002*. Pretoria: ISS.

312 Burger, M and Gould, C (2002) *Secrets and Lies*. Cape Town: Zebra Press, p 200.

313 Gould, C and Folb, P (2002) *Project Coast: Apartheid's chemical and biological warfare programme*. UNIDIR/2002/12. Geneva: UN Institute for Disarmament Research, p 8.

314 Nathan, L and Lewis, P (2002) Preface: *Project Coast: Apartheid's chemical and biological warfare programme*. UNIDIR/2002/12. Geneva: UN Institute for Disarmament Research, pp ix–x.

315 Nathan, L and Lewis, P (2002) Preface: *Project Coast: Apartheid's chemical and biological warfare programme*. UNIDIR/2002/12. Geneva: UN Institute for Disarmament Research, p ix.

316 Tutu, Archbishop DM (2002) Foreword: *Project Coast: Apartheid's chemical and biological warfare programme*. UNIDIR/2002/12. Geneva: UN Institute for Disarmament Research, p v.

317 Gould, C and Folb, P (2002) *Project Coast: Apartheid's chemical and biological warfare programme*. UNIDIR/2002/12. Geneva: UN Institute for Disarmament Research, p 207.

318 Gould, C and Folb, P (2002) *Project Coast: Apartheid's chemical and biological warfare programme*. UNIDIR/2002/12. Geneva: UN Institute for Disarmament Research, p 214.

319 Sole, S and Brummer, S (2003) Bid to hijack SA bio-stocks. *Mail & Guardian*, 25 April, p 3.

320 See Gould, C and Hay, A (2006) The South African Biological Weapons Program, in M Wheelis, L Rozsa and M Dando *Deadly Cultures*. London: Harvard University Press, pp 191–212.

321 Basson, W (1989) *Projek Coast: Moontlikhede vir privatisering* [*Project Coast: Possibilities for privatisation*], 28 November, Exhibit 23B in *The State vs Wouter Basson*, South African High Court, Transvaal Division.

322 Gould, C and Folb, P (2002) *Project Coast: Apartheid's Chemical and Biological Warfare Programme*. UNIDIR/2002/12. Geneva: UN Institute for Disarmament Research, p 153.

323 Burger, M and Gould, C (2002) *Secret and Lies*. Cape Town: Zebra Press, p 26.

324 For an overview of the appeal process, see Swart, M. 2008. The Wouter Basson prosecution: The closest South Africa came to Nuremberg? *ZaöRV*, 68: 209–26.

325 See Swart, M (2008) The Wouter Basson prosecution: The closest South Africa came to Nuremberg? *ZaöRV*, 68: 209–26.

326 Pickover, M (2005) *Animal Rights in South Africa*. Cape Town: Double Storey, p 131. Reproduced with permission.

327 See, The Centre for the Study of Violence and Reconciliation (2007) *The Violent Nature of Crime in South Africa*. Johannesburg: Centre for the Study of Violence and Reconciliation, 25 June, p 131.

328 *South African Crime Quarterly* policy on the use of racial assignations. Available at https://www.issafrica.org/uploads/SACQ_policy%20on%20use%20of%20racial%20classification_9-07-2015.pdf [Accessed March 2017].

329 Parliamentary Office of Science and Technology (2009) *POSTnote: Lessons from History* Number 323, January. Our thanks to Brian Blamer for suggesting this publication.

330 Lindblom, C and Woodhouse, E (1992) *The Policy Making Process*. London: Pearson.

331 Available at www.globalpolitics.cz/rozhovory/interview-with-anja-mihr-%E2%80%93-on-transitional-justice-democratization-and-challenges-of-post-conflict-development [Accessed 26 May 2017].

332 Nelson, M (2011) *The Art of Cruelty: A reckoning*. New York: WW Norton, p 32.

333 Von Holdt, K, Langa, M, Molapo, S, Mogapi, N, Ngubeni, K, Dlamini, J and Kirsten, A (2011) *The Smoke that Calls: Eight case studies of community protest and xenophobic violence*. Johannesburg: Centre for the Study of Violence and Reconciliation and the Society, Work and Development Institute, p 3.

334 Available at http://www.theguardian.com/world/2015/may/19/marikana-massacre-untold-story-strike-leader-died-workers-rights [Accessed 26 May 2017].

335 Olwagen, O (2012) Witch-hunt against Basson should end now, *The Star*, 19 July. Available at http://beta.iol.co.za/the-star/witch-hunt-against-basson-should-end-now-1344597 [Accessed December 2015]. Reproduced with permission from *The Star*.

336 Here we draw strongly from Rappert, B and Gould, C (2014) The Biological Weapons Convention: Confidence, the prohibition and learning from the past. ISS Occasional Paper. Pretoria: Institute for Security Studies, 14 July. Available at https://www.issafrica.org/publications/papers/biological-weapons-convention-confidence-the-prohibition-and-learning-from-the-past [Accessed 26 May 2017].

337 Meeting of Experts and Meeting of States Parties between 2007–2012, associated preparatory events in the build-up to the 7th Review Conference in 2011 (such as those in Montreux, Berlin and Beijing), and other related events (for instance, notes of meetings held under the Geneva Forum in 2009–2010).

338 For instance, see Annex I of the 2012 *Report the Meeting of Experts*, BWC, / MSP/2012/MX/3 3, August, pp 43–8.

339 See BWC (2012) Final Document of the Seventh Review Conference, BWC/CONF.VII/7 13, January.

340 To be sure, matters of some significance have been discussed, including access to the database of the CBMs and the public availability of the forms. See, for example, Canada (2010) *Proposals to Strengthen the Existing Confidence-building Measure Submission and Review Process*, BWC/MSP/2010/WP.2, 6 December.

341 Though some states have urged others to complete this part of the CBM, notably see South Africa (2011) *Confidence-Building Measures*, BWC/CONF.VII/WP.19, 25 October and the UK offered a recent update of its Form F.

342 An oblique reference to the issues of the declaration of past programmes was made in a 2011 working paper by Norway, Switzerland and New Zealand titled BWC/CONF.VII/WP.2. On p 3, it stated: 'There is very little public information on how individual States Parties use the CBM returns once they have accessed them. There is one significant exception to this: one State Party produces, through statutory requirement, a public compliance report that not only provides an assessment of its own adherence to arms control, nonproliferation and disarmament agreements, but also an assessment of the adherence of other States to their obligations. These reports state that CBMs are central to the compliance assessments made, and they regularly note whether certain States Parties have yet to submit a CBM return, that some only do so intermittently, and that while some States do submit returns these have either not declared past offensive programmes or current biological research and development activities.'

343 Isla, N (2006) Transparency in past offensive biological weapon programmes: An analysis of Confidence Building Measure Form F. Hamburg Centre for Arms Control Occasional Paper No. 1, June, p 29.

344 Isla, N (2006) Transparency in past offensive biological weapon programmes: An analysis of Confidence Building Measure Form F. Hamburg Centre for Arms Control Occasional Paper No. 1, June

345 Isla, N (2006) Transparency in past offensive biological weapon programmes: An analysis of Confidence Building Measure Form F. Hamburg Centre for Arms Control Occasional Paper No. 1, June, p 30.

346 An extract from the Wikileaks website describing the purpose and function of the organisation makes this link very clearly:

> Publishing improves transparency, and this transparency creates a better society for all people. Better scrutiny leads to reduced corruption and stronger democracies in all society's institutions, including government, corporations and other organisations. A healthy, vibrant and inquisitive journalistic media plays a vital role in achieving these goals. We are part of that media.
>
> Scrutiny requires information. Historically, information has been costly in terms of human life, human rights and economics. As a result of technical advances particularly the Internet and cryptography – the risks of conveying important information can be lowered. In its landmark ruling on the Pentagon Papers, the US Supreme Court ruled that 'only a free and unrestrained press can effectively expose deception in government.' We agree.

See http://www.wikileaks.org/About.html [Accessed 30 January 2014].

347 Hunger, I and Isla, N (2006) Confidence-building needs transparency: An analysis of the BTWC's confidence-building measures. *Disarmament Forum* 3: 27–36.

348 Interview with Beck Volker on 11 August 2013.

349 Interview with Beck Volker on 11 August 2013.

350 Argyris, C (1993) *Knowledge for Action*. San Francisco, CA: Jossey-Bass Publishers; Argyris, C, Putman, R and Smith, DM (1985) *Action Science*. London: Jossey-Bass; and Argyris, C and Schön, D (1996) *Organizational Learning II*. London: Addison Wesley.

351 Argyris, C (2006) *Reasons and Rationalizations*. Oxford: Oxford University Press, p 212.

352 See, for example, Argyris, C, Putman, R and Smith, DM (1985) *Action Science*. London: Jossey-Bass, p 230.

353 Morrison, E and Millike, F (2000) Organizational silence, *Academy of Management Review*, 25(4): 706–25.

354 Argyris, C (1999) *On Organizational Learning*, 2nd edition. London: Blackwell.

355 Note that this focus on what activities were not taking place posed certain challenges. To foster a general testing of assumptions and reasoning, Argyris advocates that the entries in maps should be based as much as possible on citable observable data. Neither of these expectations was possible to meet in this case. Because we have been *initiating* dialogue rather than *reflecting on* current organisational interaction also meant that we played a large role in framing discussions; and because our primary focus was with what had not come up within discussion in almost any respect, documenting observable behaviour proved problematic in many ways. Therefore, it was not possible to emulate all of the conditions and practices in place to follow the types of Model II interventions proposed by Argyris.

356 In contrast, for instance, it would be clear to anyone attending the BWC meetings in recent years that a verification protocol is not being discussed. This is an example of how discussion can take place about the lack of discussion.

357 For an overview on organisational studies literature relevant to this point, see Morrison, E and Millike, F (2000) Organizational silence, *Academy of Management Review*, 25(4): 706–25.

358 See Rappert, B and Gould, C (2014) Biological Weapons Convention: Confidence, the prohibition and learning from the past. July ISS Paper No. 258.

359 See also, United Kingdom (2013) *Confidence-building Measures: Next Steps to Enable Fuller Participation - Submitted by the United Kingdom of Great Britain and Northern Ireland*, BWC/MSP/2013/MX/WP.3, 29 July.

360 Australia, Canada, France, Germany, Netherlands, the United Kingdom of Great Britain and Northern Ireland, and the United States of America (2013) Getting past yes: Moving from consensus text to effective action. BWC/MSP/2013/WP.4, Working Paper submission to the 2013 States Parties Meeting, 6 December.

361 For instance, as suggested in Switzerland (2013) Confidence-building measures: Enabling fuller participation, BWC/MSP/2013/MX/WP.13, Working Paper submission to the 2013 States Parties Meeting, 9 August.

362 The Heritage Centre, Voortrekker Monument [Accessed 7 June 2014].

363 In the context of the Biological Weapons Convention, the Non-Aligned Movement refers to those countries that are part of a group not aligned with traditional Western or Eastern blocs.

364 Malan, M (2013) Dr Death close to patients' hearts. *Mail & Guardian*, 22 November. Reproduced with permission. This article was published in the *Mail & Guardian* on 22 November 2013. It was produced by the *Mail & Guardian*'s health journalism centre, Bhekisisa. The original article is available at http://bhekisisa.org/article/2013-11-22-dr-death-close-to-patients-hearts [Last accessed 8 December 2015].

365 Malan, M (2013) Dr Death close to patients' hearts. *Mail & Guardian*, 22 November. Available at http://mg.co.za/article/2013-11-22-dr-death-close-to-patients-hearts [Accessed 8 December 2015.]

366 Health Professions Council of South Africa (2013) *Professional Conduct Committee Concerning Dr W Basson*. Pretoria: HPCSA, 18 December.

367 As relayed to the authors during an anatomised interviewee on 20 February 2014.

368 Institute for Security Studies and Africa Check (2014) *FACTSHEET: South Africa's official crime statistics for 2013/14* Africa Check. See www.africacheck.org/factsheets/factsheet-south-africas-official-crime-statistics-for-201314/#sthash.3J0iuTZB.dpuf [Accessed 26 May 2017].

369 See The Centre for the Study of Violence and Reconciliation (2007) *The Violent Nature of Crime in South Africa*. Johannesburg: Centre for the Study of Violence and Reconciliation, 25 June.

370 South African Government (2013) *Police Killers will be Apprehended and Punished, says Minister Nathi Mthethwa*, Press Statement, 23 July.

371 South African Police Service website: http://www.saps.gov.za/about/tbvc_info.php.

372 Response by the Minister of Social Development to a parliamentary question, Question 899/2001, Official reply 06/07/11, 18 March 2011.

373 Pelser, E (2007) How we really got it wrong: Understanding the failure of crime prevention, *South African Crime Quarterly*, 22: 3–4.

374 For an in-depth discussion of these issues see Pearson, A, Chevrier, M and Wheelis, M (eds) (2007) *Incapacitating Biochemical Weapons*. Landham, MD: Lexington Press.

375 Dando, M (2009) Biologists napping while work militarized, *Nature*, 460: 950; and British Medical Association (2007) *Drugs as Weapons*. London: BMA House.

376 See Rappert, B (2003) *Non-lethal Weapons as Legitimizing Forces?* London: Frank Cass.

377 International Committee of the Red Cross (ICRC) (2013) *ICRC Position on the Use of Toxic Chemicals as Weapons for Law Enforcement*, 6 February. Geneva: ICRC.

378 For a historical analysis of debates about the abhorrence of chemical weapons see Price, R (1997) *The Chemical Weapons Taboo*. Ithaca, NY: Cornell University Press.

379 Moeller, S (1999) *Compassion Fatigue: How the media sell disease, famine, war and death*. London: Routledge.

380 Gould, C (2014) Editorial: Memory and forgetting. *SA Crime Quarterly*, 48: 4.

381 Letter from Dr Stuart Perkins, Defence Science and Technology Laboratory, 10 February 2014.

382 Argyris, C (2003) A life full of learning. *Organizational Studies*, 24(7): 1178–92.

383 Leitenberg, M and Zilinskas, RA (2012) *The Soviet Biological Weapons Program: A history*. Boston, MA: Harvard University Press.

384 Vogel, K (2006) Bioweapons proliferation. *Social Studies of Science* 36: 659-690.

385 MacKenzie, D and Spinardi, G (1996) Tacit knowledge and the uninvention of nuclear weapons, in *Knowing Machines*. Cambridge, MA: MIT Press.

386 See Furukawa, K (2009) Dealing with the dual-use aspects of life science activities in Japan, in B Rappert and C Gould (eds) *Biosecurity: Origins, transformations and practices*. London: Palgrave.

387 See Rappert, B (2006) *Controlling the Weapons of War: Politics, persuasion and the prohibition of inhumanity*. London: Routledge, Chapter 6.

388 Though see Falk, R (2001) The challenges of biological weaponry, in S Wright

(ed.) *Biological Warfare and Disarmament*. London: Rowman & Littlefield, for a critical analysis of the geopolitics of the BTWC.

389 'Track 2 diplomacy: Unofficial dialogue and problem-solving activities aimed at building relationships and encouraging new thinking that can inform the official process. Track 2 activities typically involve influential academic, religious, and NGO leaders and other civil society actors who can interact more freely than high-ranking officials. Some analysts use the term track 1.5 to denote a situation in which official and non-official actors work together to resolve conflicts.' Glossary of terms for conflict management and peace building, United States Institute of Peace. Available at http://www.glossary.usip.org/resource/tracks-diplomacy [Accessed 11 October 2016].

390 See Wiltshire, B (n.d.) The South African veterinary cover-up. *The Snout*, 3. Available at http://www.snout.org.za/issue3.php [Accessed October 2016].

391 Christie, N (1986) The ideal victim, in E Fattah (ed.) *From Crime Policy to Victim Policy*. Basingstoke: Macmillan, pp 17–30.

392 Available at https://www.docs.google.com/forms/d/14IJnOr-nnWuGzyVgcoM-YRrTcl2iYm91He3C3VUQIWA/viewform [Last accessed 8 December 2015].

393 See http://www.khulumani.net/khulumani/about-us.html [last accessed 21 October 2016].

394 https://www.ictj.org/news/south-africas-moral-voice (2015) (Howard Varney op-ed – first published in *City Press* and then on the ICTJ website: http://www.news24.com/Opinions/SAs-moral-voice-is-a-crying-sham-20150619) [Accessed 26 May 2017].

395 Documentary fragment, *Confessions of an Apartheid Killer* (n.d.), pp 16 and 17.

396 Varney, H (2015) South Africa's 'moral voice' is a crying sham. *City Press*, Johannesburg, 21 June.

397 Figure taken from Bruce, D (2002) Police brutality in South Africa, in N Mwanajiti, P Mhlanga, M Sifuniso, Y Nachali-Kambikambi, M Muuba and M Mwananyanda (eds) *Police Brutality in Southern Africa: A human rights perspective*. Lusaka: Inter-African Network for Human Rights and Development, Section 4.

398 Lancaster, L (2016) Measuring public and election violence in South Africa. ISS Policy Brief. Pretoria: Institute for Security Studies.

APPENDIX 1
WHO WAS AFFECTED

THE QUESTION 'Who has been affected by Project Coast?' raises important issues about how suffering is both concealed and acknowledged, and how those affected should be represented.

There are a small number of people who were almost certainly poisoned by substances produced by Project Coast front companies. But units of the police and military, which made use of poisons and drugs, may have sourced substances elsewhere.

Here, we honour all those individuals who are believed – or suspected – to have fallen victim to poisoning, those who were intended targets of failed operations, and those who were drugged during military or police actions, including those whose cause of death or injury remains a mystery. The names of many who died are still unknown.

Donald Woods

In 1977, Donald Woods, a South African journalist and anti-apartheid activist, received a shirt laced with Ninhydrin for his five-year-old daughter, Mary. The chemical was said to sting on contact and is used by police forces worldwide.

±200 unknown SWAPO members

Between 1979 and 1988, many members of SWAPO were killed by SADF soldier Johan Theron, mostly by the lethal injection of muscle relaxants. Some of these soldiers had allegedly been 'turned' and then outlived their usefulness to the SADF. Their bodies were disappeared either by being thrown from an aircraft into the sea or from armoured vehicles into the veld. Some were dumped in the Brandenberg Mountains. One victim is believed to have been a woman. The body-disposal operation was dubbed Operation Dual. The identities of these victims, and the number of victims disposed of in this way are unknown, but it is believed that nearly 200 people died this way.

4 unknown men One a Barnacle member

In 1980, four unnamed men were targeted for assassination by Barnacle member Trevor Floyd. One of these four men was also a member of Barnacle and had become a risk when it was discovered that he was making calls to Zimbabwe. Floyd gave all four of the men lethal injections.

5 POWs, Fort Rev

Soldier Johan Theron alleges that he and Dr Wouter Basson visited Fort Rev in South West Africa in 1980, where they gave five prisoners sleeping pills and then injected them with lethal quantities of muscle relaxants. Basson denies this allegation.

Joe Slovo

In 1981, ANC member Joe Slovo was a target of an assassination attempt in London. Police hit squad commander Dirk Coetzee ordered the attempt on his life and gave a security police officer a poison with which to lace Slovo's drink. The assassination attempt failed.

Gonisizwe Kondile

In 1981, political detainee Gonisizwe Kondile was given 'knock-out drops' by police hit squad head Dirk Coetzee before he was murdered near Komatipoort. The security police burnt his body.

Selby Mavuso Peter Dlamini

In 1981, police hit squad commander Dirk Coetzee poisoned, tortured and killed activist Selby Mavuso and askari Peter Dlamini.

Siphiwo Mtimkhulu

In 1981, Eastern Cape student Siphiwo Mtimkhulu was hospitalised shortly after his release from prison. He was suffering from thallium poisoning. Before he could sue the police he disappeared along with his friend Topsy Madaka. Mtimkhulu was murdered in 1982 but his remains were never found.

3 men Dukuduku forest

In 1983, three men were taken to the Dukuduku forest in Kwa-Zulu Natal. They were smeared with a substance and tied to a tree by a chain and left there overnight. The next day military doctor Kobus Bothma and soldier Johan Theron injected them with lethal quantities of muscle relaxants and threw their bodies into the sea. Their identities remain unknown.

Roland Hunter

In 1983, SADF conscript and ANC member Roland Hunter was the intended target of an assassination attempt. The plan was to inject Hunter with mamba toxin and leave a dead mamba next to his body so that it would appear he died from a snakebite. Hunter was arrested by the security police on charges of espionage before the plan could be carried out.

	**Christopher Barnacle member**	In 1983, a Barnacle operative known only as Christopher was murdered by Civil Co-operation Bureau member Danie Phaal and Barnacle member Trevor Floyd. According to Phaal, they had offered Christopher a ride to Messina, and during the trip they gave him a beer containing sedatives. After he fell asleep they injected him with the anaesthetic drug Ketalar. The intention was to keep Christopher sedated until their flight from the Zeerust airfield. However, while sedated Christopher stopped breathing.
	**5 Renamo members 1 possibly Boaventura Bomba**	In 1983, five members of Renamo who were believed to be responsible for the murder of Renamo leader, Orlando Christina, were captured by the police and taken to the Caprivi. One of the men was taken from 1 Military hospital. During the Basson trial it was alleged that the men were injected with drugs during their interrogation, after which they were killed and their bodies dumped in the sea. One of these men is believed to have been Boaventura Bomba.
	**Unknown victim, possibly a SWAPO member**	Sometime between 1983 and 1986, a prisoner believed to be a SWAPO member detained at Ondangwa, Namibia, was given orange juice laced with poison by Civil Co-operation Bureau member Danie Phaal. After drinking the juice he started bleeding from all orifices and died a short while later.
	**Garth Bailey**	In 1984, SADF 5 Reconnaissance Commando member Garth Bailey died mysteriously at 1 Military Hospital. His clinical and post mortem records state cause of death as sudden onset of myasthenia gravis, however his death might equally be explained by poisoning with botulinum toxin. His widow Daphne Potter says: 'Although it is not so uncommon these days for children to grow up without their biological fathers, it is hard to grow up without ever having had the opportunity to meet your father. To have that opportunity taken away [from Garth's child] and the "what ifs" and the "why's" never answered has been difficult. There are still so many unanswered questions that even the opportunity for proper grief has been taken away. How can you be angry when you don't know for sure what or why he died? You are left with a hole in your life that can never be filled because the questions go on.'

Peter Kalangula

In 1985, Namibian religious leader Peter Kalangula was an intended target for assassination by Barnacle member Trevor Floyd. Floyd was given a toxic substance to smear on the door handle of Kalangula's car. The attempt failed.

Victor da Fonseca

In 1986, Victor da Fonseca, a Mozambican member of 5 Reconnaissance Commando, died. According to his official death certificate he had a brain tumour and died of pneumonia. Civil Co-operation Bureau member Danie Phaal testified that on two separate occasions that he was given substances to put in Da Fonseca's drinks with the intention of killing him. Da Fonseca's body was exhumed in 1998 and examined for thallium, but the levels were found to be too low to have caused his death.

Samuel Phina Themba Ngesi

The ANC submission to the TRC lists Samuel Phina and Themba Ngesi as having died after being poisoned in Mozambique in 1986.

Ronnie Kasrils Pallo Jordan

In 1985/86, ANC leaders Ronnie Kasrils and Pallo Jordan were the intended targets of an assassination attempt in London, by way of a poison-tipped umbrella. Project Barnacle member Trevor Floyd stated that he was given the modified umbrella by bio-engineer Jan Lourens who showed him how to load the umbrella with the poison. The attempt failed.

In 1987/88, a second attempt on the lives of Kasrils and Jordan in London was planned. This time, bio-engineer Jan Lourens supplied Barnacle operative Floyd with a modified screwdriver 'applicator' and a substance that may have been phenylsilitrane. There was no opportunity to administer the toxins and Floyd discarded them in the Thames.

Mack Anderson

In 1987, Corporal Mack Anderson of Reconnaissance Commando had allegedly become a security risk. He died after fellow soldier Johan Theron administered lethal injections of Scoline, Tubarine and Ketalar. His body was loaded into a helicopter and left in the Mozambican bush.

Petrus Lubane

In 1987, ANC courier Petrus Lubane was given a beer laced with sleeping tablets before he was murdered by members of the Northern Transvaal Security Branch, who detonated an explosive strapped to his body.

Gibson Mondlane

In 1987, ANC member Gibson Mondlane (aka Gibson Ncube) was seen drinking a South African beer at a party in Maputo. By the time the party ended, his feet were paralysed. The paralysis spread through his whole body and he died eight days later.

Conny Braam

In 1987, former head of the Dutch anti-apartheid movement, Conny Braam, believed that two attempts were made to poison her, in Lusaka and Harare respectively. She became ill after trying on a jacket she found in the cupboard of her hotel room.

Jeremiah Ntuli
Jeremiah Magagula
Rooibaard Geldenhuys
Morris Nkabinde
Samuel Masilela
Abram Makolane
Stephen Makena
Thomas Phiri
Sipho Sibanyoni
Elliot Sathekge

In 1987, ten young men between the ages of 15 and 22 were recruited in Mamelodi by askari Joe Mamasela under false pretences. They were told they would be joining the ANC. They were given drinks laced with an unknown substance and their unconscious bodies were blown up in the minibus in which they had been travelling. They have become known as the Nietverdiend Ten.

**Klaas de Jonge**	In April 1988, Dutch anti-apartheid activist Klaas de Jonge left a small bag of clothes in a luggage locker at Nijmegen railway station. Returning a few hours later he found the entire door of the locker missing and the bag gone. He recovered the bag at the left luggage office, where he was told a man had handed it in. The contents were checked and everything seemed normal. The next day, after wearing clothes from the bag, De Jonge experienced severe pain and swelling of his right eye. Within a few weeks, he was completely blind in his right eye. Examination at several hospitals by a number of specialists failed to establish the cause of the infection. A second plot to murder De Jonge is suspected but was never carried out.
**Dullah Omar**	In 1989, ANC leader Dullah Omar was the intended target for assassination. Civil Co-operation Bureau member 'Slang' Van Zyl was given a powder to put in Omar's food that would induce a heart attack. The plan was never carried out.
**Reverend Frank Chikane**	In 1989, ANC and religious leader Reverend Frank Chikane was the target of an attempted assassination by the police security branch. He fell violently ill after wearing underwear that had been poisoned with organophosphates.
**Enoch Dlamini**	In 1989, ANC member Enoch Dlamini died in Swaziland. Military Intelligence member Jan Anton Nieuwoudt testified in the trial of Dr Wouter Basson that he had given poisoned beer to an agent in Swaziland to give to Dlamini. The official cause of death was recorded as acute haemorrhagic pancreatitis.
**Kwenza Mlaba**	In 1989, Durban civil rights lawyer Kwenza Mlaba was the target of an attempted poisoning. Members of the Civil Co-operation Bureau left a sealed bag of poisoned razor blades in his office in the hope that he would use them.

	**ANC meeting Soweto 1989**	In 1989, Roodeplaat Research Laboratories microbiologist Dr Mike Odendaal was asked for salmonella, which he was told would be added to the sugar at an ANC meeting in Soweto. Odendaal was later told that the salmonella had 'worked so well' that all the delegates had fallen ill.
	**Dr Allan Wellington Madolwana (aka Francis Melli)**	In 1990, Dr Allan Wellington Madolwana (aka Francis Melli), a high-ranking ANC official believed to have been a spy for the South African security forces, was found dead in his room at the Protea Inn Hotel in East London. It is suspected he had discovered information that could compromise the Directorate of Military Intelligence. The cause of his death is unknown, but the ANC suspected he was poisoned.
	**Jean Luc Curutchet**	In 1990, AECI scientist Jean Luc Curutchet was involved in a work-related accident. He attempted to sue for liability, and shortly thereafter began to experience symptoms, which he believed resulted from being given a poisoned neck-brace to wear.
	**Peter Martin**	In 1992, former British intelligence (MI6) agent Peter Martin died of a heart attack. The London Sunday Times reported on 14 July 1998 that an investigation into Martin's death had been opened after the TRC's chemical and biological warfare hearings. Martin was believed to have met with Basson in London some time before. His fiancé, Rosemary Durrant, feared he may have been poisoned. No evidence to that effect has yet been made public.
	**Samuel Khanyile (aka Solly Smith)**	In 1993, former ANC representative in London Samuel Khanyile (aka Solly Smith) was found dead in his bed under mysterious circumstances. In 1991 he had confessed to the ANC that he had been compromised by Military Intelligence, and had been feeding them information. The ANC suspected he was poisoned to prevent further exposure of its agents.

APPENDIX 2
SALES (VERKOPE) LIST

THE SALES LIST was a list of items made available by RRL to members of the security forces. The list was drawn up by Dr Andre Immelman.

ß 0000

CBI: 80

DATUM GELEWER	STOF	VOLUME	PRYS
19.03.89 JK	Phensiklidien Thallium asetaat	1 x 500mg 50g	Teruggebr.
23.03.89 JK	Phensiklidien	5 x 100mg	
04.04.89 C	Aldicarb - Lemoensap	6 x 200mg	
04.04.89 C	Asied - Whisky	3 x 1,5ℓg	
04.04.89 C	Paraoxon	10x 2ml	
07.04.89 C	Vit D	2gr	
15.05.89 C	Vit D	2gr	R300,00
15.05.89 C	Katharidien	70mg	R150,00
15.05.89 C	10ml Spuite	50	
16.05.89 C	Naalde 15Gx10mm	24	R18,00
16.05.89 C	Naalde 17Gx7,5mm	7	R7,00
19.05.89 C	Thallium asetaat	1g	
30.05.89	Fosfied tablette	30	
09.06.89	Spore en Brief	1	
20.06.89 K	Kapsules NaCN	50	
21.06.89	Bierblik Bot	3	
21.06.89	Bierblik Thallium	3	
21.06.89	Bottel bier Bot	1	
21.06.89	Bottel bier Thallium	2	
22.06.89 K	Suiker en Salmonella	200gr	
27.06.89 C	Wiskey en Paraquat	1x75ml	
20.07.89 K	Hg-sianied	~4gr	
27.07.89 K	Bobbejaan foetus	1	

- 1 -

259

VERKOPE

DATUM GELEWER	STOF	VOLUME	PRYS
04.08.89 K	Vibrio cholera	16 bottels	✓
10.08.89 ⟨	Asied 4xgr ✓	Kapsule sianied 7	
11.08.89 ⟨	Sigarette B anthracis	5 ✓	
⟨	Koffie sjokolade B anthracis	⁽¹⁾ 5 ✓	
C	Koffie sjokolade Botulinum	⁽²⁾ 5 ✓	
C	Pepperment sjokolade Aldikarb ⁽³⁾	3 ✓	
C	Pepperment sjokolade Brodifakum⁽⁴⁾	2	
C	Pepperment sjokolade Katharidien⁽⁵⁾	3 ✓	
C	Pepperment sjokolade Sianied⁽⁶⁾	3	✓
16.08.89 K	Vibrio cholera	6 bottels	✓
16.08.89 ⟨	Kapsules Propan NaCN	7 ✓	
18.08.89 K	Formalien en Piridien-naalde	50ml x 30	
	Roalole 10cm x no 16	12	
05.09.89 K	Kantharidien - poeier in sakkie	100mg ✓	→ ?
08.09.89 ⟨	Metanol	3-30ml	?
C	Vibrio cholera	10 bottels	✓
08.09.89 ⟨	Slange	2	
K	Mamba toksien	1	⅔ ᵍᵃᵇ
13.09.89 ⟨	Digoksien	5 mg	✓
18.09.89 C	Whiskey 50ml + colcnicine	75mg ✓	✓
6.10.89 ⟨	B.melitensis c̄	⁻I x 50 ✓	✓
	S.typhlmurium in deodorant	1 ✓	
11.10.89 K	Kulture vanaf briewe	2	

- 2 -

260

₤.0000

DATUM GELEWER	STOF	VOLUME	PRYS
21.10.89	B.melitensis c		
	S.typhimurium in deodorant	1	

- 3 -

261